The Mind Is Flat

NICK CHATER

The Mind Is Flat

*The Remarkable Shallowness of
the Improvising Brain*

Yale

UNIVERSITY PRESS

New Haven and London

First published in the United States in 2018 by Yale University Press.
First published in Great Britain in 2018 as *The Mind Is Flat: The Illusion of Mental Depth and the Improvised Mind* by Penguin Books Ltd, London.

Yale University Press books may be purchased in quantity for educational, business, or promotional use. For information, please e-mail sales.press@yale.edu (U.S. office) or sales@yaleup.co.uk (U.K. office).

Typeset in 10.5/14 pt Sabon LT Std by Jouve (UK), Milton Keynes.
Printed in the United States of America.

Library of Congress Control Number: 2018941452
ISBN 978-0-300-23872-3 (hardcover : alk. paper)

This paper meets the requirements of ANSI/NISO Z39.48-1992 (Permanence of Paper).

10 9 8 7 6 5 4 3 2 1

To my mother and father, Robert and Dorothy Chater, and to my wonderful wife and children, Louie, Maya and Caitlin Fooks, whose unfailing support and love has made this book possible.

Contents

Prologue: Literary Depth, Mental Shallows

> . . . when we claim to be just using our powers of inner obser-
> vation, we are always actually engaging in a sort of impromptu
> theorizing – and we are remarkably gullible theorizers, pre-
> cisely because there is so little to 'observe' and so much to
> pontificate about without fear of contradiction.
>
> *Daniel Dennett*[1]

At the climax of *Anna Karenina*, the heroine throws herself under a train as it moves out of a station on the edge of Moscow. But did she want to die? Various interpretations of this crucial moment in Tolstoy's great masterpiece are possible. Had the ennui of Russian aristocratic life and the fear of losing her lover Vronsky become so intolerable that death seemed the only escape? Or was her final act mere capriciousness, a theatrical gesture of despair, not seriously imagined even moments before the opportunity arose?

We ask such questions. But can they possibly have answers? If Tolstoy says that Anna has dark hair, then Anna has dark hair. But if Tolstoy doesn't tell us why Anna jumped to her death, then Anna's motives are surely a void. We can attempt to fill this void with our own interpretations and we can debate their plausibility. But there is no hidden truth about what Anna really wanted, because, of course, Anna is a fictional character.

Suppose instead that Anna were a historical figure and Tolstoy's masterpiece a journalistic reconstruction of real events. Now the question of Anna's motivation becomes a matter of history, rather than literary interpretation. Yet our method of inquiry remains the same: the very same text would now be viewed as providing (perhaps unreliable) clues about the mental state of a real person, not a fictional character. Lawyers, journalists and historians, rather than critics and literary scholars, might put forward and debate competing interpretations.

Now imagine that we ask Anna herself. Suppose that Tolstoy's novel was indeed an account of real events, but the great steam engine slammed on its brakes just in time. Anna, apparently mortally injured, is conveyed anonymously to a Moscow hospital. Against the odds, she pulls through and chooses to disappear to escape her past. We catch up with Anna convalescing in a Swiss sanatorium. As likely as not, Anna will be as unsure as anyone else about her true motivations. After all, she too has to engage in a process of interpretation: considering her memories (rather than Tolstoy's manuscript), she attempts to piece together an account of her behaviour. Even if Anna does venture a definitive account of her actions, we may be sceptical that her own interpretation is any more compelling than the interpretations of others. To be sure, she may have 'data' unavailable to an outsider – she may, for example, remember the despairing words 'Vronsky has left me forever' running through her mind as she approached the edge of the fateful platform. However, any such advantage may be more than outweighed by the distorting lens of self-perception. Our interpretations of our own actions seem, among other things, to assign to ourselves greater wisdom and nobility than might be evident to the dispassionate observer. Autobiography always deserves a measure of scepticism.

Might we get closer to Anna's true motivations if we asked her not in hindsight, but at the time? Suppose a journalist, employed by a scandal-hungry Moscow paper, is following Anna's every move, scenting a story. He leaps to save Anna from falling to her death, only to brandish pen and notepad, with the words, 'Now, Ms Karenina, tell me a little about why you decided to launch yourself into oblivion.' This strategy seems unlikely to succeed, to put it mildly. And a discreet query of, 'Ms Karenina, I perceive you to be about to leap to your death. Perhaps you could spare a couple of moments to answer this short questionnaire?' seems equally doomed to fail.

There are two opposing conclusions that one might draw from this vignette. The first possible moral is that our minds have dark and unfathomable 'hidden depths'. From this viewpoint, we cannot expect people reliably to be able to look within themselves and compile a complete and true account of their beliefs and motives. Explanations of behaviour, whether from observers or participants, and whether before, during or after the event, are partial and unreliable at best.

From the 'hidden depths' standpoint, then, uncovering the true motivations for human behaviour needs more than the blunderbuss of asking people directly. It requires delicacy and sophistication. We need somehow to dive deep into the inner workings of the mind, and to measure directly the hidden beliefs, desires, motives, fears, suspicions and hopes governing our actions, forces of which we may ourselves be only dimly aware. Psychologists, psychiatrists and neuroscientists have long debated how best to plumb the deep waters of human motivation. Word associations, the interpretation of dreams, hours of intensive psychotherapy, behavioural experiments, physiological recordings and brain imaging have all been popular options over the last century or so. Whatever the method, the objective is clear: to discover the feelings, motives and beliefs that lurk below the mental 'surface' of conscious awareness – to chart, in short, our hidden depths. Yet the contents of our hidden depths seem to remain perpetually elusive. Freudian psychoanalysts can speculate about our hidden fears and desires; psychologists and neuroscientists can attempt to draw subtle and highly indirect conclusions from actions, heart-rate, skin conductance, pupil dilation and the rate of blood flow in the brain. But no hidden beliefs, desires, hopes or fears are ever actually observed. Perhaps our hidden depths are an 'inner space' that is as, or more, mysterious than the depths of outer space; and to penetrate it we will need more sophisticated instruments and methods of analysis. From this viewpoint, our failure so far to reveal the hidden depths of the human mind should drive us to even greater efforts.

In this book, I will argue for precisely the opposite viewpoint: that the project of charting our hidden depths is not merely technically difficult, but fundamentally misconceived; the very idea that our minds contain 'hidden depths' is utterly wrong. Our reflections on Anna Karenina's fateful act should point us, instead, to a radically different moral: that the interpretation of the motives of real people is no different from the interpretations of fictional characters. And fictional characters can't, of course, have an inner life, because they have no life at all: there is no more a fact about whether the fictional Anna has a subconscious fear of dogs, doubts about the stability of the Tsarist regime, or prefers Bach to Mozart, than there is a fact about whether she was born on a Tuesday. There is no 'hidden' truth about fictional characters, nothing beneath the 'surface' of the words on the page.

But the picture would be largely the same had Tolstoy's novel been reportage, and Anna a living, breathing member of the nineteenth-century Russian aristocracy. Then, of course, there would be a truth (whether known or not) about whether Anna was born on a Tuesday. But, I argue, there would still be no truths about the real Anna's motivations, any more than for the fictional Anna. No amount of therapy, dream analysis, word association, experiment or brain-scanning can recover a person's 'true motives', not because they are *difficult* to find, but because there is *nothing* to find. It is not hard to plumb our mental depths because they are so deep and so murky, but because there are no mental depths to plumb.

The inner, mental world, and the beliefs, motives and fears it is supposed to contain is, itself, a work of the imagination. We invent interpretations of ourselves and other people in the flow of experience, just as we conjure up interpretations of fictional characters from a flow of written text. Each possibility can be challenged with endless alternatives. Perhaps Anna primarily despaired of her precipitous social fall, or the future of her son, or the meaninglessness of aristocratic life, rather than being tormented by love. There is no ground truth about the right interpretation of the fictional Anna, though some are more compelling and better evidenced in Tolstoy's text than others. But Tolstoy the journalist would have nothing more than interpretations of a 'real' Anna's behaviour; and the real Anna, whether at the time, or looking back months later, could do no more than venture one more interpretation of her own behaviour. We never have the last word in explaining our own actions – our interpretations of our own actions are as partial, jumbled and open to challenge as anyone else's.

The flow of Tolstoy's text can give us the feeling that we are being given sketchy reports from another world. Tolstoy could have chosen to tell us about Anna's childhood, the impact of her death on her son Seryozha, or how Vronsky (perhaps) retired from society and became a monk. These scenes would spring into being only as they were written. As he writes, Tolstoy is *inventing* more of the lives of Anna and her circle; he is not *discovering* more about them.

Yet the unfolding of a life is not so different from the unfolding of a novel. We generate our beliefs, values and actions in-the-moment; they are not pre-calculated and 'written' in some unimaginably vast memory store just in case they might be needed. And this implies that there is no pre-existing 'inner world of thought' from which our thoughts issue. Thoughts, like fiction, come into existence in the instant that they are invented, and not a moment before.

The very idea of 'looking' into our own minds embodies the mistake: we talk as if we have a faculty of introspection, to scrutinize the contents of our inner world, just as we have faculties of perception, to inform us about the external world.[2] But introspection is a process not of *perception* but of *invention*: the real-time generation of interpretations and explanations to make sense of our own words and actions. The inner world is a mirage.

Now in fiction, while some characters are 'two-dimensional', others seem to have real 'depth'. They can, indeed, assume in our imagination a vividness that may equal, or even exceed, that of some of our living acquaintances. We may attribute to them attitudes and beliefs beyond the printed page. Yet such apparent depth is, of course, 'in the eye of the beholder': there are no facts about Anna Karenina's life, save what Tolstoy gives us; no hidden motives lurking between the lines. As for fictional characters, so for real people. The sense that behaviour is merely the surface of a vast sea, immeasurably deep and teeming with inner motives, beliefs and desires whose power we can barely sense is a conjuring trick played by our own minds. The truth is not that the depths are empty, or even shallow, but that the surface is all there is.

As we have already seen, it is awfully tempting – especially for psychologists – to suspect that while our everyday, common-sense explanations of ourselves and each other, as guided by beliefs, desires, hopes and fears, may be wrong in detail, they are right in spirit. Anna's leap to her death is, one may think, guided by some beliefs, desires, hopes and fears, even though she may not be able to tell us quite which beliefs, desires, hopes and fears. Her introspection is imperfect or perhaps untrustworthy. But the problem with our everyday view of our minds is far deeper: no one, at any point in human history, has ever been guided by inner beliefs or desires, any more than any human being has been possessed by evil spirits or watched over by a guardian angel. Beliefs, motives and other imagined inhabitants of our 'inner world' are entirely a figment of our imaginations. The stories we tell to justify and explain our own and others' behaviour aren't just wrong in detail – they are a thoroughgoing fabrication from start to finish.

Our flow of conscious thought, including our explanations of our own and each other's behaviour, are creations in the moment, not reports of (or even speculations about) a chain of inner mental events. Our mind is continually interpreting, justifying and making sense of our own behaviour, just as we make sense of the behaviour of the people around us, or characters in fiction. If you cross-examine me, or any other reader, about Anna's motivations (Q: 'Did she think that jumping under the train would mean certain death?' A: 'Yes.' Q: 'Did she believe that Seryozha would be better off without her?' A: 'Possibly – though almost certainly quite wrongly'; and so on), I will generate answers, as quick as a flash. So we clearly have the *ability* to fabricate justifications at will, but these justifications cannot, of course, be conjectures about Anna's mental life, because Anna, being a fictional character, *has* no mental life.

If Anna were real, and had survived, we could cross-examine her, in her Swiss sanatorium, with just the same questions, and she too could reply, quick as a flash. And, for that matter, were you to cross-examine me about some prosaic aspect of my own life (e.g. why I took the train, rather than driving, to London), I can come back with a string of explanations (about carbon emissions, traffic congestion, parking etc.). The sheer inventiveness of our minds implies that the real Anna could be interpreting and justifying her own thoughts and behaviour, in retrospect, using exactly the imaginative powers that we are using when considering her as a fictional character (extended by the imaginative work of Tolstoy himself in creating her story). And this suggests that this very same inventiveness could underlie the stream of justifications we provide to explain our everyday lives to ourselves and each other.

In this book, I want to convince you that the mind is flat: that the very idea of mental depth is an illusion. The mind is, instead, a consummate improviser, inventing actions, and beliefs and desires to explain those actions, with wonderful fluidity. But these momentary inventions are flimsy, fragmented and self-contradictory; they are like a film set, seeming solid when viewed through the camera, but constructed from cardboard.

An improvising mind, unmoored from stable beliefs and desires, might seem to be a recipe for mental chaos. I shall argue that the opposite is true: the very task of our improvising mind is to make our thoughts and behaviour as coherent as possible – to stay 'in character' as well as we are able. To do so, our brains must strive continually to think and act in the current moment in a way that aligns as well as possible our prior thoughts and actions. We are like judges deciding each new legal case by referring to, and reinterpreting, an ever-growing body of previous cases. So the secret of our minds lies not in supposed hidden depths, but in our remarkable ability to creatively improvise our present, on the theme of our past.

The argument – and this book – has two parts. In the first, I attempt to clear away what I take to be fundamental and widespread misunderstandings of how our mind works. I then turn to present a positive account of the brain as a ceaseless improviser. More concretely, in Part One, we will explore the psychological evidence that talk of beliefs, desires, hopes and fears is pure fiction. Yet it is such convincing fiction, and so effortlessly and fluently invented by our own brains, that we take it for reality. We'll find that almost everything we think we know about our minds is false. This is not the story from the psychology textbook. According to that story, common sense is roughly on the right track, but just needs to be modified, adjusted and filled out. But these modifications and adjustments never seem to work. The common-sense mind and the mind we discover through experiment just don't seem to fit together. The common-sense story needs to be abandoned, not patched up.

Yet while the textbooks don't take a radical line, a growing number of philosophers, psychologists and neuroscientists do.[3] In Part One, I will point to the root cause of the problem with the common-sense view of the mind: that mental depth is an illusion.

We imagine that mirroring the outer world of people, objects, stars and noises there is an inner world of rich sensory experiences (the subjective experience of people, objects, stars and noises), not to mention our emotions, preferences, motives, hopes, fears, memories and beliefs. The possibilities for exploration in this inner world seem vast.[4] Just paying close attention to what we see and hear, and the states of our bodies, seems to reveal that our inner perceptual world is wonderfully rich; and that we just need to step off from direct sensory experience into the realm of the imagination that dreams, meditations and hypnosis seem to provide. Or we can explore the vast archives of our memories, perhaps reliving fragments of childhood or student life; or we can discourse with ourselves endlessly about our beliefs and values.

There are many who suspect that the scale of our inner world is far greater still – that we should add into the mix subliminal perception, which slips into our minds without our noticing; that we have unconscious beliefs, motives, desires and perhaps even unconscious inner agents (for Freud, the id, ego, and superego; for Jung, the collective unconscious). And perhaps there is a self, or many selves, or a soul. Many believe that with the right meditative practice, psychotherapy or even hallucinogenic drug, the doors to the rich inner world of the unconscious might be prised open. And, turning to neuroscience, it is natural to imagine that the contents of our inner world might one day be accessible to brain-scanners – which might 'read off' our beliefs, motives and feelings, whether conscious or not.

But all of this depth, richness and endless scope for exploration is utterly fake. There is no inner world. Our flow of momentary conscious experience is not the sparkling surface of a vast sea of thought – it is *all there is*. And, as we shall see, each momentary experience turns out to be startlingly sketchy – at any moment, we can recognize just one face, or read just one word, or identify just one object. And when, like our imagined Anna, rehabilitating in the Alps, we begin to describe our feelings, or explain our actions, we are only creating stories, one step at a time, not exploring a pre-existing inner world of thoughts and feelings. The more outré 'inner worlds' of dreams, or mystical or drug-induced states, are similarly nothing more than streams of invention – acts of the imagination, not voyages of inner discovery. And the interpretation of dreams, far from boring deep into our psyche, is no more than one creative act set atop another.

The aim of Part One is to help reinterpret our intuitions about the nature of our own minds, and to undercut misconceptions that have been repeated and even amplified in many areas of philosophy, psychology, psychoanalysis, artificial intelligence and neuroscience. But if the intuitive picture – of a rich and deep 'inner sea' of which our conscious thought is merely the glittering surface – is so utterly wrong, the obvious question is: what possible alternative story about human thought and behaviour could there be?

In Part Two, we take up this question. If the mind is flat, then our mental lives must exist purely at the 'mental surface'. Our brain is an improviser, and it bases its current improvisations on previous improvisations: it creates new momentary thoughts and experiences by drawing not on a hidden inner world of knowledge, beliefs and motives, but on *memory traces of previous momentary thoughts and experiences*.

The analogy with fiction is helpful here too. Tolstoy invents Anna's words and actions as he writes the novel. But he strives to make Anna's words and actions as coherent as possible – she should 'stay in character' or her character should 'develop' as the novel unfolds. And when we interpret the behaviour of other people, and of ourselves, the same aim applies: a good interpretation is one that does not just make sense of the present moment, but links it with our past actions, words, and indeed interpretations. Our brain is an engine that creates momentary conscious interpretations not by drawing on hidden inner depths, but by linking the present with the past, just as writing a novel involves linking its sentences together coherently, rather than creating an entire world.

Conscious experience is therefore the sequence of *outputs* of a cycle of thought, locking onto, and imposing meaning on, aspects of the sensory world. That is, we consciously experience the meaningful interpretations of the world that our brain creates, seeing words, objects and faces, and hearing voices, tunes or sirens. But we are never conscious either of the *inputs* to each mental step or each step's *internal workings*. So we can report nothing to explain *why* we see an outcrop of rock as a pack of dogs, a fleeting facial expression as condescending or kindly, or why a line of poetry conjures up a vision of mortality or reminds us of childhood. Each cycle of thought delivers a consciously experienced interpretation, but no explanation of where that interpretation comes from.

Throughout this book, my argument will be illustrated through examples from visual perception. Perceptual examples are vivid and concrete; and perception is the area of psychology and neuroscience that is by far the best understood. It makes sense to focus our attention where the evidence is clearest and most easily explained. But I have another reason for focusing on perception, namely that the whole of thought, whether chess-playing, abstract mathematical reasoning, or artistic and literary creation, is really no more than an extension of perception.

We'll see how the cycle of thought works, and point to some key pieces of evidence in support of this story. On closer analysis, the stories we tell about our stable personalities, beliefs and motives can't possibly be right. By contrast, the quirks, variability and capriciousness of human nature make sense when we realize that our brain is an incomparable improviser: an engine for spontaneously finding meaning and choosing actions that make the best sense in the moment. Thus our thoughts and actions are based on a rich tradition of past thoughts and actions, which our brain harnesses and reworks to address the challenges of the moment. Moreover, just as today's thoughts follow yesterday's precedents, so they also set precedents for tomorrow – giving our actions, words and our life a coherent shape. So what makes each of us special is, to a large extent, the uniqueness of our individual history of prior thoughts and experiences. In other words, each of us is a unique tradition, continually in the process of creation.

As the story unfolds, we will see that we are, in a very real sense, characters of our own creation, rather than playthings of unconscious currents within us. And while each new perception, movement and thought builds on our unique mental tradition of past perceptions, movements and thoughts, we are also able to build new thoughts from old in a wonderfully free and creative way. Our current thoughts can become locked into patterns of past thoughts, but they need not be: our human intelligence gives us a wonderful ability to create new thoughts from old. And such freedom and creativity does not depend on rare seeds of genius, or the occasional spark of inspiration; it is fundamental to the basic operation of the brain – how we perceive, dream, talk.

Our freedom has its limits, of course. Amateur saxophonists can't 'freely' choose to play like Charlie Parker, new learners of English can't spontaneously emulate Sylvia Plath, and physics students can't spontaneously reason like Albert Einstein. New actions, skills and thoughts require building a rich and deep mental tradition; and there is no shortcut to the thousands of hours needed to lay down the traces on which expertise is based. And for each of us, our tradition is unique: with those thousands of hours each of us will lay down different traces of thoughts and actions, from which our new thoughts and actions are created. So each of us will play, write and think in our own way – though sometimes with remarkable flexibility (musicians and poets can 'impersonate' each other; and generations of physics students can and do learn to reason in Newton's shadow). Yet the same points arise in our everyday lives – our fears and worries, our sometimes bumpy interactions with other people. Our freedom consists not in the ability magically to transform ourselves in a single jump, but to reshape our thoughts and behaviours, one step at a time: our current thoughts and actions are continually, if slowly, re-programming our minds.

The ideas in this book are drawn from a wide range of sources, ranging from cognitive, social and clinical psychology, to philosophy and neuroscience. Perhaps the most fundamental inspiration for me has come from attempts to understand the brain as a biological computing machine. Scientists have been considering how vast networks of biological neurons are able to serve as powerful computational machines since the Second World War. Such 'connectionist', or brain-style, models of computation work very differently from the familiar digital computers that have revolutionized all our lives – although connectionist computation, in the form of so-called 'deep neural networks', is currently sweeping all before it in the project of building intelligent learning machines.

Connectionist models work through a process of 'cooperation' between vast numbers of neurons: filling in, and arranging, fragments of information – rather like simultaneously jiggling the pieces of a jigsaw into place. But it is very hard to reconcile this vision of the machinery of the brain with our everyday intuitions that our minds are guided by beliefs and desires. Our common-sense psychology attempts to explain our behaviour by summoning beliefs, motives, hopes and fears, sequenced into a reasoned argument. So an everyday explanation of why I headed down to the shop on a fruitless attempt to buy a newspaper might involve beliefs (that the shop is open; that it sells my favourite paper; that I have money with me) and desires (to read this particular paper; a preference for the print rather than the online edition). And this explanation makes sense because it can be arranged into a credible justification for my actions – the type of justification I might provide to explain why my actions, though unsuccessful, were entirely reasonable. Rather like mathematical proofs, arguments are formulated step-by-step (I'd like a copy of *The Western Bugle*. I could read it online, but spend my life looking at a screen; I bet they sell it at the corner shop; and surely the shop must be open at this time of day. Oh, I'll need some cash, but luckily I just went to the bank, and so on). We introduce assumptions, draw conclusions, add more assumptions, draw further conclusions, and so on. But this step-by-step style of thinking is difficult to reconcile with the simultaneous and cooperative 'jiggling' of multiple constraints that seems to be involved in recognizing a face, a musical style or an object. Indeed, we don't have very convincing 'arguments' for why I think a cartoon is of Winston Churchill, a snippet of music is Motown, or a glimpsed shape in the water is a seal or the Loch Ness monster. In short, common-sense psychology sees our thought and behaviour as rooted in reasoning, but a lot of human intelligence seems to be a matter of finding complex patterns.

Cooperative connectionist computation does not merely appear to clash with the reason-based explanations of common-sense psychology. It is also extremely difficult to reconcile with many scientific theories of human thought, from areas as diverse as artificial intelligence, cognitive, developmental and clinical psychology, linguistics and behavioural economics – theories that have taken common-sense ideas about minds stocked with beliefs, desires and the like as their starting point. Taking account of the computational style of the brain threatens, therefore, to have some far-reaching, and potentially destructive, consequences. After thirty years working with computational and mathematical models of the mind, and surveying and gathering experimental data, I have come to accept that our intuitive conceptions of our own minds, and many of our scientific theories of the mind that have been built upon that conception, are fundamentally flawed.

From a broader perspective, perhaps this should not surprise us. The entire history of science has been a tale of one astonishing shock after another: that the Earth goes around the sun; that the chemical elements of which it was composed were expelled from dying stars; that matter can turn into energy; that life is encoded in a double helix of chemicals; and that our distant ancestors were single-celled organisms. The very idea that thought is the product of a whirr of electrical and chemical activity across a hundred billion nerve cells is remarkable enough. Indeed, in this book I will argue that almost everything we think we know about the operation of our own minds – our intuitive introspections, justifications and explanations – needs to be abandoned wholesale.

There is a rich tradition of scepticism about our common-sense view of our minds. Psychologists and philosophers, from B. F. Skinner to Daniel Dennett, have long doubted our abilities to introspect the contents of our minds or perceptions; and many have suspected that the beliefs, motives, hopes and desires with which we justify our thoughts and actions are no more real than the Garden of Eden, the four humours of Hippocratic medicine, or the principles of astrology.

Some past sceptics about those common-sense stories have a very different agenda: doubting, for example, that the brain is any kind of computer at all.[5] This has always seemed a puzzling line to me: the brain's function is surely to integrate information from perception and memory, to figure out the state of the world, and to decide what to do. In short, the brain faces spectacularly complex information-processing challenges – and 'information-processing' is really just another label for computation. I'm going to take it as uncontroversial that the brain is a biological computing machine.

What is, and should be, controversial is the proposal that our theory of the calculations that the brain carries out match up, in some fairly direct way, with our common-sense psychological explanation in terms of beliefs and desires and the like – a viewpoint that has been widely held ever since early computational models of the mind took hold in the 1950s. It would, indeed, be awfully convenient if it turned out that our mind contained a database containing the very sorts of beliefs, desires, hopes and fears that we talk about in everyday life. Building intelligent machines would be off to a flying start if it happened that we could just *ask* people what they knew – and write this knowledge directly into a computer database. So the thesis that the stories we tell ourselves about how we think are roughly true would be highly convenient for cognitive science and artificial intelligence *if true*.

But common-sense psychology *isn't true*. We'll see that a very different picture emerges from psychological experiments, the 'wiring' of brain circuits, and the processing mechanisms in modern machine-learning and artificial intelligence that are inspired by cooperative, brain-style computation. Our 'computational innards' are not a churning sea of experiences, feelings, beliefs, desires, hopes and fears, whether conscious or unconscious. Our mind spins stories about how we work – driven by motives, beliefs, percepts, moral norms, religious precepts. And they are such compelling stories that we can imagine that they are true, or partially true, or surely at least along the right general lines.

In reality, though, the rich mental world we imagine that we are 'looking in on' moment-by-moment, is actually a story that we are inventing moment-by-moment. A real Anna Karenina would no more have an 'inner mental world' than a fictional Anna Karenina. If this is right, then there is no more hope of finding a real Anna's 'inner feelings', 'deep beliefs' or 'true nature' by probing her brain, than there would be of uncovering the inner life of the fictional Anna by a scientific analysis of the ink and paper of Tolstoy's manuscript.

*

I have struggled long and hard to swallow this troubling truth, for several reasons. The first is that some of the psychological data just seem too extraordinary to believe. For example, the psychological data tell me that my brain can identify just one word at a time, but looking at the text in front of me, I have the overwhelming impression that I am simultaneously, if slightly tenuously, aware of the identities of words across entire paragraphs. The experimental data tell me that I can, roughly, identify *one object at a time*. Yet as I scan the room, I feel that I am taking in almost an entire roomful of sofas, cushions, books, glasses, plants and pieces of paper. The list of counter-intuitive experiments and strange quirks of the brain tells a story so downright peculiar that it is easy to imagine that there must be some mistake or misunderstanding. For our intuitions to be so wrong about the contents and workings of our own minds implies that we are subject to a systematic and all-pervasive illusion. I have now, somewhat reluctantly, come to the conclusion that almost everything we think we know about our own minds is a hoax, played on us by our own brains. We will see later how the hoax is done, and why it is so compelling.

The second reason for my long resistance to adopting the radical perspective outlined in this book is that it clashes, not just with common sense, but with theories of perception, reasoning, categorization, decision-making and more, which have been central to psychology, cognitive science, artificial intelligence, linguistics and behavioural economics. So much of our most sophisticated thinking in these disciplines has involved extending, modifying and elaborating our intuitive conception of our minds – an intuitive conception that is founded on an illusion. Jettisoning such a large portion of the ideas in disciplines I have been closely involved with for so long feels a little like vandalism.

The final reason I have held on so long to our everyday picture of the mind is simply the lack of a credible alternative. Yet in the light of advances in 'brain-style' computation, and machine-learning more broadly, I think that the outline of a credible alternative is beginning to emerge.[6] Increasingly, researchers are finding that the best way to make computers display intelligent behaviour is not to attempt to extract the knowledge and beliefs that people say they rely on; it is far more effective to create intelligent behaviour by designing machines that can learn from experience. So, for example, when trying to write a computer program to play world-class backgammon, chess or Go, it turns out to be unhelpful to 'program in' knowledge, insights and strategies that top human players claim they are using. It is much better to learn, bottom-up, from the experience of playing vast numbers of games – and, indeed, machine-learning programs are now able to beat the best human players in these and many other games.

This has been a delightful, though slightly unsettling, book to write. As an academic, now in the Behavioural Science Group at Warwick Business School, I have worked mostly on quite specific, though varied, aspects of the mind, from reasoning to decision-making, from perception to language. I have also worked on a wide range of practical behavioural science projects with my colleagues at Decision Technology Ltd. In both the academic and practical worlds, it pays to be circumspect and not to stray too far into unfamiliar territory. This book takes the opposite approach: throwing caution to the wind, I want to give you the most compelling story I can about how the mind works. And in truth, I don't just want to tell this story to you, the reader. I want to tell this story to myself: to zoom out from the patchwork of observations, data and theory that are my daily life and ask 'what does it all mean?' This requires joining up dots, extrapolating exuberantly from the specific to the general, and engaging in doses of outright speculation. Drawing together data and insights from more than a century of psychology, philosophy and neuroscience, the resulting picture is strange, radical and liberating. This viewpoint has, I think, been coalescing in many areas of the cognitive and brain sciences over the past few decades, even as much of the field has continued to proceed with 'business as usual'. But business as usual won't do: when we take seriously what science is telling us about the mind and the brain, we are forced to reconsider just about everything we thought we knew about ourselves. This requires a systematic rethink of large parts of psychology, neuroscience and the social sciences, but it also requires a radical shake-up of how each of us thinks about ourselves and those around us.

I have had a lot of help writing this book. My thinking has been shaped by decades of conversations with Mike Oaksford and Morten

Christiansen, and discussions over the years with John Anderson, Gordon Brown, Ulrike Hahn, Geoff Hinton, Richard Holton, George Loewenstein, Jay McClelland, Adam Sanborn, Jerry Seligman, Neil Stewart, Josh Tenenbaum and James Tresilian, and so many other wonderful friends and colleagues. Writing this book has been supported by generous financial support through grants from the ERC (grant 295917-RATIONALITY), the ESRC Network for Integrated Behavioural Science (grant number ES/Koo2201/1) and the Leverhulme Trust (grant number RP2012-V-022). My colleagues at the Behavioural Science Group at Warwick Business School have provided the perfect intellectual environment for a wide-ranging and downright speculative project such as this; and the interdisciplinary and innovative spirit of the University of Warwick has been an inspiration. This book has benefited hugely from the insights, suggestions and encouragement of my wonderful agent, Catherine Clarke at Felicity Bryan Associates, and of Alexis Kirshbaum and Laura Stickney, my editors at Penguin. I am also grateful to my wife, Louie Fooks, and our daughters Maya and Caitlin Fooks, for their unstinting support throughout this book's uncomfortable and lengthy gestation, for their critical discussions of its arguments, but most importantly for being delightful people with whom to share a life. Finally, I would like to thank my parents, Robert and Dorothy Chater: without their faith in me, and their continuous love and support, I would probably have never persisted long in research, still less written this book.

Nick Chater
Coventry, 2017

PART ONE

The Illusion of Mental Depth

I

The Power of Invention

Mervyn Peake's Gormenghast Castle is one of the strangest settings for a work of fiction – vast, misshapen, ancient, crumbling and architecturally idiosyncratic. Peake's visual imagination was wonderful – he was an artist and illustrator as much as a writer – and his sharp and striking descriptions create a sense of a world of solidity, richness and detail. As you read his novels *Titus Groan* and *Gormenghast*, Gormenghast Castle begins to inhabit your imagination. Over the years, some particularly committed, and perhaps slightly obsessive, readers have tried to piece together the geography of the castle from its scattered descriptions. Yet this appears to be an impossible task: the attempt to draw a map, or build a model, of Gormenghast Castle leads to inconsistency and confusion – the descriptions of great hallways and battlements, libraries and kitchens, networks of passages and vast, almost deserted wings can't be reconciled. They are as tangled and self-contradictory as the inhabitants of the castle itself.

Peake's verbal magic aside, this should not be surprising. Creating a fictional place is a bit like setting a crossword. Each description provides another 'clue' to the layout of the castle, city or country being imagined. But as the number of clues increases, knitting them together successfully soon becomes extraordinarily difficult – indeed, it rapidly becomes impossible, both for *Gormenghast*'s readers and for Peake himself.

Troubles with the coherence of fictional worlds go far beyond mere geography, of course. Stories have to make sense in so many ways: through consistency of plot, character and a myriad of details. Some authors go to inordinate pains to minimize such mishaps: J. R. R. Tolkien set *The Hobbit* and *The Lord of the Rings* in a world – Middle-earth – with a detailed history, mythology and geography, complete with maps, to say nothing of invented 'Elvish' languages with extensive vocabulary and grammar. At the other extreme, Richmal Crompton, author of the stories of the charmingly roguish schoolboy William Brown, sketched in the details of her stories with considerable abandon, and cheerfully admitted flagrant inconsistencies (the hero's mother is sometimes Mary, sometimes Margaret; his best friend is either Ginger Flowerdew or Ginger Merridew).

So inconsistencies are one thing that make fiction different from fact: the actual world may *seem* puzzling, paradoxical and downright contrary, but it cannot actually be self-contradictory; and while a description of a castle or a country can turn out to make no sense, an actual castle or country is, by its very existence, perfectly consistent – all the facts, distances, photographs, theodolite measurements, satellite imagery and geological soundings must yield a coherent picture – because there is just one unique, actual world. But with fictional worlds, avoiding inconsistency requires incredible vigilance. Despite the painstaking efforts of a brilliant and remarkably retentive mind, Tolkien's Middle-earth has yielded a haul of apparent inconsistencies, when scoured by its huge fanbase.

Fictional 'worlds', even the immensely detailed worlds of Peake and Tolkien, are notable too for their sheer sparseness. In real life, everyone has a specific birthday, fingerprint and an exact number of teeth. In fictional worlds, most characters have none of these properties, or any of a million others, whether significant (having a recessive gene for haemophilia) or trivial (the precise family relation to Elvis[1]).

But, of course, the scarcity of information in fiction is much more profound than this. Consider again Anna Karenina, whose public persona, relationships and, perhaps, sense of her own identity, depend on her beauty. Yet what did she look like? Artist and celebrated book-cover designer Peter Mendelsund points out that Tolstoy says astonishingly little – that she has thick lashes, a thin down of hair on her upper lip and scarcely more.[2] Is she tall or short? Blonde, redhead or brunette? Blue-eyed or brown-eyed? The astonishing thing is not that Tolstoy tells us so little, but that we don't notice and, still less, care. We can read the book with the subjective feeling that it is the story of a flesh-and-blood, three-dimensional woman, rather than a blurry stick figure, but Tolstoy tells us almost nothing about *which* flesh-and-blood, three-dimensional woman.

One might retort, of course, that literary fiction is not about the physical appearance of characters, but about the inner life of the mind. Yet the truth is that Anna's mind is just as vaguely sketched as her body: what sort of person is Anna, exactly? How would it feel to have a conversation with her? How does she view the Russian state and its vast inequalities? Is she both defiant of, and crushed by, the opprobrium she receives in pursuing her affair with Vronsky? The wonder of Tolstoy's novel is that these questions are not answered, but are tantalizingly and fascinatingly open: we can 'read' Anna in a variety of ways: as heroic, obsessive, romantic, defiant, wild, oppressed, loving, or cold, in various degrees and combinations. But this very openness implies, of course, that Anna's characteristics, whether physical or mental, are not pinned down by the text of the novel.

Consider, now, the 'real Anna' we imagined in the Prologue. Suppose, indeed, that the novel were novelized biography, rather than pure fiction. Then all those missing facts about Anna (her precise physical appearance, her genome, her relationship to Elvis) would all be completely well defined. We might be able to figure some of them out, through concerted research (e.g. careful genealogical analysis might reveal a common ancestor with Elvis in, perhaps, seventeenth-century Kiev); other facts (e.g. her height on her eleventh birthday) might be neither known nor knowable, given the surviving traces from her life. But is there a true 'reading' of Anna's life, a precise delineation of her personality traits, motives and beliefs, if we only knew more?

Recall the two characteristics of fiction we mentioned earlier – inconsistency and sparseness. If Anna were to explain her own inner life, she would surely be as jumbled, incoherent and self-contradictory as Mervyn Peake's Gormenghast Castle. Her explanations would be inherently sparse – she might have little idea of her views on many aspects of Russian society, the people around her, her own goals and aspirations, and many other topics she has scarcely considered. While the real Anna really would have a family relationship to Elvis, she would surely not have precisely defined views on the merits of different modes of Russian agricultural reform or the future of the Tsar. She could, of course, create and articulate opinions, on demand. But these opinions would themselves be both vague and liable to fall into self-contradiction. The real Anna's mind would be just as much a work of fiction as the fictional Anna's mind; our own minds are no more 'real'. Whereas the fictional Anna is a sketchy and contradictory character created by Tolstoy's brain, a real Anna would be an equally sketchy and contradictory character, created by her own brain.

The external world is quite the opposite, of course. It is specified in complete detail, whether we know the details or not. My coffee mug was bought on a particularly day of the week and fired at a particular temperature, in a specific kiln; it has a particular weight and distance from the equator. And the real world is relentlessly consistent: for facts to hold good in the same world, they cannot be contradictory.

By contrast, our beliefs, values, emotions and other mental traits are, I suggest, as tangled, self-contradictory and incompletely spelled out as the labyrinths of Gormenghast Castle. It is in this very concrete sense that characters are all fictional, including our own. Inconsistency and sparseness are not just characteristics of fiction. They are also the hallmarks of mental life.

ARTIFICIAL INTELLIGENCE AND THE 'INNER ORACLE'

It is hardly controversial that our thoughts *seem* fragmentary and contradictory. But can't the gaps be filled in and the contradictions somehow resolved? The world and mind of Anna Karenina are defined by Tolstoy's text – there is no 'ground truth' that can fill out the details. But perhaps with real people, there might be such a ground truth, if only we search hard enough. Perhaps, somewhere within us, lies a complete specification of our beliefs, motives, desires, values, plans and more. Perhaps we have rich mental depths – a complete and coherent inner realm from which our thoughts and actions consistently follow. Perhaps we can uncover the contents of such inner depths, if we only search hard enough: we can consult our 'inner oracle' by asking ourselves to outline and explain our knowledge as clearly as we can. If so, we could then try to piece together the 'wisdom' of the inner oracle, from a careful study of its utterances; through weeding out its inconsistencies and filling in the gaps.

Might this work? The only way to find out is to try. And try we have. Two thousand years of philosophy have been devoted to the problem of 'clarifying' many of our common-sense ideas: causality, the good, space, time, knowledge, mind, and many more. Science and mathematics began with our common-sense ideas, but ended up having to distort them so drastically – whether 'heat', 'weight', 'force' or 'energy' – that they were refashioned into entirely new, sophisticated concepts, with often counter-intuitive consequences. We don't intuitively distinguish between heat and temperature; common-sense doesn't distinguish weight, mass and momentum; we imagine (as did Aristotle) that if no force is acting on a body, it comes to rest – whereas in reality it keeps moving at a constant velocity; we have no intuitive idea that heat is a kind of energy; or that energy can be stored by moving objects uphill, carrying out chemical reactions, stretching elastic bands, and so on.

The laws of motion, thermodynamics and more that govern the physical world are strange and counter-intuitive. Indeed, this is one reason that 'real' physics took centuries to discover, and presents a fresh challenge to each generation of students. Whatever our inner oracle, hidden somewhere in our mental depths, might know, it can't be anything like physics.[3]

Now, of course, no one seriously proposes that each of us has an inner Newton, Darwin and Einstein – or rather inner representations of their astonishing theoretical achievements – generating our common-sense explanations of the physical world. But maybe our inner oracle has something different: a simple, intuitive, approximate physics, biology or psychology. Perhaps our thoughts are guided by common-sense theories which, while nothing like the theories painstakingly created by science, might be theories none the less.

This is a seductive idea. Indeed, starting in the 1950s, decades of intellectual effort were poured into a particularly sophisticated and concerted attempt to crystallize some of our common-sense theories. The goal was to systematize and organize human thought in order to replicate it and to create machines that think like people. This was the guiding idea in the early years of one of the great technological challenges of our time: the goal of creating artificial intelligence.

The pioneers of artificial intelligence in the 1950s, 1960s and beyond, and their collaborators in cognitive psychology, philosophy and linguistics, took the idea of mental depth very seriously. Indeed, they took it for granted that the thoughts that we consciously experience and can put into words are drawn from a vast sea, or web, or database of similar, pre-formed thoughts, which we are not currently consciously experiencing. Behind each expressed thought lies, supposedly, a thousand others beneath the surface. And all this hidden knowledge is, it was assumed, organized into theories, rather than being a hopeless jumble. So to emulate human intelligence, the starting strategy is:

> Step 1. To excavate our mental depths, and to bring to the surface as much of this supposed inner storehouse of beliefs as we can.

> Step 2. To organize and systematize this knowledge to recover our hidden 'common-sense theory'. To encode this knowledge in a computer database involves expressing it in a tidy and precise formal language that the computer can work with, rather than merely noting it down in 'plain English'.

> Step 3. To devise computational methods to reason over this database, in order to use this common-sense knowledge to make sense of new experiences, use language, solve problems, make choices, plans and conversation, and generally to engage in intelligent behaviour.

Early attempts to create artificially intelligent computer programs to replicate human intelligence took precisely this approach. There were plenty of sceptical philosophers and psychologists who felt that this method was doomed from the outset – people who suspected, in our terms, that mental depth might be an illusion. But the researchers were undeterred. If there was a *chance* that the approach might succeed, it was surely well worth attempting – the achievement of creating genuinely intelligent machines by capturing and recreating our own understanding of the world would be so spectacular.

And hopes were high. Over successive decades, leading researchers forecast that human-level intelligence would be achieved within twenty to thirty years. Yet progress seemed slower, and the challenges far greater, than had been imagined. By the 1970s, serious doubts began to set in; by the 1980s, the programme of mining and systematizing knowledge started to grind to a halt. Indeed, the project of modelling human intelligence has since been quietly abandoned, in favour of specialist projects in computer vision, speech-processing, machine translation, game-playing, robotics and self-driving vehicles. Artificial intelligence since the 1980s has been astonishingly successful in tackling these specialized problems. This success has come, though, from completely bypassing the extraction of human knowledge into common-sense theories.

Instead, over recent decades, AI researchers have made advances by building machines that learn not from people but from direct confrontation with the problem to be solved: much of AI has mutated into a distinct but related field: machine-learning. Machine-learning works by extracting information not from people, but from huge quantities of data: images, speech waves, linguistic corpora, chess games, and so on. And this has been possible because of advances on a number of fronts: computers have become faster, data sets larger and learning methods cleverer. But at no stage have human beliefs been mined or common-sense theories reconstructed.

THE ILLUSION OF EXPLANATORY DEPTH

The project of creating artificial intelligence by extracting, systematizing and reasoning with human thoughts – trying to coax out the 'theories' of our inner oracle – failed in a particularly instructive way. The very first step, drawing out the knowledge, beliefs, motives, and so on, that underpinned people's behaviour, turned out to be hopelessly difficult. People can fluently generate verbal explanations and justifications of their thoughts and actions; and, whenever parts of those explanations are queried, out will tumble further verbal explanation or justification. But analysis of these streams of verbal description, however long they continue, shows that they are little more than a series of loosely connected fragments. Chess grandmasters, it turns out, can't really explain how they play chess; doctors can't explain how they diagnose patients; and none of us can remotely explain how we understand the everyday world of people and objects. What we say *sounds* like explanation – but really it is a terrible jumble that we are making up as we go along.

This becomes all too obvious when artificial intelligence research attempts to carry out Step 2: arranging and organizing the fragments into a coherent and reasonably complete form to create the database for the artificial intelligence system. This is a hopeless task: the fragments of knowledge that people generate are both woefully under-specified and fatally self-contradictory. So it was scarcely possible to get started on Step 3: getting computers to do reasoning with any extracted human knowledge.

It turned out, indeed, that even the simplest aspects of knowledge, about the very most basic properties of the everyday world, proved completely intractable. For example, artificial intelligence researchers had hoped to extract the common-sense physics that was presumed to govern our everyday interactions with the physical world. In the 1960s and 1970s, this seemed a good place to start the project of capturing human knowledge.[4] Yet half a century later, we are still at square one.

To understand why, let us focus for a moment on a familiar aspect of common-sense physics: the knowledge that we apparently all share about the behaviour of everyday objects and substances. Specifically, let us think about what we know about the behaviour of coffee, ball-bearings and sugar when dropped onto the kitchen floor. As we all know, the coffee would splash and settle in various sized puddles and blobs; the sugar might form a shallow heap or spread more evenly across the floor; and the ball-bearings would scatter in all directions, disappearing under units and appliances.

So we know roughly how everyday things behave. But it is surprisingly difficult to explain convincingly *why* any of these things is true. We can certainly generate lengthy explanations. The coffee spreads out, we might say, because it is trying to 'find a level'. But quite why some coffee stays on the floor and some breaks free into droplets and splashes is not explained by the 'find a level' intuition. Perhaps one clue is that water, the main ingredient of liquid coffee, likes to stick together, which would explain why coffee moves through the air in streams and droplets, and why it holds together in rounded puddles and patches. This story could, as you can imagine, be extended indefinitely.

Now what about sugar? This doesn't splash like coffee for some reason; it also doesn't seem to 'stick' together. It spreads out a little on impact with the floor but not much – this must be something to do with its roughness and with some consequent friction when it tries to move. Would this be different if the sugar were super-fine or super-coarse? Is coffee behaving a little like frictionless, or nearly frictionless, sugar? Presumably the sugar wants to find a level, like coffee, but much less so – though if it is blown by a draught or a fan it can gradually create a fairly even covering over the floor. Ball-bearings are different again, being smooth, hard and having no tendency to stick together – when one ball-bearing lands on another with a glancing blow, both can shoot off in any direction. Quite how this works is not too clear. Somehow the bounciness of ball-bearings is important – balls of putty would behave very differently. And this is odd, as ball-bearings do not seem very elastic (unlikely rubber balls).

Now suppose that coffee, sugar or ball-bearings were being dropped into an empty plastic bucket – or a bucket full of water – or any of a number of variations. You can generate verbal explanations for this too. One point to note is that each explanation seems to be new, different and typically incompatible with the last one, rather than following from a single set of underlying principles – the explanations of every new scenario just seem to run off on all directions, apparently without limit. Moreover, each step in each explanation can itself be queried. Why does water tend to 'find a level?' Why do ball-bearings bounce off each other? Why does sugar change consistency as it enters the bucket of water? And so on.[5]

We have run, predictably enough, into the twin problems of sparseness and incoherence. Our explanations have holes everywhere and inconsistencies abound. Indeed, psychologists have a phrase, 'the illusion of explanatory depth', for the bizarre contrast between our feeling of understanding and our inability to produce cogent explanations.[6]

Whether explaining how a fridge works, how to steer a bicycle, or the origin of the tides, we have a feeling of understanding which seems wildly out of balance with the mangled and self-contradictory explanations we actually come up with.

Perhaps the single most important discovery from the first decades of artificial intelligence is just how profound and irremediable this problem is. The starting assumption was that our intuitive verbal explanations just need to be fleshed out and patched up – that there must be a common-sense theory in there 'deep down' if we only looked hard enough. Our assumptions need to be firmed up, and our concepts knocked into shape. The hope was that, with a bit of order and organization, verbal descriptions could be distilled into a form that could be turned into clear, comprehensive theories that could be coded up by computer programmers.

But the opposite proved to be the case. Armies of artificial intelligence researchers, with an impressive combination of raw ingenuity, mathematical firepower and sheer tenacity, struggled to squash verbal knowledge into a usable form. And they have consistently failed. Our verbal explanations of the physical world – but equally of the social, economic worlds or our moral or aesthetic judgements – turn out not to be a confused description of inner clarity, but a confused description of inner confusion.

Our verbal explanations and justifications are not reports of stable, pre-formed building blocks of knowledge, coherent theories over which we reason, deep in an inner mental world. They are ad hoc, provisional and invented on the spot. We have consulted the inner oracle of common-sense physics, psychology, ethics and much more hoping to uncover its hidden wisdom. But the oracle turns out to be a fraud, a fantasist, a master of confabulation.

TRUE BELIEVERS IN THE INNER ORACLE

We have vastly underestimated our powers of invention. Our 'inner oracle' is such a good storyteller – so fluent and convincing – that it fools us completely. But the mental depths our mind conjures up are no more real than the worlds of Gormenghast or Middle-earth. The mind is flat: our mental 'surface', the momentary thoughts, explanations and sensory experiences that make up our stream of consciousness is all there is to mental life.

The illusion of mental depth is much more pervasive than it appears at first sight. Two and a half millennia of philosophy have tried to systematize our intuitions and verbal explanations about core concepts, from 'the good' to the nature of objects and events, mind and body, knowledge, belief or causality. This only makes sense if there *is* a coherent way of fitting together our intuitions and explanations using these categories. Yet no such coherent theories are ever outlined.

In the late nineteenth and twentieth century, philosophers in what was to become the analytic tradition began to explore what became a hugely influential approach to wrestling the chaos of common sense into shape. Gottlob Frege, Bertrand Russell, the early Wittgenstein and many others attempted to regiment common sense through understanding the language in which it was expressed and, specifically, to focus on clarifying the 'logical structure' of language through exploring and systematizing intuitions about *meaning*. Getting language and meaning 'straight' was seen as a crucial stepping stone to launch an indirect attack on big philosophical questions. The idea was that many of the confusions in our thoughts would disappear if only we could clarify how those thoughts are captured in language. Yet it turned out that our intuitions about language and meaning are also hopelessly full of gaps and contradictions. Intuitions are either absent, or conflict horribly, over such elementary questions as the meaning of names (e.g. there is deep puzzlement over tricky cases such as Homer – more 'oral tradition' than author? – or Sherlock Holmes or any fictional character, people with noms de plume, multiple people with the same name, and so on). Again, the very idea that there is some inner coherent theory of meaning that can be drawn out by intuition and reflection is misguided – our use of, and thoughts about, the meaning of our language is a chaotic, incoherent jumble.

After careful reflection on our contradictory intuitions about meaning, truth, knowledge, value, mind, causality, or whatever common-sense notion is under analysis, philosophers are able to fill in a gap here and iron out a contradiction there. But new gaps and fresh contradictions continually appear. If the mind is a confabulator, not a theorist, no such theory of our common-sense intuitions about anything can be constructed, any more than enthusiastic fans would ever be able to draw a map of Gormenghast Castle.[7]

In a parallel development, linguists began to pursue the project of systematizing the structure of language, following Noam Chomsky's project of generative grammar: the goal was to systematize our intuitions about which sentences are acceptable into a mathematically rigorous theory, which was assumed to capture the nature of each person's knowledge of the language. Yet this programme too has foundered: it turns out that even the structural patterns observed in language – not just its meaning – are a jumble of inconsistent regularities, sub-regularities and outright exceptions.[8]

The same story applies in economics. Economists worked on the assumption that consumers and companies would have a complete and consistent theory of the 'world' (or the economically relevant parts anyway), including a complete understanding of their own preferences. The behaviour of markets could be seen as 'emerging' from the interaction of these 'super-rational' agents. This programme, for all its mathematical elegance, has also foundered. For one thing, countless experiments in psychology and behavioural economics have shown just how spectacularly ill-defined and self-contradictory our beliefs and preferences are. For another, the confusion of individual decision-makers (their exuberant hopes, desperate panics, their tendency to blindly follow or wildly over-react) can generate unexpected turbulence at the level of markets or of entire economies.

The idea that people have complete and consistent theories of the world, and preferences as to what they want, is also widely presupposed in business and policy. Market researchers try to work out what goods or services we want. Decision analysts attempt to distil the beliefs and preferences of the many stakeholders in complex projects such as airports or power stations. Health economists try to put stable monetary valuations on disease, disability and life itself. All of these projects are bedevilled by the same problem: the inconsistent and partial nature of our intuitions. People routinely supply wildly different answers to exactly the same question (even within a few minutes), and their answers to different questions are often inconsistent; there is the same variation in their actual choices (people can express a high valuation of their own life, but still engage in dangerous behaviour). And often we are expressing views about matters (for example nuclear power, climate change, or whether a new cancer drug should be funded by the government) where our explanations are shallow indeed – most of us understand these matters no better than we understand the operation of our fridge. We may or may not have strong opinions, but these opinions don't – and could not possibly – spring from coherent and fully spelt-out common-sense theories. There are, as the artificial intelligence 'experiment' showed, no such theories to be extracted. The problem, in short, is that our intuitions about everyday physics, psychology, morality, meaning, or what we want, are no more coherent than Peake's description of Gormenghast Castle.

Yet we are often seduced by a very different picture – that the confusions and contradictions in our thoughts and lives must represent a clash between multiple, and conflicting, selves. Perhaps, for example, we believe that we are the product of a conflict between a 'conscious self' and also a hidden, perhaps dark, atavistic 'unconscious self'. But the incoherent nature of the 'self', and the thoughts, motives and beliefs it is supposed to contain, is not explained by adding extra selves, any more than the incoherence of Peake's description of Gormenghast Castle is resolved by postulating multiple castles.[9]

PSYCHOLOGY: ART OR SCIENCE?

I've spent decades being pulled towards, and at the same time desperately resisting, the conclusions in this book, as I mentioned in the Prologue. This may strike you as puzzling. For many people, the idea that we are, at bottom, story-spinning improvisers, interpreting and reinterpreting the world in the moment, is immediately appealing for a variety of reasons.

For one thing, the fact that our thoughts don't cohere together in a way that can be replicated in a computer may seem to provide a welcome defence against the idea that human freedom, creativity and ingenuity can be reduced to mere calculation.

Moreover, the 'mind is flat' perspective can seem entirely natural – perhaps even old news – from the perspective of the arts, literature and humanities, where there is a long tradition of seeing people and their actions as the subjects of conflicting, fragmented and endlessly re-created interpretation. Indeed, many scholars would go further and argue that the right conclusion to draw from our reflections is that human nature cannot, and should not, be understood from a scientific point of view at all. Perhaps we should simply embrace our intuitive interpretations of ourselves and each other, with all their gaps and contradictions, as all there is to say about human behaviour.

According to this perspective, psychology should be aligned with the arts and the humanities rather than the sciences; perhaps understanding ourselves is inevitably just a matter of eliciting, reflecting on, analysing, challenging and reconceptualizing our interpretations of thought and behaviour; and interpretations of other people's interpretations; and so on, indefinitely. If so, then perhaps we should create a psychology in which everyone has a valid perspective on themselves and everyone else, in which any view can be re-analysed, contested, overturned or revived, which sees the understanding of mind and behaviour as an open-ended discussion, where there are no 'right answers' and never could be.

For many people, this is a thrilling and ennobling vision. I am not one of those people. I despair at the prospect that our understanding of ourselves will take us no further than our hopelessly inadequate intuitive explanations, reflected and distorted in an endless hall of mirrors of equally flawed and baseless intuitions. For me, this is not liberation but nihilism; not a freeing of psychology from the bonds of sciences, but the total abandonment of the project of understanding ourselves through the application of science.

Viewing psychology as part of the arts and humanities is to react to the illusion of mental depth in, I think, precisely the wrong way: it embraces the ad hoc, the improvised, the partial and contradictory style of everyday verbal explanation of our thoughts and behaviours, and adds endless layers of further, ever more convoluted, verbal speculation, whether about dreams, associations, complexes, multiple selves, metaphors, archetypes, phenomenology, and more. Turning a wild, creative but entirely untrustworthy imagination upon itself could scarcely be expected to lead to reliable results. This would be like explaining the origin of fairy tales by means of yet another fairy tale.

A science of the mind requires the opposite approach: understanding how the 'engine of improvisation' that is the core of human intelligence can be constructed out of the machinery of the human brain. The brain is, after all, ultimately a biological machine – specifically, a machine constructed from a network of about a hundred billion brain cells, densely wired together. It is a biological machine that creates, improvises, dreams and imagines. One of the deepest challenges in science is to figure out how this can possibly work – to understand how electrical and chemical activity in our neural circuits can somehow generate our stream of thought and actions.

Early artificial intelligence explored one tack – and initially a very appealing one – which makes perfect sense if we assume that the human brain operates according to roughly the same principles as the type of computer on which the researchers were writing their computer programs – and, indeed, on which I am writing these words. The symbolic explanations we generate in everyday language don't seem so far from the symbolic representations used in computer language and databases. We just need to knock our intuitive verbal explanations into shape a bit – fill in the gaps and iron out the inconsistencies – and, perhaps, we can turn them into the contents of our inner database, over which symbolic calculations can occur. So the researchers take the stories, justifications, intuitions and explanations that we spin at face value; and try to systematize and organize these into theories over which a machine might reason. Yet, as we have seen, this approach has never worked, and can never work: our stories are irreparably flimsy, inconsistent inventions, invented on the spot, rather than clues about deep inner theories.

But there has long been an alternative viewpoint: that biological computation is very different from the symbolic computation of conventional computers. In Part Two, we'll explore the so-called 'cooperative' style of computation used by the brain to tell a new story about how the mind works – how our continually inventive stream of thoughts arises from the machinery of the brain. But first we need to explore, and undermine, our existing intuitions about how our minds work more thoroughly. We need to clear the ground before we can build anew. It turns out that the illusion of mental depth is far more insidious and all-pervasive than we have seen so far. Unravelling our intuitions and seeing our minds afresh is the topic of the rest of Part One.

2

The Feeling of Reality

FROM WORDS TO PICTURES

Gormenghast *feels* like an entire, coherent world, even though it is nothing of the kind. Yet perhaps this is not so surprising. As we read a novel, we 'touch' the supposed fictional world, as it were, one word at a time. Glimpsing fragments through such a narrow window, it is quite likely that gaps and inconsistencies in the whole can slip by unnoticed. Invented stories are notoriously difficult to distinguish from true stories – both *feel* real. Indeed, fictional worlds, and their characters and castles, can often feel real even to their creators – who ought, one might think, to be particularly aware of their unreality. After all, authors often talk of their characters, and of the entire story, gradually taking on a 'life of their own'. But of course this is no more than a metaphor: the fictional world and its characters have no existence beyond the words committed to the page.

Now, though, consider the 'inner world' composed just of your *current sensory experience*. Rather than focusing on the unfolding chatter of your stream of consciousness, concentrate instead on your current mental 'picture' of the world, with all its colour, detail and clutter of objects. Surely our 'picture' of the sensory world isn't glimpsed, piece by piece, through a narrow window? It seems, instead, to be 'loaded' simultaneously into our mind as a coherent and unified whole. If so, surely this 'inner world' of momentary experience can't be incoherent: because we can simultaneously survey the whole, we would immediately spot any gaps or inconsistencies in our sensory experience, wouldn't we? Stories can have gaps and contradictions, but pictures can't. Can they?

Yet, as we'll see in this chapter, our sense of 'grasping' the entire visual world before us is also a hoax. Our mental 'pictures' of the world can have as many contradictions and gaps as any fictional world or common-sense explanation.

The Swedish artist Oscar Reutersvärd (1915–2002) devoted his life to the creation of 'impossible objects' of deceptive simplicity. In Figure 1, three of his famous images are shown on a rather elegant set of Swedish stamps. Each 'object', when viewed as a whole, looks like an entirely coherent and unexceptional three-dimensional geometric figure. But on closer inspection, the interpretations of the different parts of the figure just don't 'add up'.[1]

The left-hand stamp in Figure 1 has the general look of a fairly conventional geometric layout – lines of cubes floating in space. But as we consider it more closely, our brain comes to the unsettling realization that the apparent depths in different parts of the image just don't fit together. What is wrong, exactly? Disturbingly, the 3D interpretation of the parts of the image can't be made to fit together to create a unified 3D interpretation of the whole. These innocent-looking images, when interpreted in 3D, turn out to be self-contradictory. They look like 3D objects, but they are not.

The phenomenon of 'impossible objects' may seem to be no more than a momentarily entrancing party trick, but it provides deep insights into the nature of perception, and a powerful metaphor for the nature of thought.

What, then, do impossible objects tell us? I think we can draw out

Figure 1. Oscar Reutersvärd's images of impossible objects were celebrated in a series of rather beautiful Swedish stamps.

three conclusions, which will, in various forms, be recurring themes throughout this book. First of all, they tell us that there is something badly wrong with our common-sense ideas about how perception works. According to our common-sense view, the senses map the outer world into some kind of inner copy, so that, when perceiving a book, table or coffee cup, our minds are conjuring up a shadowy 'mental' book, table or coffee cup. The mind is a 'mirror' of nature.[2] But this can't be right. There can't be a 3D 'mental copy' of these objects – because they don't make sense in 3D. They are like 3D jig-saw puzzles whose pieces simply don't fit together. The mind-as-mirror metaphor can't possibly be right; we need a very different viewpoint – that perception requires *inference*.

Second, the way we experience impossible objects implies the brain 'grasps' different aspects of the image at different times. We scan the different parts of the figures, and find that each, considered in isolation, has a perfectly coherent depth. The 3D interpretations of each part (e.g. a particular strut, cube or plane) seem perfectly con-sistent. But these interpretations just don't fit together into a coherent whole. Our brain glimpses, and conceives of, the world fragment by fragment.

The third lesson concerns our misplaced confidence. When view-ing an impossible object, we have the overwhelming sense that we are looking at a 3D scene, albeit a peculiar one. But this 'feeling' of solid-ity is completely misguided – we are actually looking at a flat image that has no possible 3D interpretation.[3] This is yet another illus-tration of the illusions of depth. These illusions of depth, which can be both literal, as with impossible figures, and metaphorical, as with stories and explanations, are everywhere.

THE SPARSENESS OF SENSORY EXPERIENCE

So the visual 'world' can be contradictory. But is it also full of gaps? This isn't how things *seem*. Surveying the room, I have the *feeling* of simultaneously grasping the clutter of walls, pieces of furniture, rugs, lights, computers, coffee mugs, and scattered books and papers. Surely my intuitions about my *own sensory experience* can't be wrong. Can they?

One much-discussed reason that you should be suspicious of your sense of a detailed and multicoloured sensory world comes from basic anatomy. The sensitivity of colour vision falls very rapidly, though smoothly, as we move out from the fovea (the dense pit of specialized colour-detecting 'cone cells' in the retina which your eye 'points' at any item of interest; see Figure 2). Indeed, outside a few degrees of where you are directly looking, you are close to being completely colour blind. The 'rod' cells that dominate most of your visual field can only detect dark and light. So the basic anatomy of the eye tells us that, except for within a few degrees of where we are directing our eyes, we are seeing in black and white. Yet, of course, we have the feeling that our entire 'subjective visual world' is richly coloured. This, at least, must be an illusion.

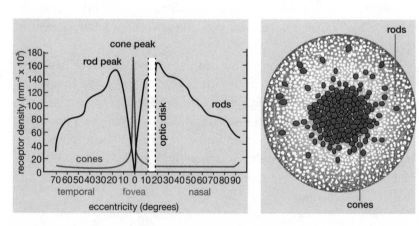

Figure 2. The density of light-sensitive cells in the eye.[4]

While we are on the subject of the retina, notice that cone cells are not just specialized for detecting colour; they are also specialized for picking up fine detail. It is for this reason that your eye directs the fovea onto the word it is currently attempting to read. Indeed, the sensitivity of vision falls rapidly, but smoothly, as we move out from the fovea; and the rate at which sensitivity declines is not arbitrary but is precisely calibrated so that, within the widest possible range, our perceptual abilities are independent of the size that objects project onto the retina. So we can recognize a friend in the distance, make sense of thumbnail pictures on a computer screen, or read a small font, but equally we can also recognize a looming face, make sense of close-ups from the front row of the cinema, or read a giant billboard from up close. To be able to zoom in or zoom out requires that the smaller the region to be analysed, the more densely our visual 'resources' are concentrated.

To see just how sharply concentrated our visual powers are, look at the graph of visual acuity (Figure 3) – a measure of the ability to see fine details that is picked up with the well-known chart of letters of diminishing size beloved of opticians – and notice how precisely it mirrors the density of cone cells in the retina (Figure 2). But this observation implies that, not only is the visual periphery colourless, it is also extremely fuzzy. Surveying the room before me, I have the sense that the entire scene is captured by my inner experience in precise detail; yet this too is an illusion – whatever I am not looking at directly is an inchoate blur.

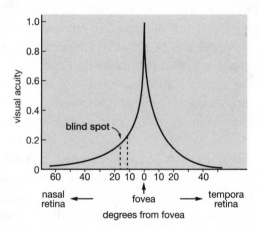

Figure 3. Visual acuity over the retina. The precision with which we see declines smoothly, but very precipitously from a peak at the fovea. Visual acuity beautifully tracks the density of cone cells, shown in the left panel of Figure 2.[5]

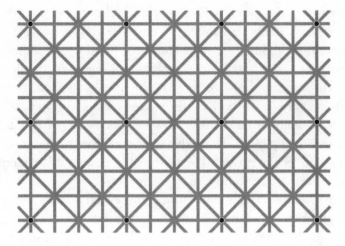

Figure 4. How many black dots can you see? As you search, the dots continually blink in and out of existence. This illusion, the Ninio extinction effect, was created by French biologist and vision scientist Jacques Ninio.[6]

Elementary facts about the anatomy of the eye, then, contradict our most fundamental intuitions about our sensory experience: we see the world through a narrow window of clarity; almost the entire visual field is colourless and blurry. And, putting anatomy to one side, we can sense that some trickery is afoot by considering some of the strange visual images which directly illustrate the 'narrowness' of vision. Consider the strange 'twelve dots' illusion in Figure 4. There are twelve black dots arranged in three rows of four dots each. The dots are large enough to be seen clearly and simultaneously against a white background. But when arranged on the grid, they seem only to appear when you are paying attention to them. Dots we are not attending to are somehow 'swallowed up' by the diagonal grey lines. Interestingly, we can attend to adjacent pairs of items, to lines, to triangles and even squares – although these are highly unstable. But our attention is in short supply; and where we are not attending, the dots disappear.

The limited visual 'window' depends, to some extent at least, on where we are looking. Yet we typically have only the vaguest sense of which part of an image or scene we are looking at directly – we have the impression that the entire visual scene is simultaneously 'grasped' in pretty much complete detail. We sense that our imagined 'mental

Figure 5. A 'scintillating' image that gives us an insight into our own eye movements. The sparkling effect is even more powerful if you rotate the image 45 degrees.[7]

mirror' appears to reflect the external world equally sharply, across the whole visual field. Figure 5 makes our eye movements visible to us: as you direct your eye across the grid, you see a patch of white dots wherever you are looking. If you turn the picture 45 degrees in either direction, you may find the dots, both black and white, begin to sparkle more intensely. Our visual experience can depend, rather dramatically, on where we are looking – and we are certainly unable to 'load up' this entire image into our minds – even though it is actually very simple and repetitive.

Thus our visual grasp of the world is not quite as precise and all-encompassing as it appears to be. Looking at the page in front of me as I type, I have the feeling that I see words everywhere. But this too is an illusion: I can see, roughly, just one word at a time. Consider the following thought experiment. Suppose that all the letters on the page apart from the very word I am currently looking at (with a few letters' margin around it) were magically scrambled. That is, as soon as I shift my eyes to a new location, only the new patch of letters my eyes 'land' on would be transformed into meaningful letters. Each local patch of meaningful text would be 'created' just at the very moment I look at it; the rest of text could just as well be meaningless strings of letters. If I can only read one word at a time, then I should be entirely oblivious to all of this scrambling and unscrambling.

The invention of the technology of so-called 'gaze-contingent' eye-tracking has made it possible to test this for real. Let us see how this works in a typical experiment. Suppose you are looking at a computer screen, reading the line of text at the top of Figure 6. Your eyes are being monitored by an eye-tracker, and jump across the text as indicated by the circles. Rather than continuously showing the whole sentence, the computer screen displays only a 'window' of text (highlighted in Figure 6 by the grey rectangles – though, of course, the rectangles aren't visible to you – all you see is unadorned text) which shifts to wherever you are looking. Inside the rectangle, the text is displayed as normal; outside the rectangle, the blocks of letters are replaced by blocks of xs.

This procedure means that the display you are looking at is 'gaze-contingent': what is displayed on the screen depends on *where you are looking* at that particular moment. So, as your eye successively hops along the line of text, the display on the computer screen you are looking at shifts, as shown by the successive rows in Figure 6. The 'window' of meaningful text follows your eye as it jumps along the line of text – everywhere else there is nothing but blocks of xs.

What, then, is the subjective experience of reading a text that is almost entirely blocks of xs, with a small island of meaningful words, created on the spot, wherever you happen to be looking? If we, in some loose sense, 'see' whole screenfuls and pagefuls of text at once, then we should notice, and be rather puzzled by, the existence of the blocks of xs. But do we?

It depends, of course, on the size of the 'window'. If the window is tiny, then your brain will have the rather bizarre experience of seeing a moving snippet of letters from 'behind' a stream of xs. But if the window is long enough, *you will perceive nothing unusual* – because the xs will be too distant for you to notice them. So you will read the text without noticing anything untoward, even though it is continually mutating before your very eyes. You might wonder if the change-detecting rod cells in the periphery might spot anything amiss – and, as it were, sound the alarm that the text is shifting and not stable. And this might indeed be the case, if it were not that the changes in the display occur while your eye is moving – when, it turns out, you are effectively blind.

So, then, the crucial question is how small can we shrink the window before people notice anything is amiss? It turns out that, remarkably, it can be shrunk to just ten to fifteen characters (as shown in the figure), shifted somewhat to the right of the fixation point[8] (the brain is 'thinking ahead' slightly, to help plan the next eye movement; so, in languages that read from right to left, such as Hebrew, the window is instead shifted to the left[9]).

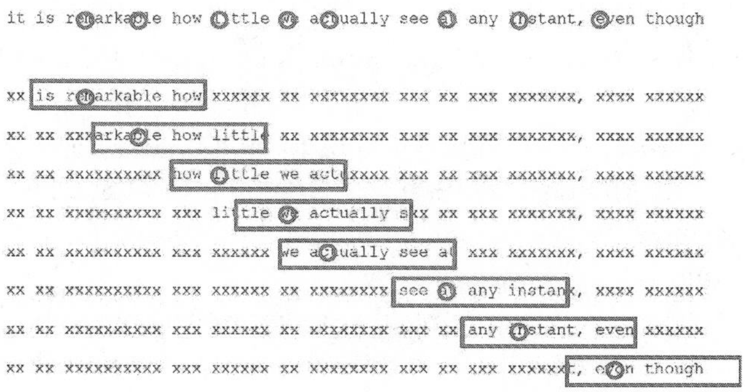

Figure 6. A schematic illustration of gaze-contingent eye-tracking.[10]

Remarkably, reading proceeds quite normally, even though the only letters you can possibly be identifying are the twelve to fifteen letters of English text that are, at that moment, visible on the screen – the rest can be strings of *x*s, or Latin, or whatever the experimenter chooses.[11] These results suggest that the eye and brain picks up little outside a very narrow 'window'. Indeed, we can go a bit further: the evidence suggests[12] that we can only read *one word at time*. Indeed, an eye-tracker monitoring your reading right now would show your eye irregularly 'hopping' along the line of text, from one word to the next. Sometimes your eyes will jump over short and predictable words, and occasionally jump back a few words when you lose the thread. But, roughly speaking, you read by hopping from one word to the next, reading one word at a time. This puts severe limits on how rapidly we can read. In particular, it implies that speed-reading is simply skimming; there is no way that the brain can 'take in' whole lines or paragraphs of text at once.

Right now, then, you are reading these very words through an equally narrow window. Aside from the small window of letters you are directly fixating on, you scarcely recognize any letters at all. And, similarly, severe restrictions apply not just to letters and words, but to our ability to make sense of faces, objects, patterns and entire scenes. Looking at a crowd, it turns out that you can only recognize one person at a time; looking at a colourful scene, you can only report colours or details of things that you are looking at directly.

This does not imply, of course, that you pick up no information at all about objects you are not attending to – just that this information is extremely sparse. While we can imagine that we see a whole page full of words at once, we are seeing just one word at a time. And we are picking up a general impression of something like 'regular lines of markings' for the rest of the page. Or when looking at a cluttered scene, we have the general impression of 'lots of objects' but can only identify one object at once.

Despite these astonishing results, many psychologists and philosophers have been unwilling to draw the conclusion that the richness of perceptual experience is an illusion – that our senses give us only a tenuous link to the external world. It is tempting to retort that perhaps we cannot *report* or *remember* more than one item at a time in the page of text or crowd of faces confronting us, but perhaps we can *see* far more than we report or remember. Perhaps, in short, there *is* an inner world of experience, which copies the external world in something close to its full complexity. But this supposedly rich subjective awareness may 'overflow' what we can report, because the inner world of experience is fleeting – it disappears even as you start to describe it.

But this reassuring picture can't be right. If it were, what people would be 'seeing' in the gaze-contingent eye-tracking experiment would be blocks of *x*s with just a narrow window of meaningful letters; and they would perceive the window of meaningful letters shifting as they moved their eyes. But this isn't what people report at all: they claim to see a completely normal sentence, composed entirely of meaningful words, and they are entirely oblivious to the existence of the blocks of *x*s, let alone the fact that letters are changing their identities as the eye scans along the line of text. So the 'overflow' story doesn't work: if we could 'see' the entire page of text, but report only one word at a time, then the gaze-contingent eye-tracker wouldn't fool us at all. The fact that we are comprehensively hoodwinked tells us that at no point do we see the full range of text in front of us – we recognize, roughly, one word at a time, and have only the vaguest sense of the rest of the text.

The sense that there is a whole text, or scene, before us arises, then, from the integration of snippets of visual information, as our eyes hop across the visual world. So our sense of a rich visual world should break down if we hold the point of contact between eye and world perfectly still. Indeed, if we could *stabilize* the visual image projected onto the eye, our perception of a scene, a word, a face, or a page of text should begin to disintegrate. Can this really be right?

We have no good intuitions about this strange situation because, of course, in daily life, our eye is continually in motion. Even when we try steadily to fixate an object, our eye is subject to a little jitter, beyond our conscious control. But what would happen if we could hold the image on our retina precisely still? Given that the eye is continually in motion, this means that the image needs to move with it in perfect synchrony, so that the pattern of light falling on each patch of retina is stabilized. Then, wherever a person looks, they see precisely the same thing.

The problem of stabilizing an image on a continually jiggling eye seems technically challenging – yet, remarkably, this technical challenge was solved as far back as the 1950s by research groups led by psychologist Lorrin Riggs at Brown University in the US, and by physicist R. W. Ditchburn at Reading University in the UK. One solution was to attach a tiny 'micro-projector' weighing just one quarter of a gram to the eyeball itself, via a contact lens. As the eye moves, the projector moves with it, so stabilizing the image precisely. And it is onto the fovea that the retinal image is projected. Through clever optics, the image appears to the viewer to be rather small and far away – in reality, though, the micro-projector is no more than an inch from the eye.

So what happens when the retinal image is suddenly made almost perfectly still? We might expect that we should see whatever is projected into our eye exactly as normal, but frozen. But this isn't at all what happens: within a few seconds, the projected image begins to disappear, either piece by piece, or in its entirety; all that is left is a uniform grey field which sometimes darkens into black. Without warning, though, the whole image or parts of it spontaneously reappear, typically to disintegrate, reorganize or entirely disappear again.[13]

Retinal stabilization sheds light on perception and, by extension, on thought. Consider, for example, what happens when a person is confronted with nothing more than a straight line. Initially, the brain locks onto and processes this line successfully, but now the brain will attempt to disengage and lock onto a new stimulus. Normally, of course, shifting the eyes will yield new visual stimulation to lock onto, but with a stabilized image, eye movements generate no new visual information. Disengaging from the line, but with nothing to re-engage with, no fresh perceptual interpretation is created – the person experiences nothing more than a blank field. Now and again, the brain re-engages with the only available 'meaningful' signal, and the straight line pops back into view. But not for long – our whirring imagination is continually straining to find new material onto which an interpretation can be imposed.

If this is right, then, we should expect simpler stimuli to disappear comprehensively and often – and, indeed, when viewing a simple straight line, people often report that they see nothing but a blank field for as much as 90 per cent of the time. On the other hand, it is possible to engage with a more complex stimulus in a variety of distinct ways, by locking onto different parts of the stimulus, potentially yielding a variety of different patterns. So more complex patterns should be visible far more of the time; they should show 'dynamic' shifts of continual disintegration and reorganization; and, crucially, because we can consciously experience only the *output* of perceptual interpretation, the visible patterns should be composed of meaningful units, rather than an arbitrary scatter of image fragments. And this is exactly what happens.

Consider, for example, the results shown in Figure 7 (opposite). In each 'strip' the left-hand picture is the image as projected into the participant's eye; the other images are a selection of the visual experiences that participants reported, as they experienced the image decompose and recompose itself. Take, first, the drawing of a head (7a), in profile: note first that the visible material tends to correspond to continuous regions of the image (e.g. the upper, lower or left-hand side), rather than a set of arbitrary fragments. Note, in particular, the 'pure' profile, disconnected from the rest of the head – it is significant that people 'lock on' to this coherent unit, rather than arbitrary outlines (e.g. the fragments of line indicating the hair).

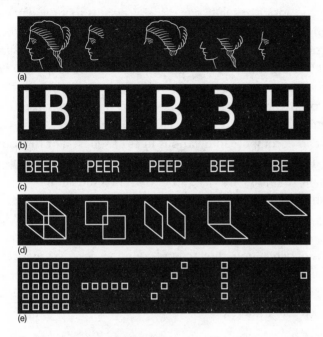

Figure 7. The breakdown of stabilized images.[14]

The focus on contiguous, meaningful units becomes even clearer when we consider (7b), where the basic stimulus is the letters H and B jammed up against each other. As might be expected, the individual letters H and B are sometimes seen alone, but also the letter H drops away completely leaving a 3; perhaps most intriguing is that it is possible to 'lock on' to a 4, and to obliterate the surrounding fragments that don't fit. This is an illustration of the delightful imaginative power of the perceptual system. It is no by means obvious, until one examines it closely, that there even *is* a 4 hidden in the HB figure. Yet the perceptual system finds this pattern spontaneously.

The same pattern is observed in 7c, where the word BEER breaks down into a number of component words, but not, for example, into 'meaningless' substrings of letters, such as EE, EER or ER. And in 7d we find that a wire-frame cube breaks down not haphazardly, line by line, but in whole chunks, so that some faces of the cube survive and others disappear. The two illustrations in which the opposite faces only are retained illustrate that the tendency to preserve discrete regions of the image is not an absolute one. Most crucial is that the patterns that the brain locks onto are themselves meaningful. Of course, these specific fragments are meaningful, but most meaningful if we assume that the line-drawing is interpreted as a 3D cube, rather than a 2D flat line-drawing. These observations at least suggest that the 'locking-on' process of attention is, in these cases, operating *after* the brain has interpreted the image in depth. Finally, in 7e, notice how a grid of squares can decompose into various lines of squares, or that our brain may focus just on a single square – notice, as ever, the brain's preference for meaningful patterns, rather than random subsets of squares.

The strange phenomenology of stabilized images has been known for more than half a century.[15] In the intervening years, such findings have largely been viewed as a puzzling curiosity, marginal to the big questions of perception, thought and consciousness. Yet they reveal the very essence of how the mind works. In particular, these phenomena suggest some fundamental principles of the operation of perception, and by extension, thought:

1. We 'see' only meaningful organizations (or at least the most meaningful organization the brain can find): visual chunks, patterns and whole letters, numbers, words, rather than a random scatter of fragments.
2. We see just one meaningful organization at a time (we can see, for example, BEER or PEEP, but we cannot have the experience of seeing both).
3. Other sensory information that is not part of this meaningful organization (though clearly and distinctly projected onto the retina at all times), is largely or even entirely ignored, to the point of becoming entirely invisible.
4. The brain is continually churning: despite the unaccustomed lack of new input, the brain is desperately attempting to disengage

from the current organization, and to find another. When it
cannot, the image entirely disappears.

The phenomenology we experience in viewing stabilized images is
the closest we have to a 'window' onto how we see – a glimpse behind
the scenes at the brain's convincing magic show. And, as we shall
explore below, perceiving is a type of thinking. Indeed, it is perhaps
the most important type; and all other types of thought are really just
extensions of perception (though powerful extensions). Following
this line, then, we shall see later in the book that evidence from retinal stabilization foreshadows a theory of thought.

These observations imply, of course, that our beliefs about what we
see, whether we are looking at text, objects, faces or colours, are systematically misleading: we see far, far less than we think we do.
Indeed, we see the world one snippet at a time; and we can tie snippets
together, just as we can link together successive sentences in a story.
So the 'inner world' of your current sensory experience is also, it turns
out, entirely fake. We are able to attend to one word, object or colour
at a time – and no more. The 'inner world of sensation' feels real, but
then so does Gormenghast Castle as we read its description, line by
line. In both cases, our brain is successfully piecing together a stream
of snippets of information, not simultaneously grasping the 'whole'.
There is no 'inner realm' which mirrors the richness and complexity
of the outer world. If there were, the gaze-contingent eye-tracker, creating tiny islands of coherence just where we are looking, against a sea
of meaningless strings of *x*s, could not possibly deceive us.

The previous chapter outlined the illusion of explanatory depth –
the verbal accounts that we give of our knowledge, motives, desires
and dreams turn out to be flimsy improvisations, invented after the
fact. In this chapter, we have seen that we are being spectacularly
fooled even about the richness and coherence of our own sensory
experience. We *think* we see a detailed, multicoloured world, but
we don't. This is a hoax so astonishing and all-encompassing that it
is sometimes known in philosophy and psychology as the 'grand
illusion'.[16]

Where does this leave us? The sensory world is no more solid than
the 'worlds' of stories and the supposed bedrock of common-sense

explanation. We have the *sense* of 'clearly perceiving' the solid 3D character of impossible objects – just as we have a vivid sense of the layout of Gormenghast Castle and a vivid 'feeling of understanding' the people and the world around us. But such understanding is riddled with contradictions. And we have seen that our experience of the sensory world is, to an astonishing degree, also full of gaps – the Grand Illusion has us in its thrall.

The unavoidable conclusion of these findings is that *the mind itself is an impossible object*: it has only the superficial appearance of solidity. Peake's visions of Gormenghast Castle, our everyday explanations of physical objects – these feel solid and coherent. But they are all hopelessly confused and contradictory. Our stream of consciousness is no more a 'projection' of an inner mental world than Oscar Reutersvärd's curious figures are projections from some alternative geometrical reality. There is nothing more to the mind than the fleeting contents of our stream of consciousness. And not only that (despite our intuitions to the contrary), consciousness is astonishingly sparse: we create sensations, beliefs and desires; and make pronouncements, carry out actions and make choices, one by one, as required.

3

Anatomy of a Hoax

We are being hoaxed: both our verbal explanations (the illusion of explanatory depth of Chapter 1) and our sensory experience (the grand illusion of Chapter 2) are vapours, masquerading as solid form. There is no mirror of nature, no inner copy of outer reality, no churning unconscious, no unfathomable depths from which our conscious thoughts break through. Beneath the momentary flow of fragmented and astonishingly sketchy experiences and even sketchier recollections from memory, there is precisely nothing. Well, of course, there is a frenzy of brain activity, but there are no further *thoughts*. The only thoughts, emotions, feelings are those that flow through our stream of consciousness.

How is it, then, that we are deceived so comprehensively? In this chapter we will focus on our senses – but the same sleight of hand underlies the apparent solidity of our explanations in terms of beliefs and desires, hopes and fears. It turns out that, as with so many convincing tricks, the grand illusion depends on misdirection. We point our fovea, and concentrate our attention, on one aspect of the visual world, and notice scarcely anything of what is happening in all the rest. If we are suspicious, even for a moment, that our perceptual representations are rather vague and monochrome in the periphery of our vision, we swivel our eyes across to check, and, sure enough, all is detailed and colourful.

Conjurors have known this for centuries – by directing our gaze and our attention to one location in the image, and then deviously slipping a coin, ball or even rabbit past our unsuspecting visual systems in some faraway location in our visual periphery. Of course, misdirection can fail – notoriously young children can be a menace to the would-be illusionist by failing to pick up the cues that are supposed to channel their attention in one direction, and inconveniently looking in some other direction – perhaps precisely where the 'magical' object is surreptitiously being manoeuvred. But there is no such danger for the perpetrator of the grand illusion. There is no possibility whatever of examining a blurry, visual location and revealing that we have no idea what words, faces or objects it contains – because the very act of examination conjures up the relevant word, face or object. The process of focusing our attention on a patch of the visual image (e.g. a face in a crowd, a word in a page of text) is the same process by which colour and detail spring into being. So the brain can fool us that we 'see' the stable, rich, colourful world before us in a single visual gulp, whereas the truth is that our visual connection with the world is no more than a series of localized 'nibbles'.

So the 'secret' of the hoax is disarmingly simple: the world around us seems sharp and colourful and full of objects, words and faces because, as soon as we wonder about any aspect of that world, our eyes can almost instantly flick across to the relevant part, fixate it and, apparently in an instant, provide an answer. The very fluency with which answer follows question gives us the impression that all the answers were already stored up, ready for use – that we have a full and precise mental representation of the world around us, to be consulted at any moment. But experiments, with gaze-contingent eye-tracking and many other experimental methods besides, show quite the opposite: that, far from drawing answers about distant parts of the visual scene from a pre-existing store, our eyes race to provide the answer in an instant.

Consider – to switch from vision to touch for a moment – the 'feel' of a tennis racket when we have our eyes shut. We get a sense of the weight and manoeuvrability of the racket from waving it to and fro; of the tautness and spacing of the strings by strumming our fingertips across them; of the oval shape of the frame of the racket by running a finger around it. But we obtained the subjective experiences of the feel of the racket one by one – we had no awareness of the strings when we wielded the racket; no sense of the racket's heft as we strummed the strings. Yet we do not have a sense of the frame springing in and out of existence – or of the strings momentarily forming and disappearing. We have the sense that the racket has an entirely stable and solid existence, even though, of course, we can only experience it one aspect at a time.

What happens, then, when we open our eyes, and examine the racket? In fact, much the same as before: our eyes will visually 'touch' different parts of the image of the racket, depending on which question we are asking – concerning its frame, strings, or overall size and weight. But our eyes shift, and report their findings, so rapidly and effortlessly that we can all too easily imagine that these findings were already loaded in our minds.

Our eyes can touch only one visual location at a time, but can dash across the visual field with astonishing rapidity to alight on whatever visual information we need in the moment. I suspect it is important too that while we are very much aware of the movement of our hands in examining some new part of the racket, we are only very vaguely aware of where our eyes are looking – so that it comes, for example, as a complete surprise that our eyes hop around when we are examining a face, continually revisiting the eyes and mouth; or that reading a line of text proceeds by a series of one- or two-word jumps, rather than a smooth glide across the text (see Figure 8). So our eyes dashing across the visual field to pick up one piece of information then another goes almost entirely unnoticed.

The step-by-step nature of perception, whether tactile or visual, goes deeper than our hopping from one 'touchpoint' with the outside world to the next. We can interpret the information from a single touchpoint in a variety of different ways, as we saw with the discussion of stabilized images in Chapter 2: the very same retinal image may at one moment be 'BEER', at the next 'BEE', 'PEEP' or 'PEER'. Our brain can lock onto different aspects of the available sensory information, but crucially it seems that we can lock onto only one interpretation of the information at a time. With normal, non-stabilized images, when we see the word 'BEER', we can fancy that we see all the other component words too, simultaneously loaded into our brains, because, after all, as soon as we wonder whether we can see 'BEE', or 'PEEP' and 'PEER' as sub-components of 'BEER', we can often provide a ready answer. But this is the same trick in another guise: rather than our eyes dashing to a different visual location, our brains are locking onto different subsets of the visual input at a

a.

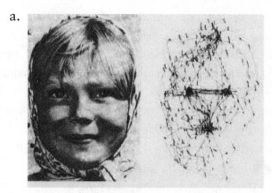

b.

When a person is reading a sentence silently, the eye movements show that not every word is fixated. Every once in a while a regression (an eye movement that goes back in the text) is made to re-examine a word that may have not been fully understood the first time. This only happens with about 10% of the fixations, depending on how difficult the text is. The more difficult the higher the likelihood that regressions are made.

Figure 8. Vision-as-touch: how we take in a picture or a text, not in a single gulp, but in many tiny 'nibbles'. (a) Alfred Yarbus, the Russian psychologist, who pioneered the use of eye-tracking in Moscow in the 1950s and 1960s, found that our eyes fixate very heavily on small portions of the image. (b) Eye-movements in reading a passage of text.[1]

particular location, but doing this quickly and effortlessly so that we can imagine we are not switching from one interpretation of the image to another, but holding all interpretations simultaneously in mind.

Thus we look at the world through a narrow window of lucidity – a tiny patch of colour and detail in a fuzzy field, but we don't notice the 'edges' of the window, or even its existence. Now imagine, by contrast, putting on a pair of glasses which blur your vision severely at the edges and drain the image of colour, except for a tiny patch in their centre. Look fixedly straight ahead through these glasses, and you will see nothing strange. The whole world will look as detailed and colourful as ever (because your retina, and so your brain, doesn't 'miss' the detail that the glasses have obliterated, because they would be unable to detect it even if it were present). But were we to move our eyes, even a little, the 'window of lucidity' allowed by the glasses would immediately become all too apparent.

Consider, for a moment, the possibility that, in some science-fiction future, it might be possible to embed a tiny eye-tracker into a pair of glasses so that the optics of the glasses would block out colour and detail except where our eyes happen to be looking. Observing this strange equipment in action, we would perhaps see a semi-opaque pair of spectacles, with a small translucent patch, which would, perhaps rather disconcertingly, continually jump around as the wearer's eyes scanned the world. Spectators would wonder how we were able to play tennis through the murk; passengers would be alarmed by the apparent near-enveloping visual fog, while wearers would nonchalantly drive through thick traffic.

Yet from our own point of view, our visual world would be much as normal. The glasses would, by design, present us with a detailed, coloured image of whichever part of the external world we happened to be looking at. The mists would part in a new location on the surface of the glasses as the eyes landed after each saccade (i.e. each jump from one fixation point to the next), and this would happen so smoothly that we would be unaware that the mists had ever been present. We would be able to scan text and report that our mug is blue (and see the detail of the hand-painted flowers on it). Every time we asked ourselves a question about the visual world, we would be able to answer it. So we would never be aware that the glasses let through, almost everywhere, only a formless colourless image – because we would see colourful detail wherever we happened to look.

On reflection, these hypothetical glasses are not entirely in the realm of science fiction; we are, in a very real sense, already wearing them. Imagine for a moment that, rather than sci-fi glasses, we decide to make sci-fi contact lenses, with precisely the same properties. Now, what would these contact lenses have to look like? Well, the handy thing about contact lenses is that they move around as your eye moves around – so we don't have to worry about clever eye-tracking technology and lens modification. All we need is a filter that blurs, and drains colour information from the periphery, and lets through colour and detail right opposite the fovea. Making a lens like this would be easy, but also pointless, because all it would do would be to block out information that we don't detect anyway. Totally clear contact lenses would do just as well; in fact, no contact lenses at all would do just as well. We don't have to build the window of lucidity into our glasses, or contact lenses, precisely because our eye and brain has done this job for us.

So, then, our sense of living in a fully colourful and detailed world is really a sense of having colour and detail available, as it were, for immediate inspection – we can 'lay our hands on' any information we wish for, with the mere flick of the eye. I have the sense of being aware of the colours of the spines of the books on the bookshelf in the corner of the room I am in now, but not of the bookshelves of the British Library, because a quick eye movement (and perhaps a turn of the head) can tell me 'thin yellow book with black bar; blue book with white writing; red oversized hardback . . .' but no amount of shifting and squinting will tell me anything about the layout of bookshelves in faraway London.

But back to the sci-fi glasses. Would their hypothetical wearers be *deluded* in thinking that they are, none the less, able to see a richly detailed and colourful world? In one sense 'Yes', but in another 'No'. Yes, they would have no idea that the glasses have a limited window of lucidity – they would imagine they were looking through completely transparent glass. But no, they would not be wrong in believing that, whatever question of detail or colour crossed their mind, they would be able to answer it, almost instantly. And perhaps this is what awareness of living in a fully coloured and detailed world really is: not that we have answers to all possible questions of colour and detail loaded up in our minds, but that we can answer any question of colour and detail almost as soon as it is asked (by, as it happens, a quick flick of the eyes to the relevant portion of the visual field).

Yet without the hoax, our subjective experience would be strange indeed: we would be tormented by the sense of the world as undergoing remarkable changes as we scan our eyes across it. Objects would suddenly snap into colourful focus, while others would, just as rapidly, be drained of detail and colour. This would, of course, be hugely misleading. Our experience would be suggesting exuberant flux even as we scan and examine an utterly still page of text, painting or scene.

When we consider the purpose of perception, then, the grand illusion is entirely appropriate – indeed, inevitable. Perception tells us about the world around us – the layout of words, faces, objects and patterns – and how to use this knowledge to guide our actions. And the external world is, of course, defined in precise detail and full colour, irrespective of where we happen to be look-ing at the time or, for that matter, whether our eyes are open or closed, or whether we are even present at all. Our perceptual experi-ence is like a narrator who wishes to remain as unobtrusive as possible – we want to know about the story, not the viewpoint of the storyteller.

The eye and brain deliver us the impression of a fully detailed and colourful world with good reason – for the world is indeed replete with detail and colour. But what the eye and brain do not do, and could not possibly do, is simultaneously deliver us the experience of all the specific colours and details. The brain 'tells us' that such col-ours and details are there – and that, by the mere flick of our eyes, we can, in almost no time at all, read off those colours and focus on those details. So, our sense of a rich sensory world is really a sense of *potential*: the feeling that we can explore the sensory world at will, uncovering whatever detail we wish.[2]

But this experience of the potential of a stable external world to yield up colours and details is easily misinterpreted as the experience of simultaneously grasping all possible colour and detail in a single sensory snapshot. So what our sense of the richness of the experi-enced world is really telling us is that we can, whenever we like, effortlessly and rapidly find out about almost any aspect of the scene before us; no sooner have we wondered about the colour of a friend's hat, the next word in the sentence, or which book is lying on the table – than, with a barely detectable jump of the eye locking the fovea onto the target of interest, combined with our wonderfully rapid visual processing, we have the answer. And so it is all too easy to fall into the trap of believing that we had the answer all along; that, moreover, we had already pre-loaded in our brains all the answers to all manner of possible questions about the scene, the face, or the text, before us.

So we are being hoaxed by our own brains for the most benign of reasons. The world is a stable place; perception is designed to tell us about the world; thus perception gives us a sense of stable awareness of colour and detail across the entire visual image. And it does so even though, outside the tiny window of lucidity, this information isn't actually captured by the eye or brain at all, but is merely available 'on demand'.

PIECING TOGETHER THE FRAGMENTS

It is easy to think of our focus of attention as a spotlight – a spatially defined blob of lucidity where our eyes are centred, surrounded by rapidly thickening darkness. But the experience of retinal stabilization tells a different story, as we saw in Chapter 2. The brain focuses on meaningful chunks of the visual image: words, letters, objects and their component parts. The meaningful units need not necessarily correspond to connected regions in space. Our attentional focus can latch onto a scatter of discontinuous items if those items can be grouped into a single 'object'. Thus we can see an animal moving through dense forest, recognize a person behind a dense wire fence, or find that we can read a distant billboard through the clutter of

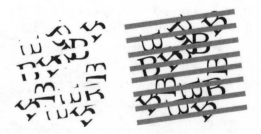

Figure 9. We can group together the scraps of black to form the letters 'B', even when chunks of the letters are missing. Notice how perceiving the shapes is much easier when the 'grill' blocking our view is plainly visible (right-hand image); having made sense of the right-hand image, it is much easier to see the Bs on the left.[3]

intervening lamp posts (our ability to group 'discontinuous' elements together is illustrated in Figure 9).

It turns out that we can also group together disconnected items that don't make coherent objects, a topic insightfully explored in theory and experiments by Liqiang Huang (now at the City University of Hong Kong) and one of the world's leading cognitive psychologists, Hal Pashler (at the University of California, San Diego). Consider, for example, the randomly coloured grids in Figure 10 (here reproduced in shades of grey). Take a few moments to check whether or not the grids in each row are linked by the relationship with which they are labelled – whether they are matching, whether they are symmetric, or whether one grid can be rotated 'in your mind's eye' to fit over the other. This is not easy – we find ourselves needing to check the coloured squares one at a time. There is, though, a shortcut: if we focus on a single colour, then we can pick out the pattern formed by squares of that colour (shown on the right side) for each grid, and compare them rapidly.

To do this, of course, we need to pick out and group together all the items of one colour – say red (represented by light grey in Figure 10) – and separate them from the rest of the image. As we do this, the red items suddenly become a discernible pattern with a clear structure (at the top right of the figure, we see that the 'red' squares approximate a

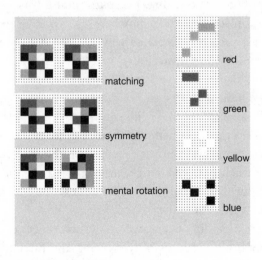

Figure 10. Transformations with patterns.[4]

diagonal line); and the structures within each pair of items can then readily be compared to see if the two figures match, are symmetric, or are rotated, for that colour. Notice, though, that as soon as we see the red squares form a unified 'figure', the colours forming the rest of the grid are no more than an amorphous 'background'. It is as if we can simultaneously 'grasp' items of a single colour, lift them free of the rest of the image, and examine them separately. So, to check possible relationships between whole grids, we do not need to check each coloured square one by one; instead, we need merely to check the patterns for each of the four colours.

Huang and Pashler propose three hypotheses from these and many related observations. Their first hypothesis, which we have already encountered in Chapter 2, is that we can 'grasp', or attend to, just one object or pattern at a time: we can hold onto the pattern in the red squares, or the green, or the yellow, or the blue. But we cannot 'hold' two patterns in mind at once, just as we can only read one word, or recognize one face, at a time. Only when we can grasp a figure, can we manipulate or transform it, looking for copies or mirror images, or twisting it through 90 degrees in our mind's eye. It is as if the visual system has a single metaphorical 'hand' that can reach out, select and manipulate just one pattern at any moment. If this is right, then perhaps the implications go beyond coloured grids to the claim that we are able only to see one object or pattern at a time, whatever the nature of that object or pattern may be.

This perspective neatly explains why we find it so much easier to relate the patterns shown in Figure 11, which are well-known pictures of animals by the great German artist Albrecht Dürer (1471–1528). These patterns are, of course, far more complex than Huang and Pashler's coloured grids, and yet we are able rapidly and effortlessly to see the links between them. But from the 'one object at a time' perspective, this is precisely what we should expect: we can easily see that such patterns match, are symmetrical, or are rotated, because each forms a single object, which can be visually grasped, and hence analysed and manipulated, as a whole.

But if we are able only to 'grasp' one visual object or pattern at a time, then our brain is successively creating and dissolving such visual objects or patterns as we flick our eyes and/or our attention, to different aspects of our visual input. Wherever we focus our attention, of course, an object or pattern is duly created. So it is so easy to succumb to the illusion that a rich, detailed, colourful visual world of objects and patterns is loaded in our minds in a single visual gulp.

If this story is right, then if we can lock onto the stimulus successfully, and we can disable, or at least impair, the ability to dissolve the pattern and find another, then the background should literally

Matching

Symmetry

Mental rotation

Figure 11. Finding simple transformations of complex objects.
We immediately have the (correct) impression that there are links between these pairs of images (animals by Albrecht Dürer). The contrast with Figure 10 is striking.

disappear. Indeed, this is precisely what happened in the retinal stabilization experiments we described in Chapter 2. Moving our eyes
provides a way to break out of the current pattern by changing the
input on which our brain must work, but when moving our eyes no
longer changes the input to our retina, then we can no longer dissolve
and reconstruct new patterns so easily, and chunks of the visual input
vanish.[5]

What would happen, then, if the brain found it difficult spontaneously to dissolve the current object of interest? Could there be a disorder
in which people might perceive just one object or pattern at a time, and
lose all sense of the existence of the surrounding items? Later we shall
see that there appears to be just such a neurological condition.

Huang and Pashler's second proposal fills out and makes specific the
notion of apprehending a pattern: visually grasping a pattern or object is
analogous to 'highlighting' the spatial pattern created by the subject (or,
as they rather nicely put it, shrink-wrapping it in plastic), so that only
that pattern or object is 'seen'. So, when we 'see' one colour in the grids
of Figure 10 (say, picking out the cross-shaped figure in 'yellow'), we are
not really 'seeing' the other colours at all. We have, of course, a general
sense of the extent and complexity of the rest of the pattern – but this is
because we can shift our attention to the rest of the pattern at will.[6]

Huang and Pashler's third suggestion is that, while our visual grasp
can lasso items at many different locations, we can only mentally
label items that are lassoed (so, for example, we can label the 'figure'
as yellow, but we cannot simultaneously label the 'background' as
having one or more colours). And more than that: all the lassoed
items have to receive the same 'label' for a particular dimension (e.g.
colour). This leads to the astonishing suggestion that, even when
looking at a multicoloured image, we are only able to perceive one
colour at a time. We can 'see' either the red, yellow, green or blue patterns in the coloured grid, but when we focus on one colour, the other
colours are 'gone'. This claim fits with another of the principles we
drew from the disintegrating stabilized images – that visual information that is not currently being attended to is largely, or even
completely, ignored. But is that right? Can it really be true that, when
confronted with a multicoloured image, we can see only one colour
at a time?

Now we have already noted that our impression that our subjective experience is fully coloured (and sharply detailed) across the entire visual field must be mistaken. But this leaves open the possibility that we can simultaneously see multiple colours, when those colours are all presented to central vision. For example, look directly at the centre of the circle shown in Figure 12. Certainly, we have the feeling that we are able simultaneously to grasp the blueness (dark grey here) of the blue quarters and the greenness (light grey) of the green quarters. Yet Huang and Pashler's theory claims that we cannot even do this: that just as we visually grasp the green segments, we must relinquish our grasp of the blue segments. And we are, they claim, unable to 'see' the colour of the segments that we are not directly visually grasping. If this is right, our attentional system must be hopping backwards and forwards between the perception of green and

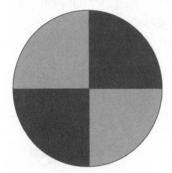

Figure 12. A two-coloured wheel. It seems 'obvious' that we can see both colours simultaneously. But our experience with the coloured grids for Figure 10 might suggest otherwise.

the perception of blue – but we are not able to grasp both colours at once.

To test this remarkably counter-intuitive prediction, Huang and Pashler modified an experimental method developed by the psychologist and cognitive neuroscientist, John Duncan.[7] As outlined in Figure 13a (see next page), Huang and Pashler studied how people perceive images presented as brief flashes which are rapidly 'overwritten' by a noisy visual pattern (a 'mask'). They varied the amount of time for which the stimulus was presented (that is, the length of the flash before it was obliterated by the mask) and measured how accurately people were able to detect whether they had seen a particular colour. The crucial comparison was between the instance when the entire pinwheel was briefly flashed up and when each 'diagonal' pair of coloured segments was presented successively. If we are able to 'see' both coloured segments at the same time, then people would be just as good at detecting, say, green, when they have just seen both green and blue for, say, 100 milliseconds, or when they have seen green and blue successively, for 100 milliseconds each. If, on the other hand, we can only load one colour at a time, then performance will be worse in the 'simultaneous' condition, because the brain will not have had time to switch between the two colours (if the brain happens to load in the blue segments initially, then there may be no time to load the green segments at all, and the green will not be seen). Remarkably, this is precisely what happens; and indeed performance in both tasks is nicely captured by the hypothesis that people are sequentially switching from one colour to the other.

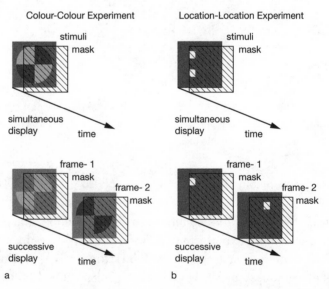

Figure 13. Can we see two colours (panel a), or two locations (panel b) at once?[8]

This pattern of results contrasts, crucially, with a variation of the experiment, in which people have to pay attention to two spatial locations, rather than colours (Figure 13b). Here, the results show that we can simultaneously 'grasp' two locations just as easily as one location. And this, of course, makes sense: the brain needs to be able to group together multiple locations, even when perceiving a single pattern or object. So while it is possible, not surprisingly, to perceive multiple locations at once, it appears not to be possible to see two colours at once: indeed, it seems that we must switch back and forth between seeing one coloured region and another, but that we do this so quickly and effortlessly that we have the illusion that we are 'grasping' two, or many, colours at the same time.[9]

This perspective has a further, intriguing and direct prediction: that we can only count colours slowly and laboriously. When we have to count spatially distinct *items* (e.g. blobs), all of which can simultaneously be grasped, we are able to answer whether there are one, two, three or four almost equally rapidly – beyond this our counting becomes slow and laborious. Roughly, this rapid counting appears to occur because we can recognize familiar patterns, for example triangles and squares. But if we are presented with a field of blobs which possess one, two, three or four colours, we do not seem to be able to grasp all these colours at once. The greater the number of colours, the slower our responses: just as if we are flipping from one colour to the next.[10]

It seems an astonishing affront to common sense to find that, even for items that we are looking at directly, the apparent richness of colour is itself a trick – that our brains seem to be able to encode no more than one colour (or shape, or orientation) at a time. But this is what the data tell us.

The sequential, fragmented view of visual awareness suggests some striking, and rather disturbing, possibilities about what might happen if our visual system is damaged. Suppose, for example, that we lost the ability to 'ask questions of' and redirect our eyes to some part of the visual field. Then we should know little about that part of the visual field – or rather, it would only ever be represented in peripheral vision, fuzzy and colourless. But the hoax will cover up this bleached fuzziness – remember that the brain aims to tell us about the world itself, not our view of it – and the brain quite reasonably presumes that the world is not blurry and colourless. So is it possible that our illusion of a rich, detailed visual field might be undisturbed, even though some significant part of the visual field might remain entirely unexplored by our fovea, and hence stay for ever in the shadows? Our perception of the richness and completeness of our subjective world could, in principle, be unchanged even if there were entire regions of the visual scene that we could no longer explore.

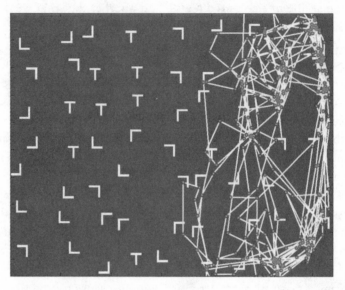

Figure 14. Eye movements for a person with left-side visual neglect, looking for Ts among Ls. The left side of the picture is completely ignored.[11]

People with the medical syndrome of visual neglect show just this pattern. They completely disregard a huge area of visual space (often the entire left side of the visual field) with no disruption in their sense of the completeness and richness of their visual world.

In Figure 14, an eye-tracker traces how a person with left-side neglect looks for Ts against a background of Ls, searching on the right-hand side and rarely scanning their fovea on the left – thus the scan paths in Figure 14 are relentlessly to the right. Copying is often also dramatically affected (Figure 15). A person with neglect typically

Figure 15. Copying in left-side neglect. The copier can be completely unaware that half the field is missing. Yet basic visual processing is typically intact.[12]

has relatively normal visual processing in the affected part of the visual field – they simple don't pay any attention to it. And, rather than sensing an alarming void which might cover fully half of the visual field, they report no change to their subjective experience. Indeed, neglect patients can sometimes feel rather doubtful that they have a visual deficit at all!

Visual neglect arises, it seems, because the brain is unable to attend to a large area of the visual field. According to the intuitive conception that our brains 'load up' a detailed and full-colour copy of the entire visual world, we should expect neglect patients to experience a huge and shocking disruption to their inner subjective world. After all, it would seem that half of it has disappeared! Yet neglect patients typically report nothing of the kind. From the point of view of the sequential, fragmentary perspective on perception, this is just what we should expect: we perceive only the parts of the image that we *are* processing, not those we are *not* processing. The unattended parts of the image no more 'feel' missing than the second half of a novel feels missing, if we never get round to reading it.

I have argued that visual neglect occurs when the brain is unable to 'question' or 'explore' anything that is in one part of the visual field. What would happen, though, if we were unable to disengage and re-engage our attention freely? Then, surely, the grand illusion would be punctured: we would be aware of the very object or pattern whose meaning we had just constructed – but that would be all we could see.

This is not merely a hypothetical possibility. Patients with the rare neurological condition of simultagnosia have exactly this phenomenology. When a comb is held in front of him, one patient correctly reports seeing a comb; when a spoon is now held up in front of the comb, forming the shape of a cross, he reports seeing only a comb; the spoon, although occupying an overlapping region of the visual field, is not seen. If the spoon and comb are held vertically, side by side, the patient reports seeing the spoon, but denies seeing the comb. The spoon and comb are now held horizontally directly in front of the patient. What does the patient see now, the experimenter asks? The patient responds that he sees what looks like a blackboard with some writing on it – both the spoon and the comb (and, we must presume, the experimenter) have disappeared, and the patient's brain has locked onto the blackboard on the wall behind.[13] So a patient with simultagnosia is able to see objects of different distances and sizes – but has no sense of the continuing existence of the rest of the visual world.

Intuitively, we may imagine that a patient with simultagnosia is restricted to perceiving one object or pattern at a time, whereas people with normal visual abilities are able to perceive any number of objects simultaneously – indeed, surveying the room around us for a moment, we may imagine that we are able to simultaneously 'take in' dozens or even hundreds of distinct objects, just as, when we glance at a page of text, we have the sense of simultaneously surveying hundreds of distinct words and thousands of letters. But, as we have seen, to think this way is, of course, to be taken in by the grand illusion: all of us perceive the world through a remarkably narrow channel – roughly a single word, object, pattern or property at a time.

Simultagnosia is a complex and varied disorder. But I wonder if it may represent what happens when a person no longer has the environment available 'on demand'. A person with simultagnosia is looking at the world through a narrow window, but is no longer able to query any part of the rest of visual world, set off the relevant eye movements, and find the required answer. If this is right, simultagnosia reveals the 'truth' about what we all see, moment by moment – it strips away the grand illusion of a cluttered, detailed world, simultaneously loaded in our consciousness.

From time to time, I have found myself wondering, somewhat despairingly, how much the last hundred and fifty years or so of psychology and neuroscience has really revealed about the secrets of human nature. How far have we progressed beyond what we can gather from philosophical reflection, the literary imagination, or from plain common sense? How much has the scientific study of our minds and brains revealed that really challenges our intuitive conception of ourselves?

The gradual uncovering of the grand illusion through careful experimentation is a wonderful example of how startlingly wrong our intuitive conception of ourselves can be. And once we know the trick, we can see that it underlies the apparent solidity of our verbal explanations too. Just as the eye can dash into action to answer whatever question about the visual world I happen to ask myself, so my inventive mind can conjure up a justification for my actions, beliefs and motives, just as soon as I wonder about them. We wonder why puddles form or how electricity circulates around the house – and immediately we find explanations springing into our consciousness. And if we query any element of our explanation, more explanations spring into existence, and so on. Our powers of invention are so fluent that we can imagine that these explanations were pre-formed within us in all their apparently endless complexity. But, of course, each answer was created in the moment.

So whether we are considering sensory experience or verbal

explanations, the story is the same. We are, it turns out, utterly wrong about a subject on which we might think we should be the ultimate arbiter: the contents of our own minds. Could we perhaps be equally or even more deluded when we turn to consider the workings of our imagination?

4

The Inconstant Imagination

Imagine a tiger, as clearly and distinctly as you can. Try to create a mental photograph, or, better still, add a third dimension and summon up a mental hologram. If your tiger moves and roars, so much the better. Our powers of imagination seem to differ a lot from one person to the next. Some of us report that we can conjure up an entire zoo of squawking and wriggling animals, while some of us (including myself) find imagining even a single animal to be something of a challenge. Oddly, though, after a little time with my eyes shut, rather compelling images of tigers do sometimes appear, at one moment leaping, at another, prowling the jungle floor.

When our visual images are at their most compelling, most of us have the impression that, perhaps only for a moment, we have created a fairly accurate, detailed, colourful, 'mental tiger' – indeed, it can feel as if we are 'watching' this creation as if projected on an inner TV screen[1] or perhaps, if we have a strong ability to create mental images in 3D, from the stalls of an inner theatre.[2] Your 'inner tiger' may not feel quite as vivid as the experience of actually facing a tiger at close quarters – but your inner tiger may feel richly detailed none the less.

According to common sense, and to the theories of many psychologists and philosophers who study our ability to form 'mental images', such an image is something like an inner picture or perhaps even a 3D copy of the world. From this point of view, examining a 'mental tiger' is rather like scrutinizing a picture of a tiger, or perhaps peering at a real tiger. Indeed, mental pictures seem to be just the kind of thing that the mind creates during perception, but in the case of the imagination, of course, there is no external object.

We have seen already that the intuition that our senses create an inner copy of the external world, rich in colour and detail, is an illusion. But if I don't have a mental picture of a tiger even when a tiger is right in front of me, then surely no such picture underlies my tenuous and rather indistinct mental images of tigers. Perhaps, then, mental imagery is no more than a visual version of creative fiction.

Consider, for a moment, the pattern of stripes on your 'inner tiger'. A warm-up task, popular among psychologists and philosophers interested in imagery, is to try to count the number of stripes on your inner tiger's tail; and then to count the number of stripes on the body. This is surprisingly difficult to do – and you may start to suspect that your image doesn't contain quite enough detail to accomplish this task. Perhaps you can 'zoom in', say, on your tiger's tail. But is the number of stripes on the 'zoomed-in' tail the same as the number of stripes on your original mental tiger? And, for that matter, I find I can't really count the stripes convincingly, even when I have zoomed in – my image just doesn't seem stable enough to give me a reliable answer. So examining a mental image, however vivid, seems very different from examining a real image (e.g. a photo of a tiger).

Let us focus instead on something more basic, concerning not the number of stripes on your 'mental tiger', but the way the stripes 'flow' over its body. Ask yourself if the stripes run along the length of the body or all round the body like hoops? And now consider how the stripes flow along the tiger's legs: do they run down the length of each leg, or, alternatively, around each leg? And finally, what happens to the pattern of stripes where the pattern on the legs (whatever that is) joins the pattern on the body (whatever that is). In fact, just so that you can be really sure that you have a crisp and precise image in your mind's eye, you might want to draw an outline of your tiger, however rough, and sketch in your pattern of stripes.

Once you've done that, take a look at the four possible scenarios in Figure 16 (opposite). Which one looks most like your drawing? Which seems most plausible? Later, we'll look at a real tiger (in Figure 21, but resist the urge to skip ahead) where the answer will be revealed.

But remember the grand illusion: even if a tiger, rather alarmingly, was standing immediately in front of you, your eyes and brain would

Figure 16. The tiger's stripes?

grasp only a sequence of visual fragments: now noticing the orangey colour of its fur, then seeing its great jaws opening in a yawn, then noticing the sheer size of its outstretched paws. Our sense of the vividness of the tiger stems from the fluency with which we can answer any question we wish about the tiger's appearance – but as we have seen, the information is created on demand, not loaded into our brains in a single visual gulp. In fact, we can't even load the perception of a simple quartered circle with alternately blue and green segments (Figure 12) into our minds, let alone an object as complex as a tiger.

Just as the visual details of a real tiger would be available on demand, so is the tiger of your imagination – as soon as you ask yourself about the shape of its teeth, the position of its tail, or whether it is longer than the sofa, an answer comes to you, quick as a flash. But this is not because you are making 'internal eye movements' across the form of the 'inner tiger' to find out how it looks; rather, your mind is *improvising* the answers, almost as soon as you ask for them. This is our subjective experience of vivid imagery: the ability to question, explore and manipulate your view of the 'tiger' at will.

The sense of vividness, of 'encompassing' a whole object or an entire scene, comes, whether in imagery or perception, from the ability to maintain the hoax. We don't 'load' vast quantities of information about an object or a scene simultaneously into our memory – but we can have the answer to any question about visual experience available just when we need it. An image is vivid to the extent that, as soon as a query crosses our mind (Are the tiger's claws retracted? Is its mouth open or closed? What are the precise locations of its front legs? What about the shape and colour of its nose?), the answer is ready to hand. If an actual tiger, or a picture of a tiger, is before us, then these questions can be fluently answered by a flick of our eyes and/or a shift of attention. If instead we are imagining a tiger, our brain needs to answer these questions not by consulting an inner mental picture, but by sketching in retracted or extended claws or by specifying the mouth or the legs in a little more detail.

The crucial clue that mental imagery is fake parallels our discussion of the fictional character of verbal explanations (Chapter 1) and sensory experience (Chapter 2): mental imagery, too, is both sparse and contradictory. For example, our mental image of a tiger, vivid or not, is incredibly sketchy – almost all the details are entirely absent. And our reports of our images are contradictory too, as we'll see shortly. The sense of vividness of an object, a text or a scene, whether in vision or imagination, doesn't come from creating a complete and precise 'inner copy' – this is just another phantom, another cleverly improvised illusion.

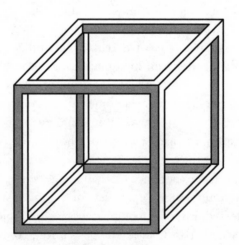

Figure 17. How easily can you imagine transformations of something as simple as a wire-frame cube?

Now let's try something much simpler than a tiger. I have a wire-frame cube on the desk in front of me (Figure 17). After inspecting it, the following seductive thought occurs to me: surely, in addition to the wire-frame cube in the outer world, the physical object on my desk, there is another cube in my mental inner world – an inner cube, as it were, in my mind's eye. Indeed, with a bit of mental effort, I can shut my eyes and imagine the cube still there on the desk; the mental 'inner cube' remains, it seems, even when its link is severed from the physical 'outer cube'.

In the case of perception, the inner and outer worlds appear to have been brought into correspondence: the inner cube of my mind's eye seemed roughly to be a copy of the physical cube on the desk. I say *roughly* because, for example, there will be details of the physical cube (e.g. discolorations on parts of the frame that are not visible from where I am sitting, and of which I am entirely unaware) which won't be present in my imagined cube. And the physical cube will be made of particular stuff (the wires may perhaps be made of copper), whereas, of course, the putative 'mental cube' is not made of a material substance of any kind. None the less, we have the intuition that the inner 'mental cube' is a pretty good copy of the real thing. Moreover, unlike the tiger's stripes, the cube seems to have rather fewer intricate details to confuse us. We seem to be on safer ground.

Interestingly, the inner cube appears to have a life of its own. Closing my eyes I can see my mental wire-frame cube before me, though admittedly rather indistinctly; and I can imagine this inner cube lifting off from the table and hovering briefly, perhaps, before setting off to my left, spinning elegantly on a vertical axis, performing a lively somersault, and dropping back onto the surface of the desk. So it seems I can explore an inner perceptual world detached from external reality. And aren't the realms of fiction, fantasy and dreams illustrations of the richness of the inner worlds that our minds can construct?

But let's cross-examine this viewpoint for a moment.

The Sceptic (S): Tell me, then, can you see the cube vividly in your mind's eye?

The Inner Explorer (E): Oh yes, very vividly.

S: And tell me, what orientation is the cube, in relation to the desk?

E: Well, that's easy – one of the faces of the cube is flush with the surface of the desk.

S: And what about shadows?

E: Shadows?

S: Well, in your perfectly vivid image, presumably there is light coming from somewhere – perhaps an Anglepoise lamp lighting the surface of the desk?

E: Oh yes, I suppose there is some sort of light. In fact, now I think about it, the light is directly overhead.

S: So there must be shadows from the frame of the cube onto the surface of the desk.

E: Yes. I suppose they were there all along – I just didn't pay much attention to them before.

S: Tell me about the shadows. What pattern can you see in your mind's eye, when you look at those shadows?

E: Umm, well, they are all rectangles and squares, a sort of inter-locking grid pattern. I can sort of see it in my mind, but it's so hard to put into words.

S: [*Handing E a pen and paper*] Perhaps it would be easier to draw.

E: Thanks, but it is actually quite tricky to draw too.

S: Perhaps I can help. Just imagine the cube balancing on one 'corner'.

E: Actually, this is not as easy as I would have thought.

S: Well, it hardly seems that this should be necessary for such a simple geometric shape, but perhaps it would help if I show you a picture (Figure 18). It's cheating, really, but just have a quick glance, and see if that helps you conjure up the cube a bit more vividly in your mind's eye.

E: OK.

S: Now there are, of course, eight corners on a cube. Let's leave aside the 'bottom' corner (the one it is balancing on) and 'top' corner (opposite to the bottom corner). Can you describe the layout of the other six corners? Imagine a horizontal plane, which intersects one of the corners. Does it intersect any of the other corners?

E: Er, well, perhaps all of them – perhaps they all lie on the same plane.

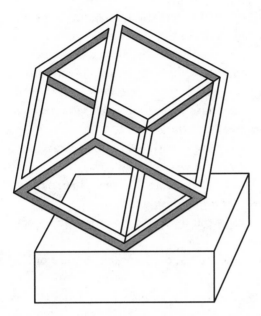

Figure 18. A cube balancing on one corner. The diametrically opposite corner lies directly above the corner on which the cube is balanced – otherwise the cube would topple over. How are the six other corners arranged? Are they all the same height as each other? All at different heights? Or arranged in 'layers'? These are challenging questions, even with the figure in front of you.[3]

S: Now that's plain self-contradictory – in fact, it's just geometrically impossible! Are you sure you're really looking at a mental copy of a cube in your mind's eye? (No looking back at Figure 18 now!)

E: OK – well, perhaps each corner is at a different height?

S: But that's geometrically impossible too.

E: Well, perhaps a plane will intersect two or three corners, then.

S: Yes, three as it happens. In fact, those six corners form two equilateral triangles, one above the other.

E: Oh yes, that sounds right. I think I can see that now – yes, I don't know what I was thinking before.

S: So if you can see that nice and clearly, you'll be able to tell me how those triangles relate to each other – you can just see them, can't you?

E: Well, not exactly. I don't think I'm going to guess – you'll just be accusing me of contradictions again.

S: OK – let's try something else with the balancing cube. Imagine that the only source of light is coming directly from above: a spotlight high above the point on the desk that the cube is balancing on. Can you see that? You can look back at the Figure 18 now and again, if you really must.

E: Yes: balancing cube, with light above. I can see that.

S: What do the shadows look like now.

E: Er, well, lots of lines at different diagonal angles; a sort of wonky grid [*becoming desperate*].

S: Do the lines of the shadow criss-cross each other?

E: They might do.

S: Do they make any kind of familiar pattern or shape?

E: Er . . .

S: [*Revealing Figure 19 with a flourish*] Does this pattern ring any bells with you?

E: [*Blanches and reels back unable to respond*]

The claim that one is able to explore, and report on, an inner mental landscape would not stand up in court. Our poor inner explorer E seems to be telling an incredible tale, and one that she is quite literally

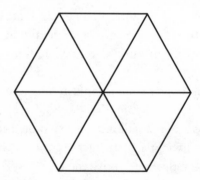

Figure 19. The shadow of a cube. Spend a little while looking at this hexagonal 'pinwheel' – you will notice that it can suddenly flip into a projection of a 3D cube. In fact, this is just what the cube looks like if we look at it from a line of sight running through two diametrically opposite 'corners'.

making up as she goes along. In the real world, wire-frame cubes have shadows, whether one notices them or not; and those shadows have definite shapes, whether one is attending to them or not; and when one's attention is drawn to those shapes, it is possible to say what they are, at least roughly. In the real world, when those shadows form a simple pinwheel, we can observe this – and report it accurately, probably with a sense of surprise.

How different this is from E's attempts to report the contents of her inner world! E's reports are the familiar confection of sparsity and self-contradiction – they seem continually to miss out crucial visual information (e.g. shadows) that surely should be present, but equally to topple easily into downright mathematical contradictions. First off, the wire-frame cube is sitting on a blank desktop; there are no shadows, and no light source to cast them. Most likely, too, the desk has no particular shape or extent; neither desk nor cube has any definite colour; the cube is of no particular size. Once light sources and

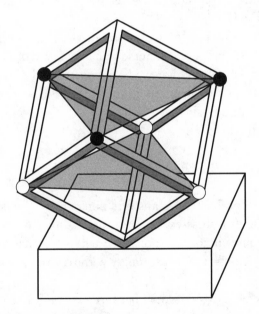

Figure 20. A cube balancing on one corner, with 'middle' corners highlighted. The lower 'white' corners form a horizontal equilateral triangle; so do the upper 'black' corners. You can see that the two triangles are 'pointing' in opposite directions: one is a mirror image of the other.

shadows are mentioned, of course, they can be sketched into our mental picture, but sketched only crudely. We have little idea what the shadows must look like, except that they must surely consist of straight lines, in some sort of slanted, grid-like pattern. Queries about the six corners reveal abject confusion – as Figure 20 shows, there is a simple and unique possible layout, as two equilateral triangles, one above the other. Any other proposal is simply geometrically impossible – yet E is happy to suggest such impossibilities (as most of us are).

We have the intuition that we can imagine the cube moving around, and perhaps a vague sense of the complex of shadows dancing beneath it. But this, too, turns out to be only the lightest of sketches. And the problem is *not* that the inner world is really there, but that it is difficult to report its flux and complexity, because even when the set-up of cube and lighting generates what should, in the outer world, be a striking, surprising and simple pattern (our pinwheel shadow), the mind's eye is entirely oblivious to this fact. Again, any other proposal is a mathematical contradiction – yet we cheerfully make such proposals none the less.

In the light of the improvised nature of visual experience, none of this should be surprising: of course our imagery will be partial and contradictory. To believe that we have constructed a 'picture' of the outer world in our own minds is to fall for the illusion of mental depth, hook, line and sinker.

THE LOST WORLD

Have we been too hasty? E's answers don't entirely make sense. But perhaps S's line of cross-examination has confused her into giving apparently contradictory responses. Such is the nature of hostile legal interrogation – the most honest witness can get into a terrible muddle.

But this defence won't work, because, as we'll see, our attempts to probe our innermost mental depths always get into a muddle, and do so in systematic and predictable ways. Our answers are full of gaps and inconsistencies. But why? Because our imagination, like visual experience, is a narrow window of lucidity, and what we see through that window is invented – creatively, subtly, intelligently – not merely reported from some fully specified, entirely coherent inner world.

Finally, back to the tiger's stripes, shown on an actual tiger in Figure 21. Most of us guess correctly that the tiger's stripes run vertically around its body, and most of us have the feeling that the stripes also run around the legs, rather than along their length, but this is perhaps less obvious (so the top left option in Figure 16 is the closest to the truth). But did you notice, by careful inspection of your mental image, that the tiger's front legs *don't have stripes at all*? Or that, for the back legs, the stripes gradually and smoothly 'rotate' from horizontal (along the leg) to vertical (along the body). The stripes on the head form a complex pattern that seems all too familiar now that one sees it, but which most of us are utterly unable to discern from our mental images of tigers. Many of us also fail to 'see' the white belly and inner legs of the tiger. You should now view your sense of a highly realistic and finely detailed 'photographic' image of a tiger cavorting in the inner landscape of your mind with great suspicion.

Yet, on reflection, perhaps these results should not come as a surprise. We have seen that we grasp the visual world one element at a time. The same is true for mental imagery. That is, just as we wonder about the shape of our imaginary tiger's tail, the shape of a tiger's tail

Figure 21. The tiger's stripes, revealed.

is immediately traced in our mind's eye; just as we ask ourselves whether its claws are extended or retracted, our imagination invents an answer to this too. When we speculate about the location of the light source shining on a wire-frame cube, we create such a light source; when asked about the shadows that it casts, we sketch a mental image of shadows (though rather unrealistic ones, as we have seen). We are not examining a fully formed, comprehensively detailed and coloured mental image in our mind's eye – at one moment zooming in, or shifting our attention to the left and right. We are, instead, *creating* our mental image, piece by piece, moment by moment, touchpoint by touchpoint.

It is worth thinking, for a moment, about what these observations imply for dreaming. Dreams seem to be naturally viewed as the successive creation and dissolution of momentary fragments; in retrospect full of holes and contradictions, however compelling they may be as we experience them. The incoherence of dreams becomes immediately evident as soon as we attempt to recall them. Scenes and even time itself shifts abruptly, people change identities, and appear and disappear without warning. The 'world' of dreams is a fiction, a jumble of fragments and contradictions. Indeed, it is a particularly inchoate fiction: there is no careful author painstakingly attempting to bring the story into some kind of order – merely a succession of capricious imaginative leaps.

Suppose, for example, we imagine meeting an old friend, Ludwig, in a dream. We may have no memory, and typically we do not, of the specific visual details of Ludwig's clothing, whether he had his glasses on or off, or had recently had a haircut. It is tempting to put down such vagueness to the weakness of memory; and perhaps especially to the rapid dissolution of the memories of our dreams. But this is not the explanation at all. We haven't forgotten these details; our brain never bothered to specify them in the first place. A plethora of further questions have no meaningful answers in this and almost any other dream encounter – What was the weather like? What sort of floor or ground were we standing on? What year was it? What was the nature and level of background noise? Were any cars or trains audible? Which trees and plants were visible? How many leaves did each tree/plant have, and how were they oriented towards the light?

Dreams are improvised stories, with few details sketched in. When our minds create them, we lock onto some specific fragments of information; almost everything else is left utterly blank. There is no more truth about whether, in my dream, Ludwig was wearing jeans or his familiar tartan trousers than there is truth about the shape of Homer Simpson's liver, or the petrol consumption of Chitty Chitty Bang Bang.

PERCEPTION AND IMAGINATION

There is a crucial difference, of course, between the work of perception and that of imagination. In perceiving the outer world, we can check and cross-check by shifting our attention back and forth; and unless we are in the grip of a devious psychological experiment, we can be fairly confident that we will obtain the same answers each time – because the outer world consists of pre-formed stable objects which we can inspect from various directions with a fair expectation that these different views will fit together. But when we consult our imagination, we can have no such assurance. The products of our minds will be as inconsistent as Oscar Reutersvärd's figures – and this should not be surprising. Even the most assiduous novelist has terrible trouble avoiding self-contradiction; even with the aid of notes on each character's back-story, invented maps and imagined family trees, still the inconsistencies creep in. But our momentary flow of improvised words and images is, of course, far more prone to confusion and self-contradiction.

Our shape-shifting 'mental image' of the wire-frame cube should also make us sceptical about inner worlds of all kinds. If we *invent* answers about the rotating cubes as we go along, perhaps the same applies to the inner world of motives and beliefs. Indeed, our storytelling about human motives and beliefs is at least as incoherent as our descriptions of the cube in our mind's eye; and here, too, the incoherence arises not because it is difficult to peer into and report back on our murky hidden mental depths, but because there *are* no hidden mental depths.

Many of us have found ourselves wondering whether we dream in colour. But dreams no more have colours than stories do. And they no more have colours than they have textures, background noises, odours or arrangements of lighting. We can have the sense of a rich and colourful dream-world, of course, because we can create sensory impressions as soon as we start wondering about them – perceptual touchpoints with our dreams are imagined, one by one. But if while we are dreaming we happen not to wonder about the colour of Ludwig's trousers, then the colour of his trousers is blank. To suspect that Ludwig's trousers may have had a colour, but we simply didn't notice it, would be as misguided as imagining that Ophelia wore sapphire earrings, bought from a particular jeweller in Copenhagen, in a specific year, even though none of this ever crossed Shakespeare's mind. It would, in short, be to confuse reality (where there are any number of facts, whether we know them or not) and fiction (where, roughly, there are no facts, beyond those that the author has set down).

The same confusion – between reality and fiction – arises when we wonder whether there are unheard sounds, unfelt pains, hidden motives or unconscious beliefs. These shadowy entities are no more real than the colour of Ludwig's trousers or the pattern of shadows projected by my supposed 'mental cube'. The inconsistent, sketchy flow of thought is not a projection of a rich and deep inner mental world. Our thoughts are not shadows of an alternative inner reality, to be charted and discovered; they are fictions of our own devising, created moment by moment.

THE CAUTIONARY TALE OF HERBERT GRAF

When the celebrated Austrian opera director Herbert Graf (1903–73) was just four years old, he witnessed a frightening event while walking with his mother. A horse, one of a pair pulling a large van through the streets of Vienna, fell and starting kicking out wildly. Herbert feared that it might be dying. This frightening incident left its mark on the sensitive child, and he expressed his fear that other horses might fall down. As a result he became afraid of the sight of horses and horse-drawn carriages (particularly large carriages, such as the one involved in the terrible incident). He also developed a more general fear of horses: not just that they would fall, but that they might bite him. Herbert explained that he was especially alarmed 'by what horses wear in front of their eyes and the black round their mouths',[4] presumably referring to the blinkers and the muzzles used by the type of working horse that he had seen fall. This fear extended into an anxiety about going out onto the streets of Vienna, with its profusion of horses and horse-drawn vehicles. These fears were severe enough to cause his parents considerable, and understandable, concern.

Why did Herbert begin to fear that horses might bite, something that he had never seen as far as we know? A natural speculation would be that the initial terrifying incident led him to feel high levels of anxiety in the presence of horses, with the associated physical symptoms – pulse racing, breath short, adrenaline coursing through him. And this has a natural interpretation: that he is afraid of horses. But the brain then needs to explain why it is afraid of horses – what harm might a horse do to a young child that would justify such a fear? A natural explanation (among other possibilities, of course) would be that the horse might bite.

Thankfully Herbert's fear of horses gradually lifted – indeed, this is quite a normal pattern with childhood phobias – though some, of course, persist. Perhaps the terrible sight and sounds of the flailing horse began to fade from memory; perhaps they were gradually overlaid by more innocuous thoughts about, and experiences of, horses.

The human ability to project imaginative and exotic stories onto relatively prosaic behaviour was beautifully illustrated by the response of Herbert's father, Max Graf, a noted music critic, to his son's fears. Immersed at the time in popular contemporary theories of infantile sexuality, Max Graf wrote to a local doctor in Vienna that he suspected that 'the ground [for the phobia] was prepared by sexual over-excitation due to his mother's tenderness' and that the specific fear of horses 'seems somehow to be connected with his having been frightened by a large penis'.[5] The doctor agreed, concluding that '[Herbert] really was a little Oedipus who wanted to have his father "out of the way", to get rid of him, so that he might be alone with his beautiful mother and sleep with her.'[6] According to this perspective,

Herbert was therefore afraid of his father, as a powerful rival for this mother's affection.

Herbert's father and the doctor began to suspect, indeed, that Herbert's fear of horses was really a fear of his father, suggesting that Herbert's particular fear of 'what horses wear in front of their eyes and the black round their mouths' might actually be a fear of his father's glasses and moustache, rather than referring to the blinkers and muzzle of the horse that felt so terrifyingly. The doctor wrote that Herbert's fear of leaving the house had, moreover, a hidden motive: 'The content of his phobia was such as to impose a very great measure of restriction upon his freedom of movement, and that was its purpose . . . allowing him to stay at home with his beloved mother.'[7] This doesn't quite hang together, even in its own terms: Herbert is not reported as having been anxious about his mother's absence (his mother leaving the home, while he remained), and he was equally afraid of being outside even when his mother was present. Herbert thus seemed to be afraid of leaving the house, rather than being parted from his mother – which would make sense if he was afraid of a repetition of the dreadful incident of the fallen horse, of course. Max Graf and the doctor were sceptical – indeed, they felt it would hardly be surprising if Herbert were to hide the true origins of his phobia, even from himself. They concluded that, while the phobia started immediately after the traumatic incident, this was merely a trigger for the phenomenon, which was assumed to have rich subconscious roots. Herbert disagreed: 'No. I only got it then. When the horse in the bus fell down. It gave me such a fright, really! That was when I got the nonsense [Herbert's name for his phobia].'

It is easy, of course, to find fanciful uses for Freudian theory to create highly elaborate and 'deep' explanations of behaviour that seems to have an all-too-obvious 'shallow' interpretation: to see a fear of horses as arising not from a frightening experience with one, but from a desire to kill one's father and sleep with one's mother. Herbert's father was a purely amateur psychoanalyst; and the doctor based his advice on the father's letters, and just one brief interview with the boy.

Yet this particular case deserves special attention, because Herbert Graf, future luminary of world opera, was known as 'Little Hans';

the local doctor, as you may have guessed, was Sigmund Freud himself; this case study (1909), for all its frailties, is one of the most important in the canon of psychoanalysis. Indeed, so celebrated did this case study become that, at the time of writing, the discussion of this relatively brief childhood phobia takes up nearly half of Herbert Graf's Wikipedia entry, given equal weight with his nearly half-century as a leading figure in the world of opera.

Max Graf and Freud were attempting to peer into the dark recesses of the mind of 'Little Hans'; later analysts have also gone over the case, producing different diagnoses. The problem with these disputes is not that they disagree about Herbert's subconscious inner mental world, but that Herbert/Hans – like the rest of us – has no inner world, just a collection of mental fragments. Asking whether Hans desired, subconsciously, to kill his father and sleep with his mother is not only wrong in detail. It is no more meaningful than wondering how many stripes William Blake's Tyger had, whether Tom Sawyer had been born on a Tuesday, or whether James Bond's lifetime grand total intake of Martinis came to a prime number. Our imaginations can fill in these details and more – but the product of our imaginations is, of course, fiction not fact.

Putting the point as starkly as possible: Graf and Freud's mistake was to confuse literary creation with psychology. They were able to invent a story about Herbert/Hans and his phobia; and they could equally easily have invented a variety of alternative stories. The key question for the creative writer is: which is the most interesting, striking and engaging story. Indeed, Freud's case notes show that he was an endlessly inventive and fascinating storyteller, drawing on a great knowledge of mythology and the arts to create intriguing new perspectives on human experience. But there is no fact of the matter regarding whether one or another of these stories is true. In short, while Graf and Freud believed psychology should be science, they practised it as a literary art form.

So much for the flimsiness of mental images and dreams. But does the story stop there? Most of us have a sense that our minds are teeming with thoughts. We may feel rather unsure exactly about the nature of the inhabitants of our 'inner world', but plausible candidates would seem to be beliefs, desires, hopes, fears, mental images, logical arguments, justifications, feelings of anxiety, delight, excitement, gloom, contentment, resignation or enthusiasm, flashes of anger or surges of empathy. Our vagueness about quite what our minds contain is by no means accidental – the solidity of our mental furniture is liable to dissolve as soon as we reach out and touch it.

5
Inventing Feelings

Lev Kuleshov, the Russian director, made his first film at the astonishingly young age of nineteen, and later successfully picked his way through the political minefield of Stalinist Russia to become a powerful figure in the Soviet film industry. He also made an astonishing psychological discovery (see Figure 22). He intercut shots of Ivan Mozzhukhin, a Russian silent film star, with three images: a dead child in an open coffin, a bowl of soup, and a glamorous young woman reclining on a divan. The audience were impressed by Mozzhukhin's subtle acting, in turn indicating grief, hunger and lust. But Mozzhukhin's acting was not so much subtle, as non-existent – the very same

Figure 22. The Kuleshov effect. The interpretation of an ambiguous facial expression is changed dramatically when intercut with different scenes.[1]

shots were used in each case; the juxtaposition of a relatively impassive face with scenes laden with emotion causes the audience to impose their own interpretations of Mozzhukhin's emotional state.[2]

The Kuleshov effect has been hugely influential in cinema – indeed, Alfred Hitchcock picks out the effect as one of the most powerful cinematic techniques in a TV interview in 1966.[3] And this type of effect is not limited to intercutting film and juxtaposing distinct images. The background of a still photograph can dramatically change how we emotionally 'read' a face (see Figure 23).

Figure 23. US Senator Jim Webb at a campaign rally. With the context stripped away, he looks angry and frustrated; in the context of a campaign rally, he looks happy and even triumphant.[4]

We think that we are 'seeing' emotions in the face, and the face alone – but context turns out to be far more important than we imagine. The power of context is certainly a ubiquitous feature of perception. Consider, for example, the patterns in Figure 24, where an isolated portion of an image which, when considered alone, can be open to more than one interpretation (just like Mozzhukhin's apparently subtle acting, or Webb's excited facial expression in Figure 23), is disambiguated by looking at the wider context. There is a general principle at work here – the brain interprets each piece of the perceptual input (each face, object, symbol, or whatever it may be) to make as much sense as possible in the light of the wider context.

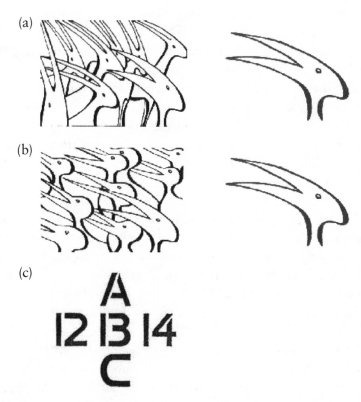

Figure 24. (a) A field of rabbits makes an ambiguous duck-rabbit look like a rabbit; (b) a field of birds makes an ambiguous duck-rabbit look like a bird; (c) the same phenomenon illustrated with numbers and letters.[5]

MAKING SENSE OF OUR AMBIGUOUS SELVES

Could the Kuleshov effect apply not just to when we ascribe emotions of others, but also to how we ascribe emotions to ourselves? In a narrow sense, this seems all too plausible. Imagine the actor Mozzhukhin being presented with the images of himself, juxtaposed with images of tragedy, food or seduction, as we saw in Figure 22. He would surely be all too likely to read his own (static) expression just as we do – gently and subtly hinting at sadness, hunger or lust. One can imagine him inwardly congratulating himself on his marvellously understated acting, of course. But one could equally imagine that, if he thought that the photos had been taken at significant moments in his own life (rather than onscreen), Mozzhukhin would read his own expression just as we would: as signifying whatever emotion made the most sense in the context.

Imagine, now, a variation of the Kuleshov effect of the following, apparently rather peculiar, form: instead of (or perhaps as well as) seeing Mozzhukhin's facial expression, we hear his heart-rate. Perhaps, with the appearance of the image (the coffin, bowl of soup, or young woman), we hear his heart-rate distinctly increase. How do we interpret this physiological signal? Just as before, I suspect it could be seen, variously, as a sign of an overwhelming despair, a sudden pang of hunger, or a surge of lust. And suppose we could hear his breathing become shallower and more rapid, and his adrenaline levels rising too: these indications would simply add colour to the same interpretation (and these signals will tend to vary in unison, of course).

Now consider how we interpret our own emotions, not in retrospect, but as they happen. We don't normally have access to our facial expressions, of course, but we do know something about our own physiological state – we can, to a degree, feel our heart racing, our breath shortening, the tingle of adrenaline racing through our arteries. These signals are, of course, highly ambiguous, just like Mozzhukhin's sphinx-like expression – they can indicate surges of feeling of many different kinds.

So perhaps we are inevitably subject to a kind of Kuleshov effect when making sense of our own emotions. Might the feeling of possessing one definitive emotion rather than another not be embodied in, or determined by, our bodily state, any more than our emotions are inscribed in our facial expressions? Indeed, isn't our bodily state just another set of highly ambiguous clues that need to be interpreted, which can be explained in many different ways depending on the situation we are in? Perhaps, in short, emotions – including our own emotions – are just fiction too.

In 1962, a remarkable, and justly famous, experiment at the

University of Minnesota provided some of the first direct evidence that this is right. Psychologists Stanley Schachter and Jerome Singer injected volunteer participants with either adrenaline or a placebo, and led them to a waiting area where they could sit for a while before the beginning of the experiment. They found that they had to share the waiting room with another participant who, so it seemed, was also waiting to be taken through to start the experimental session.

But the waiting room *was* the experiment – and the other person wasn't a fellow participant at all, but a 'stooge' of the experimenters. The stooge acted either slightly manically (making and flying paper aeroplanes) or angrily (outraged by a questionnaire they had to fill in while waiting). The artificially adrenalinized participants had stronger emotional reactions to both stooges than those who had just received a placebo. Crucially, and remarkably, their emotional reactions were stronger in opposite directions. Confronted with the 'manic' stooge, participants interpreted their raised heart-rate, shortness of breath and flushed face as indicating their own euphoria; but with the 'angry' stooge, those very same symptoms were interpreted as signalling their own irritation.

Here we can see the Kuleshov effect in another guise – one which suggests that emotions of joy or anger do not well up from our inner depths. Instead, we seem to interpret our emotions in the moment: and we appear to do this based not just on the situation we are in (the person we are confronted with is behaving, say, manically or angrily) but also on our own physiological state (e.g. whether our heart is racing, our face flushed). So if a stooge behaves a little manically, and the experimental participant experiences a high level of arousal, then the participant is likely to interpret their positive feelings as *strong* positive feelings – after all, that would explain the raised heart-rate, shortness of breath, and so on. So they infer that they must be experiencing a state of perhaps mild euphoria. Confronted with the angry stooge, by contrast, suggesting feelings of annoyance in the experimental participant, the sheer strength of their physiological reaction (caused, of course, by the adrenaline) is interpreted as indicating a powerful emotional reaction. Participants perceive themselves to be very annoyed, rather than just mildly irritated.

Schachter and Singer's experiment turns our intuitions about our own emotions on their head. We might imagine, for example, that emotions such as euphoria and anger have a distinctive physiological signal – a special state of the body, which gives them their special 'feel'. If this were right, then we would expect a physiological change, such as that generated by an injection of adrenaline, to push us towards one of these supposed emotion-specific physiological states. So we might suspect that a shot of adrenaline will make us a little happier, wherever we start out, or perhaps a little crosser. Instead, the impact of adrenaline has opposite effects, depending on our inter-pretation of our situation. Roughly, adrenaline seems to signal to us that we must feel strongly about whatever emotional reactions seems natural – pushing a positive reaction towards mania, and a negative reaction towards outright anger. It seems that we are figuring out what emotion we must be experiencing, and doing so, in part, from the state of our own body. We tend to imagine that our emotions well up from within, and cause a physiological reaction (e.g. the fact that I am angry is making my heart race). But in reality it seems that we are figuring out what emotion we must be feeling, partly based on observing our own physiological state.

Wait a second, you may say. Isn't all this talk of interpreting one's own emotions a little premature? Perhaps a shot of adrenaline does have a simple emotional effect, after all: functioning as an *intensifier*. So perhaps the emotion wells up from within, as common sense might lead us to expect (based on how the stooge behaves – whether amus-ing or annoying). But then the strength of the experienced emotion is simply amplified (or suppressed) depending on a person's level of arousal. Schachter and Singer have a clever twist in their experiment to look at this: among the people who got the adrenaline shots, some were told of the physiological effects they should expect (increased heart-rate, shortness of breath, etc.) and some were not (let's call these the Informed and Uninformed participants).

We have already described the heightened emotional reactions of the Uninformed participants in Schachter and Singer's experiment. But what about the Informed participants? If adrenaline merely acts as an emotional intensifier, then it should operate in just the same way whether we have been told about the likely effects of the shot or not. But if, instead, we are attempting to interpret our emotional experiences, in the moment, in the light of our physiological state, then our knowledge of the likely effect of the adrenaline shot should matter a lot. The Informed participants will attribute their state of high arousal to the shot; and therefore they will be less inclined to use it as a clue to the strength of that emotional reaction to the stooge (though, almost certainly, they won't be able to ignore it entirely). And, indeed, this is exactly what Schachter and Singer found.

You might find all this disconcerting. Surely our emotions burst through from our mental depths. And mustn't the emotions come first, and their physiological consequences second? Doesn't our heart race *because* of the raging power of our feelings? That is certainly the common-sense story. But what if causation can also flow in the opposite direction: that is, our sense of inner tumult is, in part, caused by our perception that our heart is racing, our body tingling, our face flushed. It is our interpretation of the state of our own body that makes us interpret the very same jumbled thoughts as desperate, hopeful or quietly resigned.

This striking inversion of common sense is by no means new. It was foreshadowed by the American psychologist and philosopher William James – author of probably the most influential textbook in the history of psychology,[6] and brother of celebrated novelist Henry James. James famously claimed that, when fleeing from a bear, we do not tremble because we are frightened, but rather, we experience the feeling of fear because we tremble. But of course, the physiological symptoms alone are not necessarily a signature of fear: we might experience the very same surges of adrenaline, raised heart rate, rapid breathing, at the starting blocks of a 100-metre race or before going on stage. Indeed, in many situations requiring concentration, effort or physical exertion, it can be difficult to tell whether we feel excited and ready to go, or nervous and fearful. When fleeing from a bear, though, few of us will interpret our physiological reactions as a thrill of excitement – the blood pumping wildly around the body and frantic breathing will unambiguously be perceived as indicators of terror.

With this in mind, I hope that Schachter and Singer's experiment with adrenaline and emotions will now make perfect sense. Just like a hard-to-read face, an ambiguous duck/rabbit, or a **13**, your physiological state is highly ambiguous. The brain receives rather crude perceptual signals from your own body, indicating that your heart is pumping, and a certain amount of adrenaline is flowing, you are breathing rapidly, and so on – but what does it all mean? The experience of those perceptions of your own internal states depends, as ever, on the interpretation that seems to make sense, given the wider context. The very same physiological state can 'feel' like irritation (when you are with the angry stooge) and 'feel' like elation (when you are with the manic stooge), just as the very same facial expression in Kuleshov's pioneering film-editing can be interpreted as grief, hunger or lust. Thus our feelings do not burst unbidden from within – they do not pre-exist at all. Instead, they are our brain's best momentary interpretation of feedback about our current bodily state, in the light of the situation we are in. We 'read' our own bodily states to interpret our own emotions, in much the same way as we read the facial expressions of other people to interpret their emotions.

And, on reflection, it could hardly be otherwise. Consider, for example, a pang of envy – perhaps of a rival's brilliant recent success or tales of her exotic holiday. The 'pang' is a physical feeling – but there can't be a special kind of bodily feeling, perfectly specific to *being envious of Edna's coming top in the exam* or perhaps *being envious of Elsa's trips to the temples and beaches of Vietnam*. The difference between various experiences of envy is in the interpretation of a physiologically similar, and perhaps even identical 'wave of feeling', depending on what has just happened (e.g. whether I've just heard about Edna's exam result, or caught a glimpse of Elsa's holiday photos).

What Schachter and Singer showed is that we interpret the same physiological state not merely as different versions of the same emotion (e.g. being envious of different things) but as examples of different emotions entirely (anger versus elation). And this is perhaps surprising because it suggests that our 'read-out' of our physiological state – that is, the bodily basis of our feelings – really is surprisingly sparse.

Psychologists and neuroscientists who study emotion differ on just how sparse those physiological signals are. According to the influential 'affective circumplex' model of Boston College psychologist James A. Russell,[7] for example, two physiological dimensions may suffice: one indicating *level of arousal* (this is the dimension that we have focused on so far), and the other indicating *like-dislike*. Russell calls this primitive monitoring of one's own physiological state 'core affect'. Our experience of having an emotion, though, involves an interpretation of 'core affect' based on our understanding of the situations we are in. So the 'pang' part of a pang of envy may be a mild kick of arousal (assuming the envy is not too extreme) and a nudge in the 'dislike' direction – but what makes me interpret this feeling as envy, rather than some other emotion, is the fact that these changes follow hearing about the exam results or spotting the holiday photos.

Our confusion about emotion has a long history. Plato has, as in so many things, helped shape our view of feelings and emotions for more than two thousand years. Sharply distinguishing thought and feeling, he conjured the metaphor that reason and emotion are like two horses pulling in opposite directions. But this viewpoint goes astray from the very outset – *having an emotion at all is a paradigmatic act of interpretation, and hence of reasoning.* We infer that we should interpret our bodily feelings as signalling anger, euphoria, envy or jealousy, based on the sparse signals from our physiology and social context. Just as we can see the face of another person as grief-stricken or lustful, angry or triumphant, just as we can see a **13** as a letter or a pair of numbers, just as we can see an ambiguous cartoon as a rabbit or a bird, we can feel the minimal signals from our body as anger or euphoria, mania or almost anything else, depending on our powers of interpretation – the very powers we use to make sense of other aspects of our lives and the world.

Now, of course, we sometimes imagine ourselves embodying Plato's metaphor. Perhaps, we might conjecture, Elsa's heart told her: Take that luxury tour of Vietnam, whereas her head said: Stop, you can't afford it! And her heart, it seems, won the day. But the two forces tugging at Elsa were not emotion and reason, *but two different types of reason.* One set of reasons is based on the attractions of the holiday (and, one might churlishly speculate, the hope of exciting a little envy in others); another set of reasons is based on financial constraints (including fear of debt, worry over paying the bills). And each set of reasons is laden with feeling and emotions (desires, hopes, fears, worries). So the clash of 'head' and 'heart' is not a battle between reason and emotions; it is a battle between one set of reasons and emotions and another set of reasons and emotions.

THE INTERPRETATION OF FEELING

But surely, you may object, I don't interpret my own feelings – I just *have* them. Well, first of all, notice that this is not really an argument – just a reiteration of common sense. And notice, too, that we have already seen that other common-sense intuitions about how we think may be highly misleading. Recall the overwhelming intuition that I see the entire visual world in full colour and detail (the grand illusion) and that the visual world of my imagination (such as Chapter 4's 'mental cube') is fully and coherently specified in 3D, rather than a mere shadowy and incoherent sketch. None the less, there seems something particularly shocking about the very suggestion that I have to interpret my own feelings.

Indeed, the 'interpretative' view of emotions has some particularly bizarre-sounding consequences, especially if we suppose that other aspects of one's body, not just one's level of arousal, could affect the interpretation of one's emotional state. Suppose, for example, that I pretend to be happy: I force a cheery smile and a cheery dance. Isn't the interpretative theory of emotions in danger of predicting that I infer that I must feel happy? And this can't be right. Apart from its patent implausibility, this would imply a panacea for all human woes – just act as if everything is fine, and you'll feel fine! And the possibility that such a panacea lies ready to hand, though strangely undiscovered or exploited for thousands of years of civilization, is surely remote indeed.

Yet perhaps taking up a 'happy' or 'sad' physical persona can affect your interpretation of your own emotions. Perhaps we can make our lives *feel* a little cheerier by *acting* a little cheerier. But push things too far and the effect may backfire: our emotion-interpreting system is highly sophisticated. We all know from personal experience how over-enthusiastic 'emoting' in other people can easily be interpreted as ironic or even mocking (and we've all experienced exuberant emoting which is disquietly ambiguous – is the other person genuinely delighted or cruelly disparaging?). So, if interpreting one's own emotions works the same way, then when the 'gap' between one's overt behaviour is too far out of line with the situation, then one's own behaviour might itself seem ironic.

This could explain an intriguing study in which people were asked to move their heads up and down or from side to side (i.e. effectively asked to nod or shake their heads) while listening to unpersuasive or persuasive messages about whether students should carry ID at all times (the head-nodding was 'justified' as a test of the quality of the headphones they were wearing).[8] People were, of course, more persuaded by the persuasive message; and, as by now you will be expecting, they were even more persuaded when nodding rather than shaking their heads as they listened to the message. The fact that they were instructed to nod didn't entirely discount the normal 'interpretation' of nodding as a signal of agreement. But here is the twist: when the message was unpersuasive, the impact of head movements reversed – 'nodders' were actually less persuaded by the message than 'shakers'. Yet from an interpretative standpoint, this makes sense. Suppose I see someone else nodding vigorously when given a patently unconvincing argument – this doesn't look like agreement; it looks like mockery, a non-verbal 'Yeah, right.' And, if we are construing our own feelings from our actions, just as we interpret other people's feelings from their actions, my own forced nodding in the context of something I obviously don't think is convincing will be interpreted *by me* as ironic disdain, not honest agreement. And once I interpret my own nodding as ironic, I infer that I must think the message is *really* unconvincing.[9]

So, there is no panacea – living one's daily life with a pencil between your teeth or otherwise maintaining a forced grin will not cause relentless cheerfulness or miraculously alleviate depression. And attempting to act cheerfully, when cheeriness is not what you are feeling, is all too likely to backfire – leading one to regard one's actions as a hollow mockery of happiness, perhaps underlining one's unhappiness even more thoroughly.

LOVE FROM A HIGH BRIDGE

In the early 1970s, the University of British Columbia campus in Vancouver was the scene of a remarkable experiment on the origins of physical attraction and romantic feeling.[10] Social psychologists Donald Dutton and Arthur Aron stationed attractive female experimenters at one end of a high, and slightly wobbly, pedestrian suspension bridge and also at the end of a second, solid, low bridge. Unsuspecting men were intercepted after crossing the bridge and asked to fill in a questionnaire; crucially, they were also handed the female experimenter's phone number, supposedly in case they had any queries they would like to ask later. It turned out that the men felt far more attracted to the woman they met at the far end of the 'scary' bridge – and were far more likely to call their number.

Perhaps, in the light of the story so far, you may be able to guess why this happened? Walking across the high bridge, the fear of heights caused a surge of adrenaline in the male bridge-crossers. And the adrenaline was still washing around each unsuspecting male's system when he met the attractive female experimenter. In the normal course of events, the extra adrenaline would probably be explained, reasonably enough, as a fear response – the bridge was conspicuously high and wobbly, after all. But now an alternative cause presented itself – the presence of the attractive female experimenter. Physical and/or romantic attraction is, undoubtedly, a possible cause of surges of adrenaline – so the men may naturally enough have interpreted their heightened physical state as generated by feelings of attraction to the young woman who was engaging them in conversation and asking them to fill in the questionnaire.

Far from knowing our own minds, we are endlessly struggling to make sense of our own experiences – and we can often jump to the wrong conclusions. Even attraction, it seems, does not well up from within from some primal source. We feel a surge of adrenaline *as attraction* rather than experiencing it as fear or anger, because of the circumstances that confront us – our brains are, moment by moment, attempting to interpret the minimal physiological feedback from our body. And, as Dutton and Aron showed, our inner interpreter can easily be fooled.

What, then, are the implications for romantic love? One slightly alarming possibility is that the very intensity of becoming close to a new potential partner causes high levels of arousal (and, possibly, high surges of positive feelings), which may be interpreted not as by-products of any new romantic encounter but as signalling the existence of a special 'bond', or as indicating particularly wonderful characteristics in the 'other'. These signals are not necessarily misleading, of course – intensity of feeling may, to some degree, reflect the strength of the 'connection' between two people, for example. But the more or less precipitous collapse of many early-stage infatuations – a staple of gossip, psychotherapy and fiction – strongly suggests that the 'signals' are much less reliable than we think. We are, as ever, attempting to explain our feelings (and the other's feelings), based on fairly sparse clues – and we are all too liable to err.

What is the 'truth' about love anyway? If we are in the grip of the illusion of mental depths, we are likely to be seduced by the idea that one's feelings of love for a partner (or hoped-for partner) arise from 'deep inside'. And, similarly, that hidden deep inside the mind of the other are feelings of love for oneself (or not, one may fear). But these inner 'feelings' are presumed to be mysterious, occult states, about which there is inevitably uncertainty and hand-wringing. So, for example, we are able to agonize endlessly, and without result, about whether and how much our beloved loves us; and, equally fruitlessly, about whether and how much we, deep down, really love him or her.

Yet, by now, we should at least treat with suspicion the idea that there is any mysterious inner state, buried deep in our lover's or our own mind, that answers such questions once and for all. As we have seen, far more prosaic questions about our supposed 'inner mental landscape' turn out not to have clear answers: questions about the lighting, shadows or even the size of the 'imagined cube' and the perceived colour or detail of one's current perceptual experience of objects viewed in peripheral vision.

Our emotions are no more real: they are creative acts, not discoveries from our inner world. So when we interpret a momentary flicker of expression across the beloved's countenance, we can't 'see' feelings of love, regret or disappointment. Rather, as victims of the Kuleshov effect, our brains will interpret an often highly ambiguous facial expression (together with any amount of background information, such as our suspicions, fears and hopes) as embodying perhaps tenderness, distraction, traces of boredom, or any number of other possibilities. And our interpretation of our own physical state as embodying our own 'feelings' for the beloved is also the result of our whirring brain actively explaining our racing pulse and shortness of breath as, in one moment, exhilarating signs of love, and at the next moment, as indicating that we are on the edge of despair.

Indeed, the parallel between emotion and imagery is exact. Just as we believe ourselves to be inspecting an inner mental 'cube' to find its shadows, so we believe ourselves to be looking deep within our innermost mental recesses to decide who we love and how much. But in each case, we are subject to an illusion – we are inventing answers to each question we ask ourselves as fast (or almost as fast) as we can ask them. So, in both cases, we have the sense that these answers are waiting, ready at our fingertips; and they are – but only because we are able to make them up, with wonderful fluidity, as we go along.

The belief that emotion is an inner revelation, rather than a creation of the moment, is, I think, not only widespread, but potentially dangerous. The illusion that words and actions generated in the heat of the moment, when our interpretations of our lives and of others are likely to be at their most incoherent, burst out from our inner core, can lead us vastly to overrate their importance. For centuries, an ill-judged intemperate word or action could, in many social circles, lead inexorably to a dual or feud; friendships and marriages can be horribly marred by the supposedly 'telling remark' or 'revealing action' that is presumed to be not a moment of momentary confusion, but an insight into the bitter truth. To believe that our capricious and inventive minds are pouring out hidden truths at moments of crisis can also lead the religious to doubt their faith, the brave to suspect their own cowardice, and the good to undermine their own motives.

The philosopher, logician and political activist Bertrand Russell writes memorably of a moment of apparent emotional insight in the autumn of 1901: 'I went out bicycling one afternoon, and suddenly, as I was riding along a country road, I realized that I no longer loved Alys. I had had no idea until this moment that my love for her was even lessening. The problem presented by this discovery was very grave.'[11] For Russell, this thought was no mere creation of the moment (perhaps a product of a frustrating morning's work, or the aftermath of argument); instead, he interpreted it as an indisputable revelation, breaking through from a hidden subterranean emotional world. This proved to be a disastrous interpretation, at least for their relationship, which foundered rapidly, though not leading to divorce until twenty years later. Of course, the marriage might have failed in any case, but once Russell had received, as he saw it, a damning and final verdict from the 'inner oracle', he became utterly convinced that the relationship was dead. And with that belief firmly established in his mind, there was probably little hope.

Giving excessive weight to one's transitory emotional interpretations is hardly the preserve of great philosophers. We all face a continual struggle to regard our thoughts and emotions as transitory creations, mere commentaries on the moment, rather than as bearers of undeniable truth. The danger is that one moment's speculative thought ('I don't love Alys', 'I'm a hopeless failure', 'the world is terrifying') becomes the next moment's incontrovertible proof – the very thought is taken as its own justification. Indeed, the problem is so widespread, and can be so injurious, that an entire approach to mental well-being, so-called 'mindfulness' therapy, is primarily focused on breaking this illusion: seeing our thoughts and feelings, including, most importantly, destructive thoughts and feelings associated with depression and anxiety, as momentary inventions that we can step away from, criticize, or choose to dismiss. Needless to say, disrupting damaging patterns of thought is not easy – techniques involve achieving a sense of distance from one's emotions by controlling (e.g. via breathing exercises) and paying close attention to one's physiological state (e.g. heart-rate, levels of adrenaline). But as with Russell's marriage, dealing with negative patterns of thought becomes so much more difficult if we are in the grip of the illusion of mental depth – if we see our emotions as infallible messengers from our inner world, rather than as products of flimsy and incoherent interpretations of the moment.

The potential for disastrous misunderstandings of emotions is even greater if we are entranced by the Freudian tradition that our words and actions can reveal inner mental truths in a highly cryptic form, which can none the less be mysteriously deciphered by the enthusiastic amateur or the 'trained analyst'. And any resistance to the proposed 'reading', such as we saw with 'Little Hans', can, of course, be conveniently explained as defensiveness – and even interpreted as confirmation that the reading is correct. But, as we have seen, the entire project of attempting to fathom the emotions, motives and beliefs driving a person's behaviour is doomed from the outset. The problem is not that it is difficult to fathom our mental depths, but that there are no mental depths to fathom.

So does this mean that love is an illusion? That the romantically entangled can do no more than spin fairy stories about each other's thoughts and feelings, and their own? Not at all! The psychology of perception and emotion suggests that we should look for the truth about love not by attempting an impossible journey into our innermost selves, but by focusing instead on our patterns of thought and interaction in the here and now. Feeling fond of the other, helping and being helped in return, sharing revelations, surges of adrenaline and positive feeling at judicious and appropriate moments, sticking with each other through thick and thin – these aren't just *evidence* of a deep, authentic inner state – the state, perhaps, of 'true love'. They *are* the essence of what love is.

FINDING MEANING IN OUR LIVES

In an ever more mechanized world, and with science revealing the hidden processes of nature with ever more precision, the desire to reassert the value of the non-mechanical, the spiritual and the emotional can seem increasingly urgent. We humans struggle to find meaning in a world apparently governed by the iron laws of Newton's (or Einstein's) physics – even if those laws are leavened with a sprinkling of utter randomness from quantum mechanics.

Puzzling over the meaning of life is a particularly pressing and personal instance of puzzles about the meaning of things more broadly. Why does the word *dog* mean (very crudely) 'furry, carnivorous, domesticated, middle-sized animal, which barks and is commonly a pet'; why do double yellow lines mean 'no parking' on British roads;

why does a dollar bill, a pound coin, or a 20-euro banknote have a monetary value (rather than being mere objects that can be weighed, thrown, burned or melted)? In these cases, it seems natural to assume that meaning comes, in some roundabout way, from patterns of relationships. The word *dog* has developed its meaning because of the way we use it – its role in the language, in our lives, in its connections to the world (e.g. the existence and nature of dogs), the way our perceptual systems classify the world, and much more. But it is clearly a hopeless strategy to look for the meaning of the word by closely scrutinizing the word itself. The same goes for money: the value of physical currency is a product of enormously intricate relationships between people. It is a remarkable mutual agreement, backed by individuals, shopkeepers, manufacturers and governments, to treat currency in lieu of goods and services; it is supported by a rich pattern of norms, laws, anti-counterfeiting strategies and trust in the economy. The last place to look for the meaning of money (at least after the demise of the gold sovereign) is 'within': it is not the paper or metal that has value – no matter how closely we examine the patterns on banknotes or the precise alloy from which the coins are minted. Words are not mere sounds; money is not just the paper it is written on.

And the same is surely true for the search for meaning in our own experiences and in our lives. Emotions, then, have their meaning, not through some elementary properties of 'raw experience', but through their role in our thoughts, our social interactions and our culture. To be ashamed, proud, angry or jealous is not to experience the welling up of some primitive feeling – we are ashamed of specific actions, proud of particular achievements, angry at individual people for concrete reasons, and so on. Of course, such feelings are associated with a bodily state (just as words have physical form, as acoustic waves or patterns of ink; and just as money is embodied in paper and metal), but the bodily state – the rushes of adrenaline, the pounding of the heart – should not be confused with the emotion itself.

The same pattern surely applies to the meaning of our lives more broadly. The meaning of pretty much anything comes from its place in a wider network of relationships, causes and effects – not from within. So wondering if you are in love, whether you really believe in God, or whether you find a sentimental pop song charming or mawkish, should be a prompt for you to consider how your thoughts and feelings fit together; how they link with your actions and the actions of other people; how they compare with situations you have experienced in the past, and more. Such questions are not answered by a futile attempt to carry out a microscopic analysis of one's inner sensations, or still less one's soul.

With hindsight, one might view feelings as inherently unstable, as being continually invented and reinvented, moment by moment. Looking for some inner mental bedrock, perhaps we should look not at what we *feel*, but what we *do*. But, as we will see in the next chapter, if our feelings help determine our choices, then our choices may be just as malleable and capricious as our emotional lives.

6

Manufacturing Choice

The tightly folded cortex of the human brain is arranged, like a walnut, in two separate halves or hemispheres. The 'left' and 'right' brains (as they are sometimes informally known) are associated with different abilities. Pop psychology and pop management theory has had a field day with the supposed distinction between left-brained thinking (supposedly logical, quantitative, analytical) and right-brained thinking (presumed to be emotional, creative, empathic), though the reality is far murkier.

In normal life, the two hemispheres of the brain work together remarkably fluently – indeed, there is a massive bundle of more than 200 million nerve fibres, the *corpus callosum*, whose role it is to exchange messages between them (Figure 25).

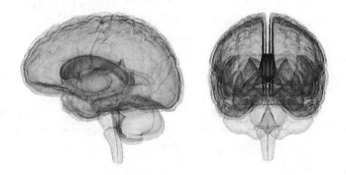

Figure 25. The corpus callosum (dark grey) links the hemispheres of the brain so that they work together as a single seamless system. People with no functioning corpus callosum, for example where it has been severed surgically, can function in daily life surprisingly well.[1]

But what would happen if the two hemispheres were truly split apart – if our left and right brains had to work in isolation? During the 1960s and 1970s, the spread of an experimental treatment for severe epilepsy provided a window into what life is like when the two hemispheres operate in isolation. Severing the corpus callosum surgically turned out to help reduce seizures, apparently by stopping the spread of anomalous waves of the electrical activity that overwhelms the brain. But what would the implications of such a drastic procedure be on the mental functioning of the patient, who is now, one might assume, divided into two distinct 'selves'? The apparent effects of the operation were surprisingly modest: people could live a normal life, reported no change in subjective experience (e.g. their sense of 'consciousness' was as unified as ever), had near normal verbal IQ, memory recall and much more.

Careful analysis in the laboratory revealed that the two halves of the cortex were, indeed, functioning independently. Consider a particularly striking study by one of the pioneers of split brain research, the psychologist and neuroscientist Michael Gazzaniga. He simultaneously showed a split-brain patient, P.S., different pictures on the left and right halves of the visual field.[2] The left-hand picture was a snowy scene; the brain's cross-over wiring pipes this information through to the visual cortex of the right hemisphere. The right-hand picture was a chicken's foot, which is sent to the corresponding area in the left hemisphere. Like most of us, P.S.'s language-processing abilities are strongly concentrated in the left hemisphere; the right hemisphere, in isolation, has minimal linguistic abilities. P.S.'s left hemisphere was able to report what it could see – and fluently describe the chicken claw, but P.S. was unable to say anything about the snowy scene that the right hemisphere could see.

For each picture, P.S.'s task was to pick out one of the four pictures which was associated in some way with the picture being viewed. Both hemispheres could do this. P.S.'s left hemisphere directed the right hand (the brain's cross-over wiring again) to pick out a picture of a chicken's head, matching up with the chicken's claw. And P.S.'s right hemisphere directed the left hand to pick out a picture of a shovel, to match up with the snowy scene in the left picture.

But how would P.S. (or rather, P.S.'s left hemisphere) explain these actions? P.S.'s language-processing left hemisphere was, after all, totally unaware of the snowy scene – so on seeing the left hand (controlled by the right hemisphere) choosing the shovel, one might expect P.S.'s left hemisphere to say nothing, or admit to being utterly mystified. Instead, P.S. explained both choices very neatly: 'Oh that's simple. The chicken claw goes with the chicken. And you need a shovel to clean out the chicken shed.' Elegant, but entirely wrong! The left hemisphere was entirely unaware of the snow–shovel association that must really have triggered the right hemisphere's choice – because the left hemisphere was totally oblivious to the snowy scene. But the left hemisphere readily invented a plausible-sounding explanation, none the less.

Gazzaniga calls the language-processing system of the left hemisphere 'the interpreter' – a system that is able to invent stories about why we do what we do. But what the experiment with P.S. shows is that the interpreter is a master of speculation. It can have no possible insight into the origin of the choice of the shovel (the snowy scene) because those causes arise in the half of the brain to which it is disconnected – yet it invents an explanation with a flourish.

In another study, Gazzaniga presented a split-brain patient, J.W., with the word 'music' in the left visual field (routed through to the right hemisphere, which has only rudimentary language) and the word 'bell' in the right visual field (routed through to the language-processing machinery of the left hemisphere). The left hand chose an 'appropriate' picture – guided by the right hemisphere, it chose a picture of a bell (the right hemisphere has some basic knowledge of word meaning). When this was queried, J.W. responded: 'Music – last time I heard any music, it was from the bells outside here, banging away' – a comment on the bells regularly ringing out from the nearby library on the campus at Dartmouth College, New Hampshire, where the study was carried out. Again J.W.'s left hemisphere interpreter was making a creditable attempt to explain the choice – but an entirely wrong one. The left hand chose a picture of a bell because the corresponding right brain had just seen the word *bell* – but of course the left hemisphere had no possible way of knowing this. But the interpreter just ploughs cheerfully onwards, even when it cannot possibly have any knowledge of what actually caused the choice.

So the left-hemisphere 'interpreter' invents 'stories' to explain the right hemisphere's choices – and does so naturally and fluently. Indeed, the very ability of the 'interpreter' to create such stories may be crucial to maintaining the sense of the mental unity for the split-brain patient. But the very existence of the interpreter suggests the possibility that, for people with normal brains, choices are also naturally and fluently explained *after the fact*. So while we may imagine that our justifications for our choices merely report the inner mental causes of those choices (the hidden plans, desires, intentions, from within our hidden depths), perhaps we should consider another possibility entirely: that our justifications for our choices are 'cooked up', in retrospect, by the ever-inventive left hemisphere interpreter.

Deciding what to say is, then, a creative act, rather than a read-out from a comprehensive inner database of my beliefs, attitudes and values. The speed and fluency with which we can often generate and justify thoughts is impressive. So quick, indeed, that it seems that at the very moment that we ask ourselves a question, the answer springs to mind – so fluent that we don't realize we are *making it up on the spot*: we can sustain the illusion that the answer was there all along, waiting to be 'read off'.

The parallel with perception is striking: we have seen how we glimpse the external world through an astonishingly narrow window, and how the illusion of sensory richness is sustained by our ability to conjure up an answer, almost instantly, to almost any question that occurs to us. Now we should suspect that the apparent richness of our inner world has the same origin: as we ask questions of ourselves, answers naturally and fluently appear. Our beliefs, desires, hopes and fears do not wait pre-formed in a vast mental antechamber, until they are ushered one by one into the bright light of verbal expression. The left-brain interpreter constructs our thoughts and feelings at the very moment that we think and feel them.

ON NOT KNOWING OUR OWN MINDS

Psychologists Petter Johansson and Lars Hall, and their colleagues from Lund University in Sweden, played a trick on voters in the run-up to Sweden's 2010 general election.[3] First, they asked people whether they intended to vote for the left-leaning or the right-leaning coalition. Then they gave people a questionnaire about various topics crucial to the campaign, such as the level of income tax and the approach to healthcare. The hapless prospective voter handed over their responses to the experimenter, who, by a simple conjuring trick with sticky paper, replaced their answers with answers suggesting they belonged to the opposing political camp. So, for example, a left-leaning voter might be handed back responses suggesting, say, sympathy with lower income tax and more private sector involvement in healthcare; a right-leaning voter might be confronted with responses favouring more generous welfare benefits and workers' rights.

When they checked over the answers, just under a quarter of the switched answers were spotted: in these cases, people tended to say that they supposed that they must have made a mistake and corrected the answers back to previously expressed opinion. But not only did the majority of changes go unnoticed; people were happy to explain and defend political positions which, moments ago, it appeared they didn't actually hold!

Now, of course the Swedish voting population don't have split brains – their corpus callosa are fully intact. But the left-hemisphere interpreter appears to be playing its tricks here too. Confronted with questionnaire responses in which she appears to have endorsed lower taxes, the prospective voter's (presumably primarily left-hemisphere) 'interpreter' will readily explain why lower taxes are, in many ways, a good thing – lifting the burden from the poor and encouraging enterprise. But this statement, however fluent and compelling, cannot really justify her original response: because, of course, her original response was completely the opposite – favouring higher taxes.

And this should make us profoundly suspicious of our defences and justifications of our own words and actions, even when there is no trickery. If we were able to rummage about in our mental archives, and to reconstruct the mental 'history' that led us to act, we would surely come up short when asked to justify something we didn't do – the story we recover from the archives would lead to the 'wrong' outcome after all. But this is not at all how the data come out: people are able to effortlessly cook up a perfectly plausible story to justify an opinion that they did not express, just as easily as they are able to justify opinions that they *did* express. And, indeed, we are blithely unaware of the difference between these two cases. So the obvious conclusion to draw is that we don't justify our behaviour by consulting our mental archives; rather, the process of explaining our thoughts, behaviour and actions is a process of creation. And, as with mental images, the process of creation is so rapid and fluent that we can easily imagine that we are reporting from our inner mental depths. But, just as we reshape and recreate images 'in the moment' to answer whatever question comes to mind (How curved is the tiger's tail? Does it have all four paws on the ground? Are its claws visible or retracted?), so we can create justifications as soon as the thoughts needing justification come to mind. (But why might tax rises help the poor? Well – they pay little tax anyway, and benefit disproportionately from public services; or conversely, why might tax rises harm the poor? Surely they are least able to pay, and are most likely to be hit by the drag taxation puts on the economy.) The interpreter can argue either side of any case; it is like a helpful lawyer, happy to defend your words or actions whatever they happen to be, at a moment's notice. So our values and beliefs are by no means as stable as we imagine.

The story-spinning interpreter is not entirely amnesic; and it attempts to build a compelling narrative based on whatever it can remember. Indeed, the interpreter works by referring back to, and transforming, memories of past behaviour – we stay in character by following our memories of what we have done before. But Johansson and Hall's results show that we can be tricked by, in effect, having the experimenter implant 'false memories' – misleading information about our past behaviour (being fooled about one's own past choices).

This phenomenon of 'choice blindness' – of defending a choice one didn't actually make – is not limited to politics. Johansson, Hall and their colleagues discovered the phenomenon in a context in which we might believe our intuitions to be deep-seated and immutable – judgements of facial attractiveness. People given pairs of faces on cards (Figure 26) chose the face they found the most attractive, and, on some occasions, by a devious card trick, were handed the non-chosen face. Mostly people didn't notice the trickery, and happily explained why they made the choice they did not actually make. Analysis of the content of these explanations (their length, complexity, fluency) found no difference between cases where the 'trick' had been performed and where it hadn't. Rather than being stopped in our tracks by being asked to explain a non-choice, the 'interpreter' blithely defended the 'opposite' point of view, noticing nothing amiss. Often, tellingly, the justifications in cases in which people had been deceived drew on reasons that were transparently post hoc: 'I chose her because of her nice earrings and curly hair' can't be a true report of past decision-making processes of a person who actually chose the picture of a straight-haired woman, without earrings. But it is just the kind of story that the interpreter would scramble together to justify its choice, with hindsight.

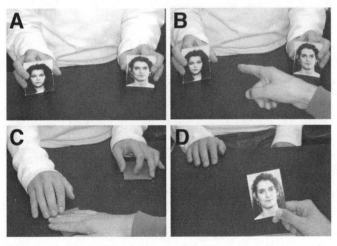

Figure 26. A magic trick with own preferences.[4]

And these results have been found not only in experiments concerning politics or faces, but also in taste tests. Setting up a stall in a local supermarket, Johansson and Hall's team asked people to choose between pairs of jams. They were able to swap the chosen and non-chosen jams by devious use of a double-ended jam jar (each end containing a different jam). The switch could be effected, unnoticed, by surreptitiously turning over the chosen jam jar before presenting it to the customer, so giving them a new taste of the jam they had rejected, rather than the jam they had actually chosen. As before, people mostly didn't notice; and, where they failed to spot anything amiss, they were just as confident in their 'fake' choices as when their choices were 'real'. Market researchers beware! Even when it comes to something as familiar as jam, most of us have only the most tenuous grasp on what we like.

SHAPED BY STORIES

So is the 'interpreter', the spinner of stories defending and explaining our thoughts and actions with such eloquence, no more than a commentator, justifying our past, but unable to shape our future? In fact, the interpreter does not merely describe our past actions, but helps shape what we do next.

Consider faces again. Some years ago, I was part of the study with Johansson and Hall's team to look at how false feedback might influence future choices. It turned out that, having been told (wrongly) that we prefer face A to face B, we are more likely to express this preference if we make the same decision later. The interpreter explained the decision we didn't make (it was the earrings, or curly hair), but that very explanation helps shape future decisions. Perhaps even more important is the aim of being consistent – to make choices that the interpreter can justify and defend. If we believe (whether rightly or wrongly) that we said that we preferred face A the first time we were asked, how can we justify having changed our minds? Given the inventive powers of the interpreter, a story could, of course, be cooked up (oh well, we hadn't noticed the friendly smile of face B . . . were distracted . . . or picked the wrong face the first time by mistake). But it is so much easier, and so much more convincing, to be consistent.[5] And with this in mind, we would be biased towards choosing face A the second time we are asked.

And how about politics? Johansson and Hall's team finished their deceptive political questionnaire study by totting up the left/right significance of people's answers in plain view of the participants; and then asked them to indicate their left/right voting intentions. So, had

the intentions changed from those they had expressed at the beginning of the experiment just a few minutes ago? Remarkably, people
who had been given false feedback that led them to the left (and,
remember, accepted and even defended some of the left-leaning opinions that they didn't originally possess) were substantially more likely
to express an intention to vote for the left-leaning coalition. It was the
same story, in reverse, for the right. And the effects were significant:
nearly half the participants had moved across the left/right boundary
as a result of the false feedback. There are, it seems, many more floating voters than pollsters might realize.

But can such momentary shifts in thinking really change how
people actually vote? We should be sceptical: after all, we might
believe that our final decision at the polling booth is the summation
of a myriad of occasions in which political issues have run through
our minds. No single moments, one might hope, should have a dis-
proportionate influence.

A remarkable study from Cornell University, in the run-up to the
2008 US presidential election, suggests, in contrast, that even apparently modest experimental manipulations can lead voters to change
their minds.[6] Participants took a web-based survey on their political
attitudes. The American flag was present in the corner of the screen
for half the sample. Prior research has suggested that exposure to the
American flag tends momentarily to bring to mind feelings of nation-
alism, concerns about security, and so on, that are most associated
with the platform of the Republican Party – and the study did indeed
show a shift to the right in people's political attitudes when the flag
was present. Such findings are interesting in themselves – further evidence that we attempt continuously to construct our preferences to fit
the thoughts that happen to be splashing through our stream of
consciousness.

Yet one might expect such effects to be short-lived. Astonishingly,
though, when the Cornell team returned to their sample after they
had voted later, the people presented with the US flag while answering part of the original survey were significantly more likely to have
backed the Republican Party. The brief presence of the American flag
in an internet survey had significantly shifted actual voting behaviour, a full eight months later! But how can this possibly be right?

After all, American voters are continuously exposed to the US flag – on buildings, billboards, on neighbours' flagpoles. Among all these hundreds of flags, surely just one more could not have tipped the balance to the Republicans. If it could, and if each flag-exposure is nudging people relentlessly to the right, then the entire political battleground in the US should surely be concerned with little more than – for the Republicans' electioneering – covering every available surface in the Stars and Stripes; and for the Democrats, discreetly blocking them from view.

In my opinion, the correct interpretation of this study is very different, and far more interesting. Exposure to the flag has an instantaneous, although limited, impact on political attitudes; and, no doubt, this impact will rapidly be overwritten by the myriad other stimuli that jostle for attention. But if you see a flag while filling in a political survey, then the flag will, of course, affect your answers in the survey – and, indeed, this is just what the researchers found. But now memory traces have been laid down which have the potential to have a long-lasting effect on behaviour. To the extent that I later recall that, when contemplating my political views, I previously found myself leaning to the right, I am a little more likely to lean to the right in future. To make the most sense of my own behaviour, I will aim to think and act as I did before.

CHOOSING AND REJECTING

Suppose that we try, despite everything, to hold onto the idea that deep down we have stable, pre-formed preferences, even if they are a bit 'wobbly'. Here is what sounds like a foolproof way to find out whether, for example, I prefer apples to oranges. Just offer me either an apple or an orange, on many occasions, and tot up which one I choose more often. That, surely, must be the fruit I prefer. And here is another apparently foolproof test: offer me an either an apple or an orange, and ask me to reject one (and hence keep the other). Now we tot up which option I reject less: that, surely, must be the fruit I prefer, mustn't it? It would be ridiculous to choose mostly apples in the first case (indicating that I prefer apples); and mostly to reject apples in the second case (indicating that I prefer oranges). Consistently deciding to choose, but also to reject, the very same thing seems to make a nonsense of the very idea of preference.

Yet remarkably, psychologists Eldar Shafir and Amos Tversky found that this paradoxical pattern does indeed occur. They asked people to decide between extreme options (with both very good and very bad features) and neutral options (where all the features were middling).[7] In one study, for example, people imagined making custody decisions between a 'parent-of-extremes' (*good*: very close relationship with the child, extremely active social life; above-average income; *bad*: lots of work-related travel, minor health problems) and a 'typical parent' (reasonable rapport with the child, relatively stable social life, and average income, working hours and health). In Shafir and Tversky's experiment, when asked to choose which parent should be *awarded* custody, people selected the parent-of-extremes most of the time. But when asked to choose which parent should be *denied* custody, they also selected the parent-of-extremes most of the time! And this general pattern was followed across many studies: when asked to choose an option, people selected the 'mix-of-extremes' more often than the 'average'. Yet when asked to reject an option, they also chose the 'mix-of-extremes' more often than the 'average'. Surely people can't think that the very same parent is both the best option and the worst option.

What is going on here? Shafir and Tversky argued that when we make choices, we are not 'expressing' a pre-existing preference at all; indeed, they would argue that there are no such preferences. What we are doing instead is improvising – making up our preferences as we go along. Improvising can take many forms – for example, we may be influenced by what we normally do, or what other people do, as we will see below. But one natural thing to do, in order to come up with a decision, is to scramble together some *reasons* for or against one option or another. But which do we focus on: reasons for or against? Shafir and Tversky argued this positive or negative focus is influenced by how the decision is described.

If we are asked to choose an option, we mostly focus on reasons *for* choosing one thing or another: and these reasons will tend to be *positive* reasons in favour of one option or the other. The extreme option has the most powerful positive reasons (e.g. a very close relationship with the child), so it wins out.

If, on the other hand, we are asked to *reject* one of the available options, then we search for *negative* reasons, which might rule out one option or the other. And the extreme option also has the most powerful negative reasons (e.g. lots of work-related travel). So now the extreme option loses out.

My colleagues Konstantinos Tsetsos, Marius Usher and I decided to look at this strange phenomenon – of choosing and rejecting the very same thing – in a highly controlled setting.[8] The participants in our experiment had to choose between gambles. In each trial, a gamble would produce a number, corresponding to a monetary reward. People saw the kinds of rewards generated by a gamble over

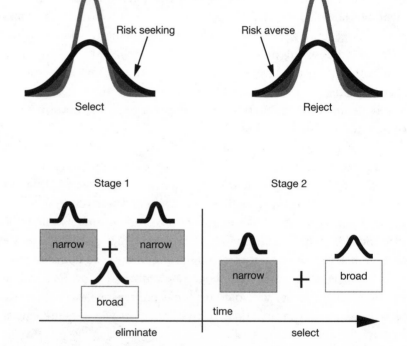

Figure 27. Rejecting and choosing the risky option. In Stage 1, people eliminate a gamble with a broad distribution of outcomes; and, moments later, at Stage 2, they select the very same option.[9]

many trials, before deciding whether to select it – a bit like looking over another player's shoulder as they play a slot machine, before deciding whether to take the plunge oneself. As it happens, people were able to see two or three gambles being played out on a computer screen in each trial – they saw 'streams' of numbers at different locations. The question for the players in our experiments was: which type of gamble – which stream of numbers – should they choose?

People watched sequences of numbers representing the possible outcomes of gambles, corresponding to the rectangular boxes. The gambles either had a relatively broad range of outcomes (the black bell curve in the upper row of Figure 27) or a narrow range of outcomes (the grey bell curve in Figure 27). The average pay-off for both types of gamble was exactly the same. So which gamble did people prefer? If people were asked to *select* either a broad and narrow gamble, then, we suggested, they might focus on positive reasons for selection – that is, on 'big wins'. If so, they might prefer the broad gamble – in economic terminology, this is known as 'risk-seeking' behaviour (top left of Figure 27). But if people were asked to *eliminate* a broad or narrow gamble, then they might focus on reasons for rejection – i.e. on big losses. But the broad gamble also has the greatest number of big losses, so now that very same option might be rejected – this is known as 'risk-averse' behaviour. And, indeed, this is precisely how people behave (lower panel of Figure 27). People were initially presented with three gambles (one broad, and two narrow), which they observed over many trials; they were then asked to eliminate one of the gambles (lower left panel); then they were exposed to further samples from the two remaining gambles, and asked which one of these they would like to choose. As expected, the typical pattern of results was that people were especially likely to *reject* the broad gamble, more than either of the narrow gambles, at the first stage, but at the second stage they were more likely to choose a broad gamble (which was deviously added back in by us, even though it had initially been rejected). So at one moment people shy away from risk; yet at the next moment they embrace it. This makes no sense if we make our choices by referring to some inner oracle, but it makes perfect sense if we are improvising: conjuring up reasons, in the moment, to justify one choice or another.

Choosing and rejecting the same thing seems peculiar. But it is hardly an isolated incident. Indeed, entire fields of research, including Judgement and Decision-Making, Behavioural Economics, and large areas of Social Cognition have found countless examples of such inconsistencies.[10] Ask the same question, probe the same attitude, or present the same choice in different ways and, almost invariably, people provide a different answer. Take our attitude to risk. We just noted that people are risk-seeking when deciding which of two gambles to choose, but risk-averse when deciding which of two gambles to reject – using a particular way of presenting the gambles as streams of numbers. But if we just ask people to choose gambles based on descriptions (e.g. a 50 per cent chance of £100 compared to a certain chance of £50), then people are mostly risk-averse. If we describe the gambles in terms of losses not gains, people typically become risk-seeking. If the gambles are 'scaled down' so that the chances of winning big (or losing big) are tiny, then things flip again: people become risk-seeking for a tiny chance of a big win (and therefore like to play lotteries), but risk-averse for a tiny chance of a big loss (and therefore buy insurance).

And it gets worse! People make wildly different choices when the same financial risk is described in a variety of superficially different ways (in terms of losses, gains, investments, gambling, etc.).[11] And when we compare risk attitudes for money, health, dangerous sports, and so on, these also turn out to be only weakly related.[12] To a good approximation, every new variation on the 'same' question gets us a systematically different answer – the brain conjures up a new 'story' each time; and if we prod the storyteller in a slightly different way, the story will, more than likely, be a little altered.[13]

If these variations were not the products of creative licence, but merely wobbly measurements, then taking more and more measurements and triangulating them carefully would eventually produce a consistent answer. But the variations in the story are systematic – so that no amount of measuring and re-measuring is going to help. The problem with measuring risk preferences is not that measurement is difficult and inaccurate; it is that there are no risk preferences to measure – there is simply no answer to how, 'deep down', we wish to balance risk and reward. And, while we're at it, the same goes for the way people trade off the present against the future; how altruistic we are and to whom; how far we display prejudice on gender or race, and so on.

If mental depth is an illusion, this is, of course, just what we should expect. Pre-formed beliefs, desires, motives, attitudes to risk lurking in our hidden inner depths are a fiction: we improvise our behaviour to deal with the challenges of the moment rather than to express our inner self. So there is no point wondering which way of asking the question (which would you like to choose, which would you like to reject) will tell us what people really want. There are endless possible questions, and limitless possible answers. If the mind is flat, there can be no method, whether involving market research, hypnosis, psychotherapy or brain scanning that can conceivably answer this question, not because our mental motives, desires and preferences are impenetrable, but because they don't exist.

PART TWO

The Improvised Mind

7

The Cycle of Thought

Despite being a pudgy bundle of fibres powered by a modest 20 watts of energy, the human brain is by far the most powerful computer in the known universe. Our brains are, it is true, forgetful, error-prone, and can struggle to sustain attention on anything for more than a few minutes. Indeed, we struggle with elementary arithmetic, let alone logic and mathematics, and we read, talk and reason painstakingly slowly. But our brains have stunning abilities too: they can interpret a bafflingly complex sensory world, perform a huge variety of skilled actions, and communicate and navigate a vastly complex physical and social world. And our brains do all this at a level that far exceeds the power of anything yet created in artificial intelligence. Our brain is a remarkable computer, but it is a very unconventional computer.

The power of the familiar digital computers – including our PCs, laptops and tablets – comes, largely, from carrying out simple calculation steps at phenomenal speeds: many billions of operations per second. By comparison, the brain is dreadfully slow. Neurons – the basic computational unit of the brain – calculate by sending electrical pulses to each other across hugely complex electro-chemical networks. The very highest rate of neural 'firing' is about 1,000 pulses per second; neurons, even when directly recruited to the task in hand, fire mostly at far more leisurely rates, from five to fifty times per second.[1] So our neurons are leisurely compared with the astonishing processing speed of silicon chips. But while neurons may be slow, they are numerous. A PC has one or at most a few processing chips, processing at a phenomenal rate, while the human brain has roughly one hundred billion sluggish neurons, linked by roughly one hundred trillion connections.

So the spectacular cleverness of the human mind must come not from the frenzied sequences of simple calculations that underpin silicon computation. Instead, brain-style computation must result from *cooperation* across the highly interconnected, but slow, neural processing units, leading to coordinated patterns of neural activity across whole networks or perhaps entire regions of the brain.[2]

But it is hard to see how a vast population of interconnected neurons can coordinate on more than one thing at a time, without suffering terrible confusion and interference. Each time a neuron fires, it sends an electrical pulse to all the other neurons it is linked to (typically up to 1,000). This is a good mechanism for helping neurons cooperate, as long as they are all working on different aspects of the same problem (e.g. building up different parts of a possible meaningful organization of a face, word, pattern or object). Then, by linking together, cross-checking, correcting and validating different parts of an organization (the parts of a face, the letters making up a word), it is possible gradually to build up a unified whole. But if interconnected neurons are working on entirely different problems, then the signals they pass between them will be hopelessly at cross-purposes – and neither task will be completed successfully: each neuron has no idea which of the signals it receives are relevant to the problem it is working on, and which are just irrelevant junk.

So we have a general principle. If the brain solves problems through the cooperation computation of vast networks of individually sluggish neurons, then any specific network of neurons can work on just one solution to one problem at a time. To a rough approximation, the brain seems to be pretty close to one giant, highly interconnected network (although the connections between different regions of the brain are not equally dense). So we should expect, then, that a network of neurons in the brain should be able to cooperate on just one problem at a time.

This gives us the beginning of an explanation of the slow, step-by-step nature of perception and thought that we came across in Part One: our ability to process one word, face, or even colour, at a time. Attending to a set of information to be explained is *setting the problem* that the brain has to solve. The problems can be very diverse: to find the 'meaning' in a pattern of black and white shapes; to figure out what is being said in a stream of speech; to visualize a cube balanced on one point; to recall the last time you went to the cinema, and so on. We can think of this as specifying the values of some subset of the population of neurons. Each step in a sequence of thoughts then involves cooperative computation to find the most meaningful organization of everything else we know to find an answer that best fits that 'question'. A single step may take many hundredths of a second, but the computational power achieved by drawing on the knowledge and processing power across a network of billions of neurons can be enormous.

The computational abilities of the brain are, then, both severely limited and remarkably powerful. The problem of interference implies that the cycle of thought is limited to proceeding one step at a time, and working on just one problem at a time. Yet by cooperatively drawing on a vast population of interconnected neurons – each contributing only a little to the overall solution to the problem in hand – each step has the potential to answer questions of enormous difficulty: for example, decoding a facial expression, predicting what will happen next in a complex physical and social situation, integrating a fast-flowing input of speech or text, planning and initiating the spectacularly complex sequence of actions to return a tennis serve thundering down at more than 100 mph. Each of these processes would, to the extent that it can ever be successfully simulated on a conventional computer at all, correspond to millions or even billions of tiny steps, implemented with almost unimaginable speed, one after the other. But the brain takes a different tack: its slow neural units split up the problem into myriad tiny fragments and share their tentative solutions in parallel across the entire, densely interconnected network.

What is important is that the very fact that the brain uses cooperative computation across vast networks of neurons implies that these networks make one giant, coordinated step at a time rather than, as in a conventional computer, through a myriad of almost infinitesimally tiny information-processing steps. I shall call this sequence of giant, cooperative steps, running at an irregular pulse of several 'beats' per second, *the cycle of thought*.[3]

The comparison between conventional computers and the brain

can, therefore, be highly misleading. We can write a document, or watch a movie, on our PC, while in the background it is searching for large prime numbers, downloading music, crunching away on astronomical calculations, or any number of tasks. So the notion that, as our conscious mind is focused on making breakfast or reading a novel, all manner of profound and abstruse thoughts might be running along below conscious awareness, seems plausible. But brains are very different from conventional computers – rather than being able to time-share a super-fast central processor, the brain works by cooperative computation across most or all of its neurons – and cooperative computation can only lock onto, and solve, one problem at a time.

If each network of cooperating neurons in the brain can only focus on a single problem, then we should be able to consider only one chess move at a time; read one word at a time; recognize one face at a time; or listen to one conversation at a time. Thus the cooperative style of computation used by the brain imposes severe limitations upon us – limitations that are indeed evident in the light of decades of careful psychological experiments.

If each brain network can take on a single task at a time, a crucial question becomes how far the brain may naturally be divided into many independent networks, each with its own task; whether such divisions are fixed or whether the brain can actively reconfigure itself into distinct networks to address the challenges in hand. But whatever the nature of the division of the brain into cooperating networks of nerve cells (and we shall briefly touch on the question of how flexibly this can be done later), the key point is that each cooperative network of neurons can address precisely one problem at a time.

Moreover, analysis of brain pathways, through tracing the 'wiring diagram' of the brain as well as monitoring the flow of brain activity when we engage in specific tasks, suggests that the networks for the brain are highly interconnected. One consequence of this is that multitasking will be the exception rather than the rule.

It turns out that whichever object or task is engaging our conscious attention will typically engage large swathes of the brain.[4] Accordingly, there will typically be severe interference between any two tasks or problems that engage our conscious attention – because the cooperative style of brain computation precludes a single brain network carrying out two distinct tasks. This means not only that we can consciously attend to just one problem at a time, but also that if we are consciously thinking about one problem, we cannot *even unconsciously* be thinking about another – because the brain networks involved would be likely to overlap. Tasks and problems needing conscious attention engage swathes of our neural machinery; and each part of that machinery can only do one thing at a time. In particular, the unconscious cannot be working away on, say, tricky intellectual or creative challenges, while we are consciously attending to some other task – because the brain circuits that would be needed for such sophisticated unconscious thoughts are 'blocked' by the conscious brain processes of the moment. We shall return to the far-reaching implications of 'no background processing' below, leading us to revise our intuitions about 'unconscious thoughts' and 'hidden motives', and eliminate any suspicion that our behaviour is the product of a battle between multiple selves (e.g. Freud's id, ego and superego).

The brain is a set of highly interconnected, and cooperative, networks, but the *structure* of these networks turns out to be particularly revealing: there is a relatively narrow neural bottleneck through which sensory information flows. This bottleneck restricts the possibility of doing too many things at once – but, as we shall see, it also gives some fascinating clues about the nature of conscious experience.

PRODDING THE CONSCIOUS BRAIN

The eminent neurosurgeon Wilder Penfield pioneered brain investigations and brain surgery on people who were wide awake.[5] From the patient's point of view, a little local anaesthetic to deal with any pain of the incision through the skull is all that is required. Though the brain detects pains of many and varied types throughout the body (pokes, abrasions, twists, excesses of heat and cold), the brain has no mechanism for detecting damage to itself. So Penfield's brain operations were entirely painless for his patients.

The purpose of Penfield's surgery was to relieve severe epilepsy by attempting to isolate, and remove, portions of the brain from which the seizures originated. In an epileptic attack, the cells across large areas cease any complex cooperative computation to solve the problem of the moment and start instead to 'fire' in slow synchronized waves and hence, being entrained by each other, become disengaged from their normal information-processing function. A slightly fanciful parallel is to imagine the population of a busy city suddenly dropping their varied and highly interconnected activities (buying, selling, chatting, building, making) to join in a single, continuous, coordinated, but entirely involuntary Mexican wave – wherever the wave spreads, work will come to a complete halt. In severe epileptic attacks, the whole, or large areas of, the cerebral cortex become entrained and hence entirely non-functional, until the brain is somehow able to reset itself; people with severe epilepsy can suffer such debilitating attacks many times each day. The entrainment in epilepsy typically starts in a specific region of the cortex. It is as if the inhabitants of one district are particularly prone to spontaneously launching into Mexican waves – and the nearby neighbourhoods are

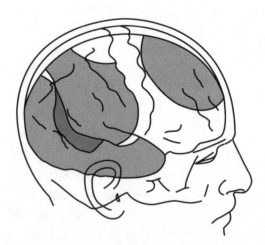

Figure 28. The areas of cortex removed in three of Wilder Penfield's epileptic patients, shown on a single diagram. The area removed at the front of the brain is here shown on the right-hand side for visibility, but was actually on the left, in mirror-image.[6]

then drawn in, and the wave spreads inexorably across the city. Penfield's logic was that, if only the troublesome district could somehow be isolated from the rest of the city, the Mexican wave would be unable to spread – and normal life would continue unhindered. In practice, Penfield found that the most effective treatment often turned out to be rather extreme: rather than a few subtle surgical cuts to key regions of the cortex, the equivalent of closing a few bridges or main roads, Penfield was often driven to remove large regions of the cortex, analogous to flattening huge areas of a city (see Figure 28).

I can scarcely imagine anything more alarming than having areas of one's brain removed with nothing more than a local anaesthetic. But the use of a local anaesthetic turned out to be crucial: the electrical stimulation of different parts of the cortex meant that the awake patient was able to communicate a good deal of information about the function of that area; some areas of the cortex are more crucial than others, and Penfield was therefore able to operate, as far as possible, without inadvertently causing paralysis, or loss of language. The surgeon was in the uncanny position of being able to converse with patients throughout the period that substantial areas of their brains were being removed. The patients not only maintained consciousness throughout, but typically maintained a fluid conversation, neither exhibiting nor reporting any disruption to their conscious experience.

One might conclude that perhaps these areas of cortex are simply not relevant to conscious thought. But a wide range of other considerations ruled out this possibility. For example, recall that the visual neglect patients we described in Chapter 3 frequently had no conscious experience of one half of the visual field – and the area of absence of consciousness maps neatly onto the area of visual cortex that had been damaged. Similarly, patients who have, often through a localized stroke, suffered damage to cortical regions known to process colour, motion, taste, and so on, show the consequences of such damage in their conscious experience: they no longer perceive colour normally, may view the world as intermittently frozen and moving jerkily, or report that they have lost their sense of taste. In short, the cortical processing machinery we possess seems to map directly onto the conscious phenomenology we experience. Penfield himself was able to collect new and very direct evidence of the close connection between cortex and consciousness, through his electrical stimulation of different parts of the cortical surface. Such stimulation often did intrude on conscious experience, and in very striking ways. Depending on the area and the stimulation, patients would often report visual experiences, sounds, dreamlike strands, or even what appeared to be entire flashes of memory (most famously, one patient volunteered the strangely specific 'I can smell burnt toast!' in response to a particular electrical probing of the brain).

So how could it be that stimulating a brain area leads to conscious phenomenology, but removing that very same area appears to leave conscious experience entirely unaffected? Penfield's answer was that consciousness isn't located in the cortical surface of the brain, but in the deeper brain areas into which the cortex projects – in particular, to the collection of evolutionarily old 'sub-cortical' structures that lie at the core of the brain and which the cortex enfolds.

The anatomy of the brain gives, perhaps, an initial clue. Sub-cortical structures (such as the thalamus) have rich neural projections that fan out into the cortex that surrounds it, and these connections allow information to pass both ways. Intriguingly, most information from our senses passes through the thalamus before projecting onto the cortex; and information passes in the opposite direction from the cortex through to deep sub-cortical structures to drive our actions. So what we may loosely call the 'deep' brain serves as a relay station between the sensory world and the cortex, and from the cortex back to the world of action. Here, perhaps, somewhere in these deep brain structures, is the crucial bottleneck of attention; and whatever passes through the bottleneck is consciously experienced.

Penfield's viewpoint was more recently elaborated on and extended by Swedish neuroscientist Björn Merker.[7] Merker highlights a number of further observations that fit with Penfield's suspicion that conscious experience requires linkage between diverse cortical areas and a narrow processing bottleneck deep in the brain. If conscious experience is controlled by the deep, sub-cortical brain structures, for example, then one might expect those structures to control the very presence of consciousness; in particular, to act as a switch between wakefulness and sleep. Indeed, such a switch does appear to exist – or, at least, electrically stimulating highly localized deep brain structures in animals (specifically the reticular formation) can lead to a sharp reduction in activity across the whole of the cortex. The animal lapses into a quiescent state.[8] Moreover, if this brain area is surgically removed, the animal is comatose – as if unable to wake up. By contrast, wakefulness is unaffected in either animals or humans by removal of large areas of cortex.

Might temporary disruption deep in the human brain cause the switch momentarily to be thrown – so that consciousness ceases abruptly, perhaps just for a matter of seconds or minutes? Following Penfield, Merker points out that so-called 'petit mal' or absence epilepsy seems to have just this character. A petit mal episode involves a person, during everyday activity, suddenly adopting a vacant stare and becoming completely unresponsive to their surroundings. If the patient is walking, she will slow and freeze in position, while remaining upright; if she is speaking, speech may continue briefly, although typically slowing and then ceasing entirely; if eating, a forkful of food may hover in space between the plate and the mouth. Attempts to rouse the patient during a period of 'absence' are usually ineffective, although they can on occasion cause the patient to 'awake' suddenly. Usually, though, consciousness returns spontaneously, often within seconds. The sufferer typically has no immediate knowledge of having suffered an epileptic episode – conscious experience appears, bizarrely, to pick up uninterrupted from where it left off, as if time, from the point of view of the patient, has stood still. Patients experience, in particular, complete amnesia during the period of 'absence'.

Recordings of the electrical activity in the cortex during periods of 'absence' show the typical slow-wave pattern – but this pattern appears to synchronize simultaneously across the cortical surface from the very beginning of the episode, rather than, as with many other forms of epileptic seizure, propagating from one area to the next. It is as if a Mexican wave were to begin across the entire city, rather than rippling from one district to the next – and this would suggest some external communication signal, perhaps a radio broadcast, simultaneously instructing the population to act in unison. Penfield's conclusion is that the deep sub-cortical brain structures, with their rich fan of nervous connections to the cortical surface that enfolds them, play precisely this role.

A further clue from Penfield's neurosurgical investigations comes from results obtained by electrical stimulation as he operated. Such electrical stimulation would frequently trigger epileptic episodes. Patients were, after all, suffering epileptic attacks of the most extreme and frequent form – or they would never have been referred to Penfield for such radical surgery – and so it is not surprising that their brains were readily triggered into an epileptic state. Yet Penfield reports that the one form of epilepsy that was never induced, whichever region of the cortex was stimulated, was 'absence' or petit mal epilepsy – no electrical stimulation of the cortex itself could trigger the crisp, immediate, total shutdown of the cortical system, because, he suggested, the 'switch' of consciousness lies not in the cortical surface but deep within the brain.

When we think of the human brain, and the astonishing intelligence it supports, we conjure up an image of the tightly folded walnut-like surface of the cortex, lying just beneath our skull. Indeed, in humans, the cortex is of primary importance. While in many mammals, such as rats, the cortex is of rather modest size in comparison with other brain regions, in primates such as chimpanzees and gorillas it dominates the brain; and it is expanded spectacularly in humans. But the cortex receives its input, and sends its output, through deeper, sub-cortical brain structures – and these sub-cortical structures may determine the contents of the 'flow' of consciousness and, indeed, whether we are conscious at all.

To see how this might work, the link between perception and action may be especially illuminating. Suppose that we are picking apples from a tree. Our brain needs to alight on the next apple to be picked, determine whether it is sufficiently ripe and not yet rotten, perhaps identifying it through a veil of foliage, and then needs to plan a sequence of movements which will successfully grasp the apple and twist it from its stem. Or, in the case of a person, the action might consist merely of suggesting that someone else pick the apple, or describing it, perhaps inwardly. But in any case, it is crucial that the action is connected to the visual input concerned with this particular apple, and that the different pieces of the visual input (the different fragments of apple visible through foliage, perhaps) are integrated into a whole. If we reach out to the apple and touch it, then inform-ation about the location of our arm, and the sensations as we brush through the leaves and then feel the surface of the apple we grasp, must be linked up with our visual input (so that we know that we are reaching and grasping the very apple that we are looking at). And all of this information must be linked, in turn, to memory: of our earlier decision to pick apples (and, perhaps, only particularly ripe apples), our memory of past visual experience which allows us to identify apples, leaves and branches; and we may, in turn, be reminded of apple-picking incidents in our childhood, agricultural or biological facts about apples, and so on. The action of reaching and grasping an apple is itself potentially complex, requiring not just coordination of a single arm and hand, but of potentially stretching actions, standing on tiptoe if necessary, and making a suite of postural compensations to maintain balance.

Now actions occur, roughly, one at a time; but each action requires the integration of potentially large amounts of information from the senses, from memory, and from our motor system. So perhaps the role of one or more structures deep in our brains is to serve as the focal point for such integration; to probe the diverse areas of the surround-ing cortex, devoted to the processing of sensory information, memory or the control of movement, and to bring them to bear on the same problem. Thus, the sequential nature of action will be mirrored by the sequential flow of thought.

While deep brain structures, rather than the cortex, may be the bottleneck through which conscious experience flows, the activation of the cortex, for example by stimulation using an electrode, should be able to intrude on conscious experience: connections between cor-tex and deep brain areas are two-way. A sudden surge of activity in a particular area of the cortex may lead to signals into deep brain areas which disturb, and even override, their current activity, generating, for example, strange sensory experiences and fragments of memory. But crucially, the complete disappearance of an area of cortex, unless it happens to be engaged directly in some current mental activity, will pass entirely unnoticed, without even the merest ripple in conscious experience. And this is, of course, precisely what Penfield observed:

patients reported strange fragments of conscious experience, such as the smell of burnt toast, when a piece of cortex was electrical stimulated, but no anomalous conscious experience at all as Penfield removed entire areas of brain.

This perspective explains, too, why patients with visual neglect, where the cortex corresponding to a large area of the visual field may be damaged or entirely inoperative, can none the less be entirely unaware of their deficit. We are consciously aware, perhaps, only of the specific task on which we are currently focused. So, if engaged in fruit-picking, a person with visual neglect will focus their attention only on visual information in parts of the visual cortex which are intact, and link with memory and action systems through the coordinating power of structures deep in the brain, just as for a person with normal visual processing. In deep brain areas, conscious experience may be entirely normal. They will not, of course, pick or describe fruit whose visual positions project into the 'blind' area of visual cortex – so their visual phenomenology, while entirely normal moment by moment, will be restricted to, say, the right half of their visual field.

Our brain is fully engaged with making sense of the information it is confronted with *at each moment*. Consciousness, and indeed the entire activity of thought, appears to be guided, sequentially, through the narrow bottleneck: deep, sub-cortical structures search for, and coordinate, patterns in sensory input, memory and motor output, one at a time. The brain's task is, moment by moment, to link together different pieces of information, and to integrate and act on them right away. Our brain will, of course, lay down fresh memories as this processing proceeds; and draw on the richness of memories of past processing.

So our *no background processing* slogan is reinforced. Or, at least, if there are brain processes which are scurrying about behind the scenes, contemplating, evaluating and reasoning about matters that we appear not to be thinking about at all, then neuroscience has found no trace of them. The brain appears, instead, be concentrating on making sense of immediate experience, and generating sequences of actions, including language (whether spoken aloud or inner speech), through the narrow bottleneck of conscious thought. This is why it can only integrate and transform to solve *one problem at a time*.

We now have some tentative answers about how the cooperative style of brain computation operates. In the Penfield/Merker vision of the brain, both the questions that the brain faces and the answers that it provides are represented in sub-cortical structures, including

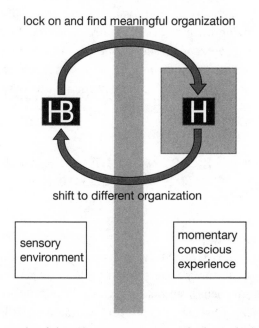

Figure 29. The cycle of thought. *Upper arrow*: The brain locks onto and organizes a fragment of the visual stimulus; we are conscious of, and can report, this organization. *Lower arrow*: But the brain – and the eye – is restlessly struggling to break free of its current organization and lock onto a different fragment of the image. This cycle is so rapid and fluent that we can have the sense of awareness of a complex object – or even an entire scene, in full detail and colour. Our stream of consciousness is of successive sensory organizations – consciousness is entirely confined to the shaded box. We have no conscious access to the information being picked up by our senses (the left-hand side of the figure) or how that information is interpreted (the curved arrows); or how our brain shifts to lock onto different information, e.g. by shifting our attention (with or without moving our eyes).

the thalamus, which serves as a relay station between the cerebral cortex and our sensory and motor systems – essentially as a gateway between the hemispheres of the brain and the outside world. And, we might suspect, both the questions and their answers are concerned primarily with the organization of sensation and movement; and the rich interconnections between these structures and the cortex provide the networks of cooperative computation that are able to solve the problems posed by these sub-cortical structures. Yet while the cortex is crucial in processing visual information, planning movement and drawing on memories, we are aware of the results of the vast cooperative enterprise across the brain only in so far as the results of such computations reach the sub-cortical 'gateway' structures – these, and not the cortex itself, are the locus of conscious experience.

FOUR PRINCIPLES OF THE CYCLE OF THOUGHT

Here is an outline of how the mind works, in the form of a picture (Figure 29) and four proposals. The first principle is that *attention is the process of interpretation*. At each moment, our brain 'locks onto' (or, in everyday terms, pays attention to) a target set of information, which the brain then attempts to organize and interpret. The target might be aspects of sensory experience, a fragment of language, or a memory.[9] Figure 29 illustrates a case where the brain has momentarily locked onto the 'H' in complex stimulus. Moments later, it might alight on the 'B'. Crucially, our brain locks onto one target at a time. This implies that the line shared between the 'H' and 'B' in the stimulus is, at any given moment, interpreted as belonging to one or the other – but not both. Following Penfield and Merker's conjectures, we might suspect that such information is represented in sub-cortical structures buried deep in the brain, with connections across the entire cortex, so that the full range of past experience and knowledge can be brought to bear on finding meaning in the current target. Remember that we can lock onto, and integrate, information of all kinds. We can use any and all pieces of information and great leaps of ingenuity and imagination to find meaning in the world, but we can only create one pattern at a time.

Our second principle concerns the nature of consciousness and is that our only conscious experience is our interpretation of sensory information. The result of the brain's 'interpretations' of sensory input is conscious – we are aware of the brain's interpretation of the world – but the 'raw materials' from which this interpretation is constructed, and the process of construction itself, are not consciously accessible. (Conscious experience is the organization represented in deep brain structures, with inputs from across the cortex – we are not directly conscious of cortical activity itself.) So in Figure 29, we perceive the 'H' or the 'B', but have absolutely no awareness of the process through which these were constructed.

Perception always works this way: we 'see' objects, people, faces as a result of a pattern of firing from light-sensitive cells triggered by light falling on our retina; we 'hear' voices, musical instruments and traffic noise as a result of picking up the complex patterns of firing of vibration-detecting cells in our inner ear. But we have no idea, from introspection alone, where such meaningful interpretations spring from – how our brain makes the jump from successive waves of cacophonous chatter from our nervous system to a stable and meaningful world around us. All we 'experience' is the stable and meaningful world: we experience the result, not the process.[10]

So far, we have focused on our consciousness of meaning in sensory information. The third principle is that we are conscious of nothing else: *all conscious thought concerns the meaningful interpretation of sensory information.* But while we have no conscious experience of non-sensory information, we may be conscious of their sensory 'consequences' (i.e. I have no conscious experience of the abstract number 5, although I may conjure up a sensory representation of five dots, or the shape of symbol '5'). Deep brain regions are, after all, relay stations for conveying sensory information to the cortex – so if they are locations of conscious experience, then we should expect conscious experience to be sensory experience, and nothing more.

The claim that we are aware of nothing more than meaningful organization of sensory experience isn't quite as restrictive as it sounds. Sensory information need not necessarily be *gathered* by our senses, but may be invented in our dreams or by active imagery. And much sensory information comes, of course, not from the external world but from our own bodies – including many of our pains, pleasures, and sensations of effort or boredom. We are conscious of the sounds or shapes of the words we use to encode abstract ideas; or the imagery which accompanies them. But we are not conscious of the abstract ideas themselves, whatever that might mean. I can imagine (just about) three apples or the symbols '3', 'iii' or 'three'; and I can imagine various rather indistinct triangles and the word 'triangle'. But I surely can't imagine, or in any sense be conscious of, the abstract number 3; or the abstract mathematical concept of 'triangularity'. I can hear myself say 'Triangles have three straight sides' or 'The internal angles of a triangle add up to 180 degrees' – but I surely don't have any additional conscious experience of these abstract truths.

Similarly, as we have seen already, it is a mistake to think that we are conscious of any of our beliefs, desires, hopes or fears. I can say to myself 'I'm terrified of water' or I can have visions of myself struggling desperately as a rip-tide pulls me out to sea. But it is words and images that are the objects of consciousness – not the 'abstract' belief. Just in case you doubt this viewpoint, reflect on what beliefs you are conscious of *right now*. How many are there, exactly? Can you feel when one belief leaves your consciousness or a fresh belief 'comes into mind'? I suspect not.[11]

Now we can tie together our three proposals into a fourth principle. I have proposed that an individual conscious thought is the process of the creation of a meaningful organization of sensory input. So what is the stream of consciousness? Nothing more than a succession of thoughts, an irregular cycle of experiences which are the results of sequential organization of different aspects of sensory input – the shifting contents of the right-hand box in Figure 29. This fits with the Penfield/Merker story about the brain: sub-cortical structures deep in the brain form a 'crucible' onto which the resources of the whole cortex can be focused to impose meaning on fragments of sensory information – but only one pattern can be placed in the crucible at a time.

Note, in particular, that the cycle of thought is sequential: we lock onto and impose meaning on one set of information at a time. Now of course your brain can control your breathing, heart-rate and balance independent of the cycle of thought – to some extent at least (we don't topple over when particularly engrossed in a problem). But the brain's activities beyond the sequential cycle of thought are, we shall see, surprisingly limited – we can manage, roughly speaking, just one thought at a time.

From this point of view, many of the strange phenomena we saw in Part One fall into place:

- The brain is continually scrambling to link together scraps of sensory information (and has the ability, of course, to gather more information, with a remarkably quick flick of the eye). We 'create' our perception of an entire visual world from a succession of fragments, picked up one at a time (see Chapter 2). Yet our conscious experience is merely the output of this remarkable process; we have little or no insight into the relevant sensory inputs or how they are combined.

- As soon as we query some aspects of the visual scene (or, equally, of our memory), then the brain immediately locks onto relevant information and attempts to impose meaning upon it. The process of creating such meaning is so fluent that we imagine ourselves merely to be reading off pre-existing information, to which we already have access, just as, when scrolling down the contents of a word processor, or exploring a virtual reality game, we have the illusion that the entire document, or labyrinth, pre-exist in all their glorious pixel-by-pixel detail (somewhere 'off-screen'). But, of course, they are created for us by the computer software at the very moment they are needed (e.g. when we scroll down or 'run' headlong down a virtual passageway). This is the sleight of hand that underlies the grand illusion (see Chapter 3).

- In perception, we focus on fragments of sensory information and impose what might be quite abstract meaning: the identity, posture, facial expression, intentions of another person, for example. But we can just as well reverse the process. We can focus on an abstract meaning, and create a corresponding sensory image: this is the basis of mental imagery. So just as we can recognize a tiger from the slightest of glimpses, we can also *imagine* a tiger – although, as we saw in Chapter 4, the sensory image we reconstruct is remarkably sketchy.

- Feelings are just one more thing we can pay attention to. An emotion is, as we saw in Chapter 5, the *interpretation* of a bodily state. So experiencing an emotion requires attending to one's bodily state as well as relevant aspects of the outer world: the interpretation imposes a 'story' linking body and world together. Suppose, for example, that Inspector Lestrade feels the physiological traces of negativity (perhaps he draws back, hunches his shoulders, his mouth turns down, he looks at the floor) as Sherlock Holmes explains his latest triumph. The observant Watson attends, successively, to Lestrade's demeanour and Holmes's words, searching for the meaning of these snippets, perhaps concluding: 'Lestrade is jealous of Holmes's brilliance.' But Lestrade's reading of his own emotions works in just the same way: he too must attend to, and interpret his own physiological state and Holmes's words in order to conclude that he is jealous of Holmes's brilliance. Needless to say, Lestrade may be thinking nothing of the kind – he may be trying (with frustratingly little success) to find flaws in Holmes's explanation of the case. If so, while Watson may interpret Lestrade as being jealous, Lestrade is not experiencing jealousy (of Holmes's brilliance, or anything else) – because experiencing jealousy results from a process of interpretation, in which jealous thoughts are the 'meaning' generated, but Lestrade's mind is attending to other matters entirely, in particular, the details of the case.

- Finally, consider choices (see Chapter 6). Recall how the left hemisphere of a split-brain patient fluently, though often completely spuriously, 'explains' the mysterious activity of the left hand – even though that hand is actually governed by the brain's right hemisphere. This is the left, linguistic brain's attempt to impose meaning on the left-hand movements: to create such meaningful (though, in the case of the split-brain patient, entirely illusory) explanation requires locking onto the activity of the left hand in order to make sense of it. It does not, in particular, involve locking onto any hidden inner motives lurking within the right hemisphere (the real controller of the left hand) because the left and right hemispheres are, of course, completely disconnected. But notice that, even if the hemispheres were connected, the left hemisphere would not be able to attend to the right hemisphere's inner workings – because the brain can *only* attend to the meaning of perceptual input (including the perception of one's own bodily state), not to any aspect of its own inner workings.

We are, in short, relentless improvisers, powered by a mental engine which is perpetually creating meaning from sensory input, step by step. Yet we are only ever aware of the meaning created; the process by which it arises is hidden. Our step-by-step improvisation is so fluent that we have the illusion that the 'answers' to whatever 'questions' we ask ourselves were 'inside our minds all along'. But, in reality, when we decide what to say, what to choose, or how to act, we are, quite literally, *making up* our minds, one thought at a time.

8

The Narrow Channel of Consciousness

If thoughts are a cycle, then it follows that we have thoughts one at a time. More specifically, we can only focus on, and attempt to impose meaning on, just one set of information at a time. But the brain does many things at once. Most of us can, as the saying goes, walk and chew gum at the same time; and also walk, chew gum and be shocked by an overheard conversation. But if our mind is locked onto the conversation, it will not simultaneously be locked onto the walking or the gum-chewing: these activities, like the control of our breathing and our heart-rate, will, in a very real sense, be mindless. These processes are precisely those that do not involve interpretation (i.e. our best attempt to imaginatively apply anything and everything that we know in order to make sense of the information that is currently in our mental 'focus'). Such mindless, automatic processes turn out to be very limited, both in what they can do and how well they can perform (though with the occasional surprising exception, as we'll see later).

Yet if the mind is able only to lock onto one set of information at a time, does this mean that we are effectively oblivious to anything we are not currently paying attention to? Not quite. First, automatic processes such as gum-chewing and walking can continue uninterrupted, and these require the processing of some sensory information – about the terrain in front of us, our posture, limb positions and muscle activity to make sure that we don't topple over, or sensory information about the inner world of our own mouths, if we are not inadvertently to bite our own tongues. Secondly, there is the question of vigilance, even for information we are not currently attending to. Remember that the periphery of the retina is continually monitoring the signs of motion, flashes of light, or other abrupt changes; our auditory system is alert, to some degree at least, to unexpected bangs, creaks or voices; our bodies are 'wired' to detect unexpected pains or prods. In short, our perceptual system is continually ready to raise the alarm – and to drag our limited attentional resources away from their current task in order to lock onto a surprising new stimulus. But these 'alarm systems' don't themselves involve the interpretation and organization of sensory input; instead they help *direct* our attempts to organize and interpret sensory input. So we do not know what it is that has attracted our attention until we have locked onto the unexpected information and attempted to make sense of it.[1]

This means that we are sometimes oblivious to information to which we are not attending, even though it may be in plain view. Such 'inattentional blindness' seems highly counter-intuitive, but turns out to be all too real. The perceptual psychologists Arien Mack and Irvin Rock asked the participants in their experiments to fixate on a small cross in the centre of a computer screen. Then, a much larger cross appeared on the screen – and the task was to judge whether the horizontal or vertical arm of the large cross was longer. As can be seen in Figure 30, this is a fairly subtle discrimination, requiring careful attention. The large cross disappeared after one fifth of a second, before being replaced by a random black-and-white 'mask' pattern (on the right in Figure 30). Previous studies have shown that the mask will obliterate further visual analysis of the cross. The mask was just used to control the amount of time that people could look at the cross. If no mask was used, and the screen simply went blank, the participants would still potentially have access to an after-image of the cross on their retinas.

The viewer initially fixates on a small central cross; then comes the 'critical stimulus', with its large central cross. The viewer's task is to report whether the vertical or horizontal 'arm' of the cross is the longer. After one fifth of a second, the critical stimulus is obliterated by a 'mask'.

The key moment in Mack and Rock's experiment came on the third or fourth trial, when they introduced an additional object, for example a black or coloured blob a couple of degrees away from the point of fixation (and hence projected near to, although not actually

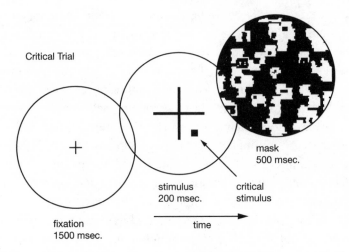

Figure 30. Three successive stimuli in Mack and Rock's experiment.[2]

within, the fovea). In this crucial trial, Mack and Rock simply asked their participants whether they had seen anything other than the large cross.

Rather remarkably, about 25 per cent of people reported seeing absolutely nothing: even though the blob was fairly large, had strong contrast and was positioned as close to the fovea as the ends of the two lines that are being compared. This flagrant 'inattentional blindness' suggests that if people were not attending to the blob they simply didn't see it.

One might suspect that the blob's slight offset from the fovea, where our visual processing is most acute, is part of the problem. If so, then there is a simple remedy: to move the large cross away from the fixation point (where the fovea is centred) and to put the blob on the fixation point – so that the participant is looking directly at the blob where their eye has the greatest possible acuity (see Figure 31). Yet incredibly, when this was done, Mack and Rock found that the rate of inattentional blindness *rose*, from 25 per cent to 85 per cent!

Is the strange phenomenon of inattentional blindness particular to vision? One way to find out is to replace the unexpected black blob with an unexpected sound.[3] Participants carried out the visual task wearing headphones which played a continuous hissing white-noise

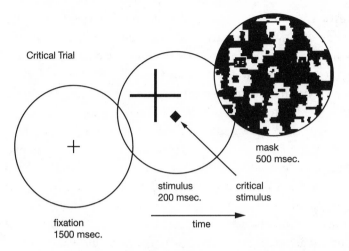

Critical Trial

mask
500 msec.

stimulus
200 msec.

critical
stimulus

fixation
1500 msec.

time

Figure 31. A key variation. As before, the viewer initially fixates on a small central cross; then comes the 'critical stimulus', this time with a central blob and the large peripheral cross. As before, the viewer's task is to report whether the vertical or horizontal 'arm' of the cross is the longer, and after one fifth of a second the critical stimulus is obliterated by the mask. Now the rate of inattentional blindness to the blob increases dramatically, even though the participant is now looking right at it.[4]

sound – in the crucial trial, precisely at the point at which the cross-shape appeared, there was an additional, extended 'beep'. Without any additional task, the beep was loud enough to be clearly audible – but, when people were focusing on which arm of the cross was longer, nearly 80 per cent of them denied that they had heard any such beep or, indeed, anything else unusual. So focusing on a tricky visual judgement can lead not only to inattentional blindness (even for a stimulus we are looking at directly), but also to inattentional deafness.[5]

Inattentional blindness is by no means a mere curiosity. Indeed, it can be incredibly dangerous. NASA researcher Richard Haines used a realistic flight simulator to explore how pilots with many thousands of hours of flying experience were able to handle the information on the heads-up display – a transparent display on which information was presented, overlaid across the visual scene. The virtue of the heads-up display is that the pilots should, in principle, be able to take in the visual scene and read off crucial instrumentation while scarcely moving their eyes. By contrast, of course, conventional dials, screens and meters require a potentially disruptive and time-consuming shift in gaze.

Haines set the simulator so that the pilots had to land their 'virtual plane' at night in conditions of low visibility and hence rely almost exclusively on their instrumentation. Late in their descent, though, the plane suddenly broke through the bottom of the cloud cover, revealing a clear night-time runway scene, as shown in Figure 32. In the context of landing a plane, Figure 32 shows a mildly terrifying prospect: another plane is turning to taxi on the runway directly ahead. The majority of the pilots took rapid and drastic evasive action. A minority, though, did not – they continued their descent and landing entirely oblivious to the presence of a large, distinct, though thankfully virtual, passenger jet right in the centre of the visual field. Just like the experimental participants looking closely at the cross and missing the blob, these pilots were paying close attention to their heads-up display: attending, integrating and using this information to guide their actions. But by locking onto the heads-up display information, they were inadvertently tuning out safety-critical scene information, even though they were looking directly at it – and this was on a task with which they had hundreds of hours of practice.

Figure 32. Inattentional blindness in action. Focusing their attention on the symbols and lines of the heads-up display (shown), a significant minority of pilots were oblivious to the rest of the image and continued with a normal landing.[6]

The phenomenon of inattentional blindness is, in fact, familiar to all of us. Look out of the window from a brightly lit room at night. Notice how you can look at the world outside, seeing nothing of the reflections of the room; or you can examine the reflections, and find the world outside temporarily disappearing from view. Sometimes, of course, your visual system can struggle to determine which parts of the image are outside, which parts a reflection: for example, seeing a reflected light from the room as hanging in the sky (perhaps one potential source of UFO 'sightings'). And it can create strange hybrids from bits of the exterior and interior of your home or office. But what the visual system cannot do is simultaneously 'see' two separate scenes at once: we can lock onto and impose meaning on (parts of) the reflected world, or the exterior world, or even a strange amalgam of the two, but we cannot do both at once. The pilots operate with the same limitations: attending to 'display-world' can entirely eliminate the external visual scene.

This is not necessarily disastrous news for heads-up displays, though. To the extent that the heads-up display augments, and meshes with, the external world, then the two may potentially be integrated together into a single meaningful whole, like a photograph adorned with highlights, arrows and other annotations. But if the display and external world are disconnected, rather than richly interconnected, then there is a real danger that seeing one will obliterate the other.

Consider now a path-breaking study led by one of the pioneers of cognitive psychology, Cornell University's Ulric Neisser, participants watched videos of three people throwing a ball to one another.[7] They had to press a button each time a throw occurred. But matters were not quite this simple: Neisser and his colleagues had created two different videos of the ball-passing game, and overlaid them. So now there were two teams of people (distinguished by having two different coloured shirts), and hence two types of ball-passing, one of which was to be monitored with the button pressing, the other of which was to be ignored.

Neisser's first intriguing finding was that, from the start, people found this apparently substantial complication of the task no problem at all – they were easily able to lock their attention onto one stream of video and ignore the other. The brain was able to monitor one video almost as if the other superimposed video was not there at all. By contrast, for current computer vision systems, 'unscrambling' the scenes, and attending to one and ignoring the other, would be enormously challenging.

But Neisser's second finding was the real surprise. He added a highly salient, and unexpected, event during the course of the video: a woman carrying a large umbrella strolled into view among the players, walked right across the scene, before disappearing from view. To a casual viewer of the video (i.e. to someone not counting the passes of one team or the other), the woman and her umbrella were all too obvious – indeed, her sudden appearance jumped out as both striking and bizarre. But less than one quarter of the people monitoring the ball-passes noticed anything untoward at all, even though, in following the passes, their eyes were criss-crossing the screen, passing and landing close to the large and, one would imagine, highly salient figure of the woman and her umbrella.[8]

What all these studies reveal is that our brains lock onto fragments of sensory information, and work to impose meaning on those fragments. But we can only lock onto and impose meaning on one set of fragments at a time. If our brains are busy organizing the lines on a heads-up display, we may miss the large aircraft turning onto the runway in front of us, in the same way that, peering through a lighted window into the garden, we can be utterly oblivious of our own reflection.

THE 'FATE' OF UNATTENDED INFORMATION

There is, according to the cycle of thought view, only one way information can enter into consciousness: through being directly attended to. But is there also a 'back door' to the mind, bypassing the cycle of thought, and hence conscious awareness, entirely?[9] To my knowledge there is no experimental evidence for the existence of any such back door. Rather than being simultaneously able to piece together a number of distinct perceptual jigsaws, the brain is able to process only one jigsaw time.[10]

A single step in the cycle of thought operates, then, along the following lines. Early in each processing step, there may be some uncertainty about which information is to be locked onto and which should be ignored. The brain will initially find some basic 'meaning' to help pin down which information is relevant and which is not. That is, where our perceptual jigsaws have been mixed together, we need initially to look at, and analyse, pieces of both jigsaws before we can pin down which pieces are relevant to us, and which should be ignored. But as the brain's processing step proceeds, the effort of interpretation will narrow ever more precisely on the scraps of information that helped form whatever pattern is of interest, and the processing of other scraps of information will be reduced and, indeed, abandoned. By the end of the processing step, the interpretative effort has a single outcome: the brain has locked onto, and imposed meaning upon, one set of information only. In terms of our jigsaw analogy, each step in the cycle of thought solves a jigsaw and only one jigsaw. We may, if reading text, or flicking our eyes across an image, or being subjected to a rapidly changing stream of sounds or pictures, solve several 'jigsaws' a second (though frequently there are hints from one jigsaw that help us solve the next – e. g. when we are scanning a scene, or reading a book, we build up expectations about what we're likely to see, or read, next; if our expectations are confirmed, then solving the next mental jigsaw will be more rapid). But our brain is still subject to a fundamental limitation: analysing one set of information at a time. And, as we have seen, the meaning that we impose in each step in our cycle of thought corresponds with the contents of our stream of conscious awareness. So the sequential nature of consciousness is no accident: it reflects the sequential engine that is the cycle of thought.

So what is the evidence for this view of conscious experience? In particular, how do we know that the brain attempts to make sense of just one set of information at a time?[11] Looking back, all the evidence we have examined for the grand illusion gives us a strong hint. We have the impression that we see pages of words, roomfuls of people, scenes full of objects rich in colour and detail – and we saw that this impression is entirely mistaken. Recall, for instance, as we discussed in Chapter 1, that when subjected to the trickery of the gaze-contingent eye-tracker, people can read fluently and normally, while entirely oblivious of the fact that, at each fixation, just twelve to fifteen letters are presented onscreen, and the rest of the text has been replaced by *x*s or by Latin.

If the brain was 'secretly' processing all, or some, of those other 'words', even if unconsciously, one might imagine that there would be some, and perhaps a rather dramatic, effect on reading. To my knowledge, no such effects have been reported.[12]

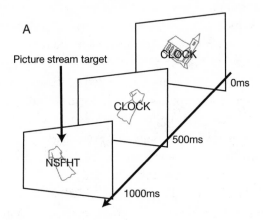

Figure 33. Visual displays in Rees et al.'s experiment.

In the grip of the grand illusion, we imagine that we simultaneously perceive great seas of words, faces and objects, all in high definition and full colour; and that we can 'take in' a rich soundscape of voices, music and clinking of glasses in a single perceptual gulp. The grand illusion tricks us into believing that our focus of attention is far wider than it actually is.

So we can attend to much less than we imagine; and unattended information can change dramatically (from *xxx*s to text to *xxx*s again) without our noticing. So it seems both that our attention is severely restricted, and that we have little or no access to information that is not attended to. Yet could it be that unattended information is processed elaborately, but is rapidly forgotten? Could it be that some of the apparent richness of subjective experience is real enough – but that the reason we can never reveal such experience in experiments is because the memory of all those unattended objects, colours and textures is so fragile?

Geraint Rees, Charlotte Russell, Chris Frith and the late Jon Driver, working at one of the world's leading brain imaging labs at University College London, found a beautifully elegant way to look at this question, by monitoring the online activity of the brain (see Figure 33).[13] People were settled into a brain scanner and shown images involving a line drawing of a familiar object, overlaid by strings of letters in block capitals. These strings of letters were meaningless in some blocks of trials, but formed familiar words in others. Prior research has established that there is a characteristic frisson of brain activity associated with reading a word in contrast merely to a meaningless string of letters. So we can use this burst of activity (as it happens, towards the back left of the brain, in the left occipital cortex) as a tell-tale objective indicator that a word has been recognized – and this indicator is, of course, completely independent of subjective awareness.

Rees and colleagues showed people streams of stimuli consisting of letter strings (which might be meaningless or might form familiar words) and pictures overlaid (see Figure 33). People's attention was directed to the word or the picture by giving them a simple task, which involved looking at just one of type of information: specifically, people were asked to monitor for immediate repetitions (i.e. pairs of successive identical stimuli) *either* for words, or for pictures. They could tell that people were paying attention to one type of information (letters or pictures) by checking that they successfully picked out the repetitions when they occurred. The images were presented sufficiently rapidly that people were able to report repetitions accurately only by locking their attention purely onto one type of stimulus or the other – there was no time for their attention to 'hop' back and forth between the letters and pictures.

When answering questions about, and hence attending to, the letter strings, the distinctive word-specific frisson of activity was present when the letter strings made familiar words – but the presence of the unattended pictures did not change the results. So far, so good. But what happened when people monitored, and hence paid attention to, the pictures? If the brain was still recognizing the unattended words as normal (i.e. if unattended information is analysed, but then ignored), then the tell-tale word-specific frisson should still be present. If, on the other hand, the brain failed to distinguish between arbitrary letter strings and words – because unattended words aren't read at all – then the distinctive, word-specific pulse of neural activity should be absent. And, indeed, the latter possibility turned out to be correct.

The results showed that the participants were simply not reading the unattended words at all, even though they were looking directly at them. And they were not reading the words because, crucially, they were paying attention to something else: the overlaid pictures. So, roughly speaking, if you don't pay attention to a word, you just don't read it. Indeed, from the brain's point of view, it isn't there. It seems reasonable to conjecture that the same is true wherever the cycle of thought operates, not just in reading: without attention, there is no interpretation, analysis or understanding.[14]

DIVIDING THE BRAIN

I have argued that the cooperative style of brain computation is what forces us to think one step at a time. But this viewpoint has a further implication: those distinct, non-interacting networks of neurons should, in principle, be able to work independently, with each network cooperatively solving its own problem, without interference. As it happens, the brain is densely interconnected – and almost any moderately complex problem, from understanding a sentence to recognizing a face or seeing a constellation in the night sky, will typically involve activity across large swathes of the cortex. So our ability to carry out several mental activities 'in parallel' will be severely limited.

There are, though, tasks for which our neural 'machinery' is, conveniently, largely separate. One clear-cut example is the operation of the 'autonomic' nervous system, which runs our heart, breathing, digestion, and so on. These neural circuits are only loosely coupled with the cortex – so that, thankfully, our heart can keep beating, our lungs breathing, and our stomachs digesting, even while we focus our attention on a tricky problem or a good book. But what about more complex tasks? Perhaps if the tasks are sufficiently different, they might not use overlapping networks in the brain – and if so, perhaps they could operate independently and hence simultaneously.

This situation is rare, but it can occur. A remarkable study[15] by the Oxford psychologist Alan Allport and colleagues looked at this question, asking pianists who were skilled sight-readers to combine sight-reading a new piece of music with 'shadowing' speech delivered through headphones (repeating the flow of speech that one is hearing, often with as little as one quarter of a second delay). Amazingly, after a fairly modest amount of practice, there was very little interference between the two tasks: people could shadow and sight-read fluently at the same time.

Shortly afterwards, a follow-up experiment by Henry Shaffer at the University of Exeter pushed this result a step further, showing that highly trained typists were able to shadow and type unseen texts with almost no interference.[16] This seems particularly remarkable, as both the shadowing task and the typing task involved language – so one might imagine they would be especially likely to become entangled. But surprisingly, the typists appeared to carry out both tasks at close to normal speed and accuracy.

So it seems that the networks of neurons involved in carrying out the two tasks are indeed separate, or at least can be kept separate with practice. So, for example, perhaps a mapping from visually presented letters or words to finger movements (required for typing) can be kept distinct from a mapping between auditory words and speech (required for shadowing). If this is right, then at most one of the streams of language flowing through the participant as they simultaneously touch-type and shadow speech in Shaffer's experiment can be processed for grammar and meaning. Indeed, this would imply that the participant can fluently touch-type and shadow speech where the linguistic material being communicated is nonsense rather than meaningful. The conscious, meaningful interpretation of language would, accordingly, apply to either the material that is being read or heard, but not to both (so that, for example, the meaning of just one stream of input would be encoded and stored in memory). It should not be possible to make sense of both linguistic inputs simultaneously any more than it should be possible to see each of two visual patterns, one superimposed upon the other or, for that matter, to see an ambiguous item as both a rabbit and a bird (see Figure 24). This line of reasoning leads logically to the prediction that people should be able to recall at most one of the linguistic inputs they were working with – only one of which can have been processed for meaning.

If this general theory is correct, the brain can carry out multiple tasks if each of those tasks draws on non-overlapping networks of neurons. But given the dense connectivity of the brain, and the multiplicity of elements involved in carrying out many tasks, this is rarely possible for tasks of substantial complexity. Usually there is some overlap in the neural networks each task recruits, which will snarl up our ability to do both tasks simultaneously. It may be that the neurons involved in walking and chewing gum are relatively distinct from each other, and from, say, doing complicated pieces of mental arithmetic (although when we need to concentrate really hard on a tricky multiplication or a crossword clue, we may find ourselves, perhaps tellingly, slowing or stopping walking, pausing our gum-chewing, and perhaps even closing our eyes).

Almost any demanding pair of tasks, then, will involve overlapping neural circuits – so that perception, memory and imagination can only proceed one step at a time. Each step may be a 'giant' step, making sense of a complex visual image or a rich musical pattern, or solving a crossword clue – and will draw on the cooperative efforts of networks containing billions of neurons; but the inner workings of each step are, of course, utterly inaccessible to conscious awareness.

In this chapter, we have seen how, special cases aside, the cycle of thought provides a single channel through which we make sense of the world, step-by-step; and if the cycle of thought is locked onto one aspect of the visual world, other information (blobs, aircraft, words) can be ignored, even when in plain sight. If this is right, then the sequential nature of the cycle of thought seems to imply that conscious thought on one topic blocks out thought (whether conscious or unconscious) on any other topic (assuming, as will typically be the case, that these streams of thought would depend on overlapping brain networks). The slogan we have already encountered in Chapter 7 remains true: 'no background processing in the brain.'

The existence of unconscious thought can therefore be considered a crucial test case for our entire account. Does it stand in opposition to the cycle of thought account? Or is it just one more mirage that disappears on closer inspection?

9

The Myth of Unconscious Thought

The great French mathematician and physicist Henri Poincaré (1854–1912) took a particular interest in the origins of his own astonishing creativity. His achievements were impressive: his work profoundly reshaped mathematics and physics – including laying crucial foundations for Einstein's theory of relativity and the modern mathematical analysis of chaos. But he also had some influential speculations about where many of his brilliant ideas came from: unconscious thought.

Poincaré found that he would often struggle unsuccessfully with some mathematical problem, perhaps over days or weeks[1] (to be fair, the problems he got stuck on were difficult, to say the least). Then, while not actually working on the problem at all, a possible solution would pop into his mind. And when he later checked carefully, the solution would almost always turn out to be correct.

How was this possible? Poincaré's own suspicion was that his unconscious mind was churning through possible approaches to the problem 'in the background' – and when an approach seemed aesthetically 'right', it might burst through into consciousness. Poincaré believed that this 'unconscious thought' process was carried out by what might almost be a second self, prepared and energized by periods of conscious work, yet able to work away on the problem in hand entirely below the level of conscious awareness.

The notable twentieth-century German composer Paul Hindemith, in a well-known passage from his book, reports a similar belief, with a striking metaphor:

> We all know the impression of a very heavy flash of lightning in the night. Within a second's time we see a broad landscape, not only in its

general outlines but with every detail. Although we could never describe each single component of the picture, we feel that not even the smallest leaf of grass escapes our attention. We experience a view, immensely comprehensive and at the same time immensely detailed, that we never could have under normal daylight conditions, and perhaps not during the night either, if our senses and nerves were not strained by the extraordinary suddenness of the event. Compositions must be conceived the same way. If we cannot, in the flash of a single moment, see a composition in its absolute entirety, with every pertinent detail in its proper place, we are not genuine creators.[2]

Taken literally, Hindemith's claim would seem to imply that the entire process of composition is the work of the unconscious – the complete score is, it seems, worked out by subterfuge by unconscious processes, only to break forth into consciousness in a moment of spectacular incandescence. The unconscious work complete, the composer needs merely to go through the laborious process of transcribing the already finished work onto paper, a humdrum activity indeed, given that the creative labour has already been done. Hindemith's conception of the composing of processing is all the more remarkable in the light of the extreme complexity and idiosyncrasy of the musical system governing his own pieces.[3]

Let us, for contrast, consider 'insight' of a much more prosaic kind, in our struggle to make sense of apparently baffling images. You may have seen one or both of the pictures in Figure 34 before. If you have, you will immediately know what they represent. If not, they will

Figure 34. Any idea what these are?[4]

almost certainly seem to you to be nothing more than a baffling jumble of speckles, marks and smudges. If initially these make no sense, spend a minute or two inspecting them closely – if you are lucky, you may experience a rather delightful feeling when, suddenly, their interpretation 'pops out' (spoiler alert! don't read on until you have finished examining the images in Figure 34). If you haven't seen these pictures before, don't give up too soon. You may find that, even after a minute or two of bafflement, you find the pictures suddenly make sense – and when they do, the pattern will seem so obvious that you may wonder how you could possibly not have spotted it right away. If you are still mystified after a couple of minutes, you can turn to Figure 35 (page 164), in which all is revealed.

The left image shows a Dalmatian dog sniffing the ground; the right-hand picture is a 'portrait' of a cow. Obvious once you see them – and once seen, they can't be unseen. These images will be easy to make sense of, if you next see them years or decades in the future.

When the object does suddenly 'pop out', we have a sense of sudden insight, but no idea how to explain where it came from. Without warning, order emerges from chaos. We have no sense of getting 'warmer' or 'colder' before insight suddenly hits us – we have a sense of floundering aimlessly, followed, if we are lucky, by what feels like a 'bolt from the blue' of sudden understanding. The problem is solved not by a sequence of steps, getting ever closer to the answer. Quite the opposite: the cycle of thought churns on and on, exploring different possible organizations with no sign of progress until, suddenly, and within a single step, it chances upon the solution.

Now, imagine that, rather than allowing you to inspect these images continuously for many seconds or minutes, I had shown them briefly (perhaps just a few seconds at a time) once a week. Eventually, on one of these occasions, a Dalmatian would spring into view; on another, you would be confronted with the sad and steady gaze of the cow. These moments of sudden insight might seem to demand an explanation: you would ask 'why does the image make sense now, when it made no sense before?'

A natural answer might suggest itself: 'I must have been unconsciously working away on these images – and solved or partially solved the mystery without even knowing it. Then the answer "broke through" into consciousness, when I saw the image again.' Yet this would be quite wrong – the same sudden 'pop out' occurs when we continuously contemplate the image, and there has been no opportunity for unconscious background pondering. The phenomenon of sudden insight stems not from unconscious thought, but from the nature of the problem: searching for a meaningful interpretation with few helpful and unambiguous clues.

These sudden flashes of 'visual insight', which could so easily be misattributed to unconscious thought, should make us sceptical of the unconscious origins of other flashes of insight in mathematics, science or music. Introspection, even the introspection of geniuses, is not to be taken at face value.

The brain is, as we have seen, a cooperative computing machine – large networks of neurons collectively piece together the solution to a single problem: the cycle of thought proceeds one step at a time. And the brain's networks of neurons are highly interconnected, so there seems little scope for assigning different problems to different brain networks. Here, the contrast with Allport's and Shaffer's demonstrations of remarkable dual task performance, outlined in Chapter 8, is telling. Their studies suggested that people could do two things at once *when distinct mental calculations – presumably associated with non-overlapping networks of neurons – were involved* (e.g. for sight-reading music and taking dictation). And such specialized brain networks can sometimes be developed for highly practised and repetitive tasks. But solving difficult problems, whether mathematical, musical or of any other kind, is the very antithesis of a routine, specialized problem with a dedicated brain network: on the contrary, thinking about such problems will need to engage most of the brain. So the idea that profound unconscious thought can be 'running in the background' as we go about our everyday lives is fanciful indeed. Routine and highly practised activities aside, the cycle of thought can attend to, and make sense of, only one set of information at a time.

Poincaré and Hindemith cannot possibly be right. If they are spending their days actively thinking about other things, their brains are not unobtrusively solving deep mathematical problems or composing complex pieces of music, perhaps over days or weeks, only to reveal the results in a sudden flash. Yet, driven by the intuitive appeal

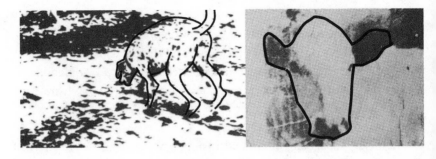

Figure 35. All is revealed.

of unconscious thought, psychologists have devoted a great deal of energy in searching for evidence for unconscious mental work. In these studies, they typically give people some tricky problems to solve (e.g. a list of anagrams); after a relatively short period of time, they might instruct participants to continue, to take a break, to do another similar or different mental task, or even get a night's sleep, before resuming their problems. According to the 'unconscious work' perspective, resuming after a break should lead to a sudden improvement in performance, compared with people who just keep going with the task. Studies in this area are numerous and varied,[5] but I think the conclusions are easily summarized. First, the effects of breaks of all kinds are either negligible or non-existent: if unconscious work takes place at all, it is sufficiently ineffectual to be barely detectable, despite a century of hopeful attempts. Second, many researchers have argued that the minor effects of taking a break – and indeed, Poincaré's and Hindemith's intuitions – have a much more natural explanation, which involves no unconscious thought at all.

The simplest version of the idea comes from thinking about why one gets stuck with a difficult problem in the first place. What is special about such problems is that you can't solve them through a routine set of steps (in contrast, say, to adding up columns of numbers, which is laborious but routine) – you have to look at the problem in the 'right way' before you can make progress (e.g. with an anagram, you might need to focus on a few key letters; in deep mathematics or musical composition, the space of options might be large and varied). So ideally, the right approach would be to fluidly explore the range of possible 'angles' on the problem, until hitting on the right one. Yet this is not so easy: once we have been looking at the same problem for a while, we feel ourselves to be stuck or going round in circles. Indeed, the cooperative computational style of the brain makes this difficult to avoid.

Mental cul-de-sacs of this kind occur when our brains fail to find a satisfactory analysis or interpretation. Conscious attempts to clear the cul-de-sac can, of course, often be successful: we jettison some information, and focus instead on slightly different information. We focus on different parts of a cryptic crossword clue (perhaps the word 'jumble' means this is some kind of anagram). We actively dredge up different pieces of knowledge that we think might help us. ('Oh – this looks like a geometry problem with circles and angles; I learnt about circle theorems at school; what were they all about?') All too often, though, such deliberate attacks on a problem fail. Indeed, we can find ourselves endlessly going down the same mental cul-de-sacs, such as when I try to think of the word *artichoke*, for which my typical internal dialogue is something like: 'No, not *avocado*! Not *asparagus*! Not *aubergine*! And certainly not *aspidistra*! Oh, this is ridiculous! Help!'

Breaking out of mental cul-de-sacs is precisely what a break will give us. Starting afresh with a relatively clear mind is more likely to succeed than a mind filled with partial solutions and suggestions which, after an increasingly frustrating struggle, have clearly failed. And, by sheer chance, we might even get a clue that helps us. But probably the most important aspect of setting a problem aside is that, when we return to it, we see it afresh unencumbered by our previous failed attempts. Often, our new perspective will be no more successful than the old, but, now and again, the answer will suddenly snap into place.

But what is not happening, despite our intuitions to the contrary, is hidden background thought mulling over our problem beneath the level of conscious awareness, and taking no part in the cycle of thought. Unconscious problem-solving, and unconscious thought of all kinds, is a myth.

Poincaré's description of his particular method of solving mathematical problems suggests why he was particularly susceptible to brilliant flashes of insight. His normal strategy for solving a problem was to work out the outlines of the solution entirely in its head, without pen and paper; and only then to, somewhat laboriously, translate his intuitions into the symbolic language of mathematics, to be checked and verified. But what is crucial is that, for Poincaré, mathematical problems were transformed into perceptual problems: and with the right perceptual intuition, the process of creating a 'proof' acceptable to fellow mathematicians would be relatively routine, if slow. A perceptual problem is just the kind of problem that can be solved in a single cycle of thought – provided that we happen to lock onto just the right information and 'see' the pattern in that information in just the right way like the Dalmatian and doleful cow of Figure 35.

From this point of view, Poincaré's mathematical brainwave is of precisely the same type as the 'insight' we experience when we glance back at our Dalmatian or cow images to find that, finally, for some reason, order has mysteriously emerged from chaos. Crucially, in neither case is the sudden revelation the product of hours or days of unconscious thought. Instead, the solution is found in a single cycle of thought when we contemplate the problem again. Having broken free of our previous and incorrect analysis, by happy chance our brains alight upon the correct solution. The mental fragments are recombined in just the right way, click delightfully together, and the problem is solved.

This viewpoint is nicely illustrated by one of the most celebrated stories of scientific insight: the discovery of the structure of benzene by the great nineteenth-century chemist August Kekulé. The brainwave struck as he was having a daydream in which a snake began to swallow its own tail. It suddenly struck Kekulé that benzene might itself have a circular structure (the kind of metaphorical leap that our elastic minds are prone to, as we shall see later); and before long he had worked out his detailed analysis of the chemical structure of the benzene ring.

We might wonder, of course, how it is that the right perceptual interpretation happens to come to mind, helping to solve what seemed to be an intractable problem, almost in the moment. Could it be, perhaps, that the unconscious has been working away furiously on the details of the solution for hours or days,[6] and finally decides to communicate with the 'conscious mind', not simply by telling it the answer, but by conjuring up a cryptic image? Despite the charm of this story, it isn't very plausible. There is no mystery about how just the right perceptual image comes to mind to lead to the starling scientific insight – because almost all the perceptual images that flash through our minds are *not* the right kind of images to spark a brilliant insight. Only the extraordinarily rare cases in which, by happy accident, the appropriate image or collision of images happens to unlock some important discovery turn into stories told to the next generation of mathematicians and scientists.

Thus, insight may indeed occur in a flash (i.e. in a single cycle of thought) when our minds lock onto a problem afresh and see it from a subtly different perspective. But there is no reason to believe that it bursts through from the deliberations of a second, unconscious self.

Hindemith's claim that entire pieces of music come to their creators in their entirety should similarly not be taken at face value. His potent image of the sense of grasping the full detail of a night-time scene lit up by a flash of lightning is itself telling. After all, in Part One, we found that our sense of a detailed and vivid visual world is itself illusory: we have the illusion that the information that we can create on demand already lies, pre-formed and within reach (e.g. with a flick of our eyes and/or a shift of attention). And surely the same is true for musical composition. What Hindemith surely means is that, after the flash of inspiration has occurred, creating the piece (and writing it out in musical notation) it proceeds with fluency. Indeed, the piece flows out of the composer in a way that feels inevitable and predetermined. Hindemith explains:

> This does not mean that any f sharp in the six hundred and twelfth measure of the final piece would have been determined in the very first flash of cognition. If the seer should in this first flash concentrate his attention on any particular detail of the whole, he would never conceive the totality, but if the conception of this totality strikes his mind like lightning, this f sharp and all the other thousands of notes and other means of expression will fall into line almost without his knowing it.[7]

So the flash of insight is not the sense of the entirety of the piece, written out in some inner brain code by an inner 'unconscious composer'; instead, in composing as in mathematics and science, the flash of inspiration represents no more than the revelation of a new and promising direction to explore – it is the *starting point* for a long period of creation, perhaps even creative struggle. Of course, if the struggle ultimately proves successful – the symphony is written, the mathematical proof is found – it is easy to imagine that all this subsequent work was an inevitable consequence, a mere 'working out' of that initial moment of revelation. But this is just loose talk: no more true than the thought that the entire Western philosophical tradition is merely the 'working out' of the details of Plato and Aristotle; or that more than half a century of rock music is merely the inevitable consequence of the first accentuated backbeat rhythm or the inspired idea to attach an electrical 'pick-up' to amplify a guitar.

ONE TASK AT A TIME

Imagine you are driving through crowded city streets, chatting to a friend over the music from the car radio. This might seem to you a miracle of multitasking. Surely, you are aware of the road and adjusting the steering and applying the brakes when needed; you must be aware of any conversation you are actively engaged in; and you are aware of the music (otherwise, why bother to play it?). And it seems that you must simultaneously be making sense of the road, conversation and music, to juggle the three activities successfully.

Yet remember the grand illusion. You 'feel' you are aware, simultaneously, of the car in front of you, the buildings flowing past, the markings on the road, the trees and sky. But, as we saw in Part One, you very definitely are *not*. Of course, just as you can flick your eyes across the visual scene to answer any query that occurs to you, so you are able rapidly to shift your attention from the conversation to the radio, or to your surroundings, conveying the impression that each is ever present. But if a lorry pulls out in front of you unexpectedly, and you brake, honk or swerve, the flow of conversation will be abruptly halted. Shaken, both driver and passenger may, indeed, be left with no idea even of what they were talking about.

Could it be that we are not multitasking at all? Might we, instead, merely be hopping from one task to the next? Is multitasking a myth?

Hal Pashler, whose work we discussed in Chapter 3, provided a fascinating insight into the severe limits of multitasking while driving with his co-authors Jonathan Levy and Erwin Boer.[8] They asked people to engage in a simple simulated driving task – rather like driving in a video game. The participants' main objective was simply to follow the car in front along a moderately winding road, using a steering wheel and the right foot to control the accelerator and brake pedals (as in normal driving). In addition, though, they had to carry out what we'll call a 'detection' task.[9] Now and again, easy-to-spot perceptual events would occur. Participants had to detect either one or two beeps; or whether the colour of the rear window of the car in front changed once or twice (that is, they had to respond to auditory or visual stimuli). If either of these events occurred, the driver had to report whether the event occurred once or twice – and these reports could also take one of two forms: pressing a button or simply saying the words 'one' or 'two' (call these the manual or vocal responses respectively). They had, of course, to do this while continuing to 'drive' safely – following the car in front, and braking where necessary.

One might imagine that experienced drivers would be more or less unaffected by carrying out such a simple additional task – after all, intuitively we often feel that we are driving on autopilot, and when we do react, we feel that we have done so almost as a matter of reflex, and certainly without prior conscious deliberation.

It would be reassuring if this were true – but the reverse is the case. In particular, when the person has to detect and respond to a 'signal' (colour changes or beeps) at the same time as the car in front begins to slow down, braking is badly affected. Indeed, the average increase in braking time when there is a signal to respond to, compared to when there isn't, is about one sixth of a second: an amount of extra time that could, of course, be all too significant if we were braking for real (e.g. the time it takes a car travelling at 60mph to travel roughly an additional 15 feet before the brake is applied).

It seems reasonable to suspect, too, that the different variants (manual versus vocal; auditory versus visual) of the additional task would have different effects. Surely, speaking one's answer aloud should interfere less with a desperate scramble to the brake pedal than pressing a button with the hand. Perhaps a signal directed at different limbs (moving the foot versus the hand) might get confused, but surely not signals between the leg and the machinery of speech – the lips, tongue and voice box. And wouldn't one expect that reporting two beeps would interfere less with braking than reporting two flashes, on the reasonable grounds that the braking task involves visual analysis to see when the vehicle in front is slowing. In fact, all these different combinations slow down braking *to the same degree*.

Moreover, the negative effect of even a simple additional task is very difficult to eliminate. For example, in a further study, Levy and Pashler checked what would happen if people were expressly told to focus on braking as fast and as safely as possible and simply to abandon any additional task if they happened to be in the middle of it.[10] Often people did indeed abandon the additional task, but their braking was still significantly slowed.

This should make you worry about having a conversation while you are driving. Of course, driving while holding a mobile phone to your ear is a bad idea – apart from anything else, you have just one hand on the wheel. But experiments have consistently shown that 'hands-free' phone conversations turn out to be almost as dangerous – the flow of conversation and the flow of driving interfere with each other much more severely than one might expect. Although we imagine that we can 'see' everything around us when we are driving, that we could brake or swerve if we needed to, independently of our chatter, these intuitions are entirely wrong. We 'see' only a minute fraction of the road flowing past us (recall the pilots obliviously landing 'through' a plane taxiing across the runway; and the invisible lady with the umbrella) – and it requires active vigilance to direct our limited window of attention where it is most needed (to scan the next junction, to track a pedestrian who might step out into the road). And worse, our driving actions (and reactions) can get badly entangled with other actions, as Pashler and colleagues' studies show.

Conversation with a passenger, as well as by phone, has many of the same dangers. Thankfully, though, passengers and drivers tend to slow or stop their conversation when road conditions get dangerous – driving simply takes precedence over speaking. A particular danger of speaking by mobile phone is that this doesn't happen, because the person on the other end of the line has no idea what hazardous manoeuvres may be demanding the attention of the driver, and the driver feels socially obliged to maintain a flow of conversation if at all possible. So the driver is all too likely to keep focusing on the conversation, unaware that she is significantly increasing the likelihood of an accident.

ONE MEMORY AT A TIME

Could it be, though, that while we may be unable actively to pay attention to more than one thing at a time, our brains might be able unconsciously to search our mental archives, pulling out, as it were, useful files for later use? If this is right, then Poincaré's unconscious could perhaps have been running through potentially relevant bits of higher mathematics, stored over a lifetime of study. Then, when Poincaré returned to a problem, some of the vital clues to the solution might have been ready to hand – and a flash of insight would result. According to this viewpoint, the brain might not be able to solve a problem unconsciously, but unconscious activation of relevant memories might prepare the ground for finding the solution.

So, can we find evidence for unconscious memory search? With my colleagues Elizabeth Maylor and Greg Jones at the University of Warwick, I carried out an experiment some years ago that tested whether unconscious memory searches can help out the conscious mind.[11]

Rather than choose deep mathematical reasoning, we chose the simplest possible task: retrieving familiar words from memory. Suppose, for example, that I ask you to name as many foods as you can. Despite the vast range of food vocabulary at your disposal, you will almost certainly find yourself slowing down surprisingly quickly, with flurries of fruits, bursts of baked goods, and surges of seasonings, punctuated by surprising, and ever longer, silences. Suppose, instead, I ask you to name as many countries as you can. Although there are 200 or so countries recognized by the United Nations, most of which will be familiar to you, you will, again, find yourself struggling sooner than you might expect.

But what if I asked you to name as many food items *or* countries as possible? The only way to do this is to focus on foods for a while, and then move over to countries when foods are getting tricky, and then back to foods again when you are running out of countries – and so on. This is interesting in itself – perhaps indicating that our memories are organized so that foods are linked to other foods, and countries are linked to other countries. But this switching strategy is also interesting for another reason: it provides a way of finding out how far we are able to continue to search for the category we are not currently generating.

According to the cycle of thought perspective, any unconscious racing around our mental archives is entirely ruled out. That is, if we are scouring our memories for foods, we are not able to simultaneously search for countries, and vice versa. If so, we should generate foods *or* countries more rapidly than we can generate one or the other alone, although not by much.

Suppose, instead, that while focusing our conscious minds on generating foods, unconscious mental search processes can work away, in the background, unearthing a string of countries. Then, when we switch to countries, we should be able rapidly to 'download' these – they would not need to be found afresh, because the unconscious search process would have identified them already. If it is indeed possible to search for foods or countries simultaneously (even though we can consciously report the results of only one search at a time), then the rate at which we generate answers in both categories should be substantially greater than the rate at which we can generate answers from either category alone.

Across a wide range of test stimuli, the results were unequivocal: there is absolutely no sign that we can search for *x*s when we are currently thinking about *y*s; or search for *y*s, when we have been thinking about *x*s. As soon as we switch from searching one category to searching another, all search processes for that first category appear to cease abruptly. While it would be hugely advantageous for an unconscious process to keep running in the background, there is absolutely no evidence that this occurs. This is particularly striking, when we consider how useful such ability would be to us in daily life. We are continually faced with a welter of tasks that somehow we have to interleave: keeping track of the current conversation, reading the newspaper, planning what we're going to do next/tomorrow/with our entire lives, pondering tricky philosophical questions ... How useful it would be if, while focusing on one task, our unconscious mind could be making progress with other tasks by bringing to light relevant pieces of information! Sadly, though, when our conscious mind is focusing on problem A, 'research' on problems B, C, D and so on seems to come to a complete standstill.

Now and again, thoughts do 'pop into our minds' – names we had struggled to remember, things we have forgotten to do, and occasionally even insights into tricky problems with which we have been struggling. But this isn't the product of unconscious, background thought. It arises when we flip back to thinking about an old problem for a moment and, now free of the unhelpful mental loops which got us stuck in the first place, we see a solution that had evaded us before – or, in some cases, dimly suspect where such a solution might lie.

The distinction between *suspecting* a solution and *finding* a solution is a rather slippery one, and leads to considerable overestimation of the evidence for unconscious mental processes. Recall Kekulé's daydream in which a snake began to swallow its own tail. His momentary insight was surely a *suspicion* that the structure of benzene might be a ring or circle; and surely he must have followed endless false trails before alighting on the correct answer. Indeed, Kekulé only knew he *had* the correct answer after carefully piecing together the detailed structure of the benzene ring, and checking that it worked. So the 'flash of inspiration' is perhaps better termed a 'flash of suspicion'. On those rare occasions when the flash of suspicion turns out to be justified, it is so easy to have the illusion that one's brain had somehow worked out the complete answer, and checked it in detail, before 'suggesting' it to the conscious mind in the first place. And if that were true, this chain of events would, of course, require unconscious thought, and lots of it. But in reality the checking and analysis comes *after* the momentary mental flash, not before.

On reflection, this is just yet another variation on the grand illusion, and the trickery that underpins it. Just as we have the sense that the whole perceptual world is loaded into our minds, because it is available whenever we need it, so it is easy to imagine that the entire solution to a problem is loaded into our minds (in the moment of inspiration) just because we find the solution easy to grasp. If the 'flash of suspicion' turns out to be the key to solving our problem, then the checking will flow easily; each question we ask will readily have an answer and all the pieces of the intellectual puzzle will start to fall into place.

10

The Boundary of Consciousness

If we are conscious of one thing at a time, and the brain is a network of 100 billion neurons communicating by streams of electrochemical pulses, we must necessarily be unconscious of almost everything our brain does. This should not surprise us. As we have seen, we are only ever conscious of the *results* of our brain's attempts to make sense of the world – or rather, to make sense of some small part of it. Yet these results arise from a hugely complex cooperative computation, the cycle of thought, involving a substantial fraction of those 100 billion neurons and drawing on vast amounts of information from our senses and our memories.

Consciousness is, then, analogous to the 'read-out' of a pocket calculator, a search engine, or an 'intelligent' computer database. When we 'feed in' a sum (43 + 456), a search term ('Fife fishing villages'), or a query ('What is the capital of France?'), the 'read-out' gives us an answer, but it gives us absolutely no explanation or justification of where this answer came from. We have not the faintest idea of the algorithms for binary arithmetic lurking deep within the calculator, the vastness of the web that our search engine is exploring, or the clever inferences and huge 'knowledge-base' embodied in our intelligent database. When we attend to an image, word or memory, we are, in essence, asking 'What sense can I make of that?' The conscious read-out springs to mind – an interpretation of what we are seeing or thinking about. Yet behind that read-out is a welter of electrical signals sparking across rich and complex networks of neurons, responding to current sensory input and past memory traces. This is the real nature of the unconscious: the vastly complex patterns of nervous activity that create and support our slow, conscious experience.

The neural processes within each cycle of thought are, crucially, not the kind of thing that *could* be conscious. They are, after all, hugely complex patterns of cooperative neural activity, searching for possible meanings in the current sensory input by reference to our capacious memories of past experience. But we are only ever conscious of *particular interpretations* of current sensory input. We could no more be conscious of our mental processes than a pocket calculator could 'read out' the design and operation of its own computer chip. Similarly, we could no more be conscious of the flow of cooperative neural activity by which we make sense of the world than we could be conscious of the biochemistry of the liver.

We *are* conscious of, and could only ever be conscious of, the meanings, patterns and interpretations that are the *output* of this cooperative computation. Consciousness is limited to awareness of our interpretation of the sensory world; and these interpretations are the *result* of each cycle of thought, not its inner workings.

CONSCIOUSNESS IN PERCEPTION

To reinforce the conclusion that conscious experience reports the brain's *interpretation*, rather than providing direct access to the input to our senses or the processes by which the interpretation is created, consider the lovely image on the left-hand side of Figure 36, created by Japanese vision scientist Masanori Idesawa. The vividness of the smooth white billiard ball, radiating black conical spines, is quite astonishing; the white spherical surface is bright, smooth and shiny and it floats a little above the white background of the page, seemingly a slightly brighter white. Look closely at the boundary of the sphere and the white background, and you may get a sense of a discernible curved edge, marking the boundary between sphere and background. Some of the black spines loom somewhat ominously towards us; others point away from us. Yet this entire construction is pure interpretation – a product of your imagination. The figure is no more than a few flat black geometric shapes on a white background; the shapes look innocently two-dimensional when randomly rearranged, as in the right-hand panel. Yet we 'see' the spiky sphere,

Figure 36. Idesawa's spiky sphere (*left*) and the same black shapes jumbled up.[1]

not the flat patches of which it is composed. Our conscious experience is determined by what the brain thinks is present – the output of the cycle of thought, not its input.

What, then, are the underlying (and unconscious) calculations that our brain networks are carrying out in order to generate the conscious experience of a spiky white sphere? Introspection is, of course, of no avail here. But we can get some sense of the nature and complexity of the calculations by considering how we would write a computer program to mimic our brain's ability to 'create' Idesawa's 3D spiky sphere from a scatter of 2D shapes.

What principles might be required to do this? For a start, the computer program will need to calculate how 3D figures project into 2D: how, for example, a black cone, pointing towards us, may project a 'triangle', with its shortest side bulging slightly outwards. And it will need to calculate that a solid white sphere would block our view of the spines pointing away from us – so that, for example, some might project smaller, chopped-off, triangles, with the shorter side curving slightly inwards, following the line of the sphere. Our program will somehow have to capture the fact that a spike pointing towards us is shorter and stubbier than one perpendicular to our viewpoint; and to work out the 3D location and orientation of the join between the black cone and the white sphere, from observing its 2D position in our image. Moreover, the program would need to be able to piece together these different 3D locations, realizing that they are all consistent with a single curved surface – namely the surface of an (invisible) white sphere. In short, the calculations involved are nothing less than an exquisitely subtle and complex web of geometric inferences.[2]

When trying to work out the interpretation that best fits the web of inferences, the ideal approach is to consider *all* the constraints simultaneously – and continue to 'jiggle' the interpretation until it fits this full set of constraints as well as possible. To the extent that the brain focuses on just a few constraints, satisfies them as well as possible, and then looks at the remaining constraints, there is a real danger of heading up a cul-de-sac – the next constraints may not fit our tentative interpretation at all, and it will then have to be abandoned. The task of simultaneously matching a huge number of clues and constraints is just what the brain's cooperative style of computation is wonderfully good at. But these are the calculations that our imagined computer vision program would have to carry out – and which, we can conjecture, the brain must carry out in order to create Idesawa's spiky sphere.

It turns out, in fact, that the brain may be particularly well adapted to solving problems in which large numbers of constraints must be satisfied simultaneously. One influential account suggests that different aspects of the sensory input (and their possible interpretations) are associated with different brain cells, and the constraints between sensory fragments and interpretations can be captured by a network of connections between these brain cells. Subsequently the neurons cooperate to find the 'best' interpretation of the sensory data (or, at least, the brain settles on the best interpretation it can find) by exchanging electrical signals.[3] The details of the process are complex, and only partially understood. But it seems clear that the network-like structure of the brain is perfectly designed for the kinds of cooperative calculation needed to weave together the many clues provided by our senses into coherent objects.

So the calculations the brain needs to carry out are clearly going to be rather complex. It is tempting to imagine that the brain must have found some clever shortcut to avoid all these complex calculations. But the current consensus in artificial intelligence, machine vision and perceptual psychology is that no such shortcut exists. Computer vision systems, from recognizing faces, scenes or even handwriting, typically work using roughly the 'web of inference' approach I've just outlined.[4] It is even more tempting to think that no calculation of any kind is required – we just 'see' what is there.[5] This apparent immediacy of perception has even led some psychologists to suggest that perception is, in some not entirely clear sense, *direct*, rather than emerging from incredibly complex and subtle hidden inferences.

However, this idea of direct contact between our conscious experience and the 'real world' can't be right – because we see the white spiky sphere, even when there is no white spiky sphere. There are just lines and shapes: the circles and spheres are constructions – perceptual conjectures to make sense of the 2D patterns projected onto our retina.

This line of reasoning implies that, when our brain pieces together a 'puzzle' from sensory fragments (e.g. a pattern of flat black shapes), the glue which sticks the different fragments together is *inference*: in this case, geometric reasoning about how spikes and the invisible surface will interact to generate a part of our 2D sensory input. And the puzzle will be 'solved', and a coherent interpretation will arise in our conscious experience, when the network of inferences has a solution: here, the spiky sphere elegantly explains the entire layout, size and shape of the black geometric shapes.

Perception, then, is a process of incredibly rich and subtle inference – the brain is carefully piecing together the best story it can about how the world might be, to explain the agitations of its sense organs. Indeed, attempts to interpret sensory input, language or our own memories typically involve inference of great subtlety to figure out which 'story' weaves together the data most compellingly. This viewpoint has a long history: it was discussed by the brilliant German physician, physicist and philosopher Hermann von Helmholtz as far back as 1867, before psychology had even resolved itself into a distinct field of study.[6] Helmholtz realized that our experience of the world is not merely a copy of the light flowing into our eyes, or the sound waves flowing into our ears – he came to understand that perception requires puzzling out the significance of a set of clues, each of which has little significance when considered in isolation. Helmholtz was ahead of his time by an entire century – the inferential nature of vision has only come to dominate thinking in psychology, neuroscience and artificial intelligence since people have started to build computer models of vision.

Moreover, perception is not merely inference – it is, of course, *unconscious* inference. The subtle patterns of reasoning that our perceptual processes go through are invariably opaque to us, whether in 'constructing' Idesawa's 'invisible' sphere (Figure 36), suddenly 'seeing' a Dalmatian or cow (Figure 34), or 'reading' the emotional expression of Ivan Mozzhukhin, the Russian silent film star who demonstrated the Kuleshov effect (Figure 22) . We can conjecture the kind of reasoning the perceptual system might go through, but we can't report it, as it were, 'from the inside'. All we know is the interpretation that is the result of perceptual inference, not the clues and chains of reasoning that our brain has used to reach that interpretation.

Yet, with regard to conscious awareness, perception is no different from any other type of thought, whether composing a tune, diagnosing a patient, choosing a holiday, having a daydream, losing oneself in a novel, formulating a mathematical proof or solving an anagram. In each of these cases, the cycle of thought can take us forward, step by step, and create meaning, but we are conscious only of the results of each step. Or consider, when deep in a novel, how our flow of experience is taken over by the story – while we have no awareness at all of the mysterious process by which the brain transforms sequences of printed letters into images and emotions. Or, more prosaically, when struggling with the rather baffling anagram '*ncososcueisns*', I may eventually find myself wondering, perhaps after many failed attempts – could it be *consciousness*? I'm aware of the various possible words that popped into my mind; I have no awareness of the sources of these possibilities – how the different letters, and for that matter the various things I have recently been reading or thinking about, somehow trigger those words rather some others. This is because mental processes are *always* unconscious – consciousness reports answers, but not their origins.

According to the cycle of thought account, then, we are only ever conscious of the results of the brain's interpretations – not the 'raw' information it makes sense of, or the intervening inferences. So there is nothing *especially* unconscious about perception. In perception, as in any other aspect of thought, the result is conscious; the process by which the result was achieved is not.

THE STREAM OF
CONSCIOUSNESS, REVISITED

The very intuition that we experience a continuously flowing stream of consciousness must, according to the cycle of thought viewpoint, itself be an illusion. Rather, our conscious experience is a sequence of steps, of irregular length, in which the cycle of thought continually attends to, and makes sense of, fresh material.

But if so, shouldn't we have some sense of discontinuity between one thought and the next – some subtle hint of the turning of our mental engine? As so often, eye movements are a crucial clue: scanning a perceptual scene or reading a text, our eyes jump, on average, three to four times a second. During a typical eye movement, the eye will be in motion for between about 20 to 200 milliseconds, depending on the angle through which the eyes 'jump'. During this period, we are in effect almost completely blind. And each time our eyes 'land on' and stick to a new spot, the image projected onto our retina, and hence onwards to our brain, is a fresh snapshot, abruptly discontinuous with what we have seen before. So our visual input is a sequence of distinct 'snaps' of the scene or page, rather than a continuous flow – and when the eye lands on its target, a new cycle of thought begins, locking onto elements of the snapshot and making sense of it (recognizing an object, reading a facial expression, identifying a word).

It is rather astonishing that we are, from the point of view of conscious experience, entirely oblivious to the highly discontinuous process by which our eyes gather information. Look at your surroundings for a moment, and ask yourself as you explore the world around you, how often you are moving your eyes. When you flick your attention dramatically from one side of the room to the other, you can reasonably infer that your eyes must have shifted. Most of the time, though, it is incredibly difficult to tell whether one's eyes are moving at all; whether they are moving in discrete jumps or roving smoothly across the image (in case you're wondering, your eyes never rove smoothly, except when you're tracking a moving object such as a passing car; aside from these specialized 'smooth pursuit' eye movements, your eyes always move in discontinuous jumps). Indeed, it is surprisingly difficult even to tell exactly where one is looking at any given moment – such is the power of the grand illusion that the entire visual field is simultaneously present in all its richness.

In particular, notice that, when viewed from outside (with the eye-tracker), the process of picking up visual information is clearly discontinuous: we lock onto a piece of the scene and impose meaning upon it; we shift our eyes to another piece of the scene and impose meaning on that, and so on, following the cycle of thought. But from the inside, the flow of thought feels entirely seamless. So we cannot trust introspection to reveal the step-by-step, cyclical nature of thought: even in vision, where the discontinuities can be read off directly in our eye movements, we are entirely unaware of them – the cracks between one thought and the next are, as it were, smoothly papered over.

But why does thought feel smooth, if it is actually 'lumpy'? The explanation is the same as that for the grand illusion more generally. The brain's goal is to inform us about the world around us, not about the workings of its own mechanisms. Were we consciously aware of the continually flickering snapshots as our eyes jump from place to place, we would be all too aware of how our eyes are moving, but completely unable to figure out whether the world itself is like the changing set of images in a slideshow or a single unitary scene.

It is, of course, only the stable world that matters – not our wildly unstable view as our eyes dash here and there. In order to decide how to act, we need to know what the world is like; our brains don't care about the complex process of gathering and knitting together our stable world. We're like military officers reading a message in a cipher that has been broken: in order to decide our next move in battle, all we care about is what the message says; the process by which the code was broken, with whatever teams of brilliant analysts and banks of computers, is entirely invisible and irrelevant.

So, in short, our sense that seeing and hearing seem continuous arises because the brain is informing us that the visual and auditory world are continuous; and subjective experience reflects the world around us, not the operations of our own minds. And it follows, of course, that the cycle of thought will, more generally, be imperceptible – we cannot 'beat time' following the irregular pulse of the cycle of thought. Conscious awareness tells us of the state of the *world* (including, of course, our own bodies), not the process by which we perceive it: as ever, our internal narrator wants us to focus on the 'story' and to remain as unobtrusive as possible.

CONSCIOUSNESS OF THE INNER SELF?

According to the cycle of thought viewpoint, our conscious experience is of the meaningful organization of *sensory* information. If this is right, then talk of being conscious of one's *self* is incoherent nonsense – 'selves', after all, aren't part of the sensory world. And all 'higher' forms of consciousness (being conscious of being self-conscious; or being conscious of being conscious of being self-conscious), though beloved of some philosophers and psychologists, are nonsense on stilts.

We can be conscious of the sound of the words expressing such thoughts running through our mind, or conscious of the words as they appear on the screen or on the page in front of us as we type. But we are not conscious of the *thoughts* behind the words, only the words themselves. Still less are we conscious of the 'mind' behind the words. The great eighteenth-century Scottish philosopher David Hume put the point with his characteristic elegance: 'For my part, when I enter most intimately into what I call *myself*, I always stumble on some particular perception or other, of heat or cold, light or shade, love or hatred, pain or pleasure. I never can catch *myself* at any time without a perception, and never can observe any thing but the perception.'[7]

Think about your conscious awareness of the number seven – clearly something, as a mathematical abstraction, that can't be picked up by our senses. Possibly you have a shadowy mental image of the number, or of arrangements of patterns of seven dots, or perhaps you hear yourself 'saying' the word *seven*. Various properties of the number may come to mind. You may say to yourself 'it's my lucky number'; 'it's an odd number', 'it's a prime', and so on. But here what we are conscious of is not the number itself, but sensory impressions pertaining indirectly to the number, such as sensory impressions of the sound of things we might *say* about the number. The more we reflect, the more the very idea of being conscious of the number itself seems increasingly peculiar. We know lots of facts about seven, of course; surely what we are conscious of are not the facts themselves, but sensory impressions – most notably of rather abbreviated snippets of English, running through our minds. The consciousness of 'seven' is really rather fake and second-hand. But none the less, we know lots about 'seven': we can count to seven, decide whether there are more or less than seven people in a room, run through our seven-times table, and so on.

The same is true, I suggest, of supposed higher-order consciousness. I can hear myself 'saying' internally: 'I'm know I'm conscious.' And for that matter, 'I must be conscious of being conscious', and I may perhaps have a vague visual image floating through my mind. But it is these sensory impressions, and their meaningful organization into images and snippets of language that I am conscious of – and no more.

We can conclude that consciousness is not at all directly connected to belief, knowledge or similar notions. I know that Paris is the capital of France, but I'm not conscious of this fact or any other fact – except in the ersatz sense that I may be conscious of intoning the words 'Paris is the capital of France' in my imagination. But then I'm conscious of the words not the fact – my conscious experience will be different if I formulate the same fact in a different language. Or consider what, if anything, it means to be conscious of the fact that Inspector Lestrade was jealous of Sherlock Holmes – I can be conscious of my inner speech, articulating these words; but I can't possibly be, in any sense whatever, conscious of the actual people, let alone one's putative jealousy of the other, because they are not actual people at all, but fictional characters. Similarly, my conscious experience of perceiving a really convincing hologram of an apple might be exactly the same as my conscious experience when confronting a real apple. The sensory input, and my brain's organization of that sensory input to interpret it as an apple, is identical in both cases. But there is nothing in my conscious experience that signals my real contact with the actual apple, rather than the entirely non-existent, holographic image of an apple. Consciousness is, in this sense, necessarily superficial: it is defined by the interpretations through which we organize sensory experience.

So, except in a rather uninteresting sense, we aren't really conscious of numbers, apples, people, or anything else – we're conscious of our interpretations of sensory experience (including inner speech) and nothing more.[8]

In this light, the tower of levels of consciousness, each built on the last, collapses. It is one more trick played on us by the brain. So we have another sense in which the mind is 'flatter' than one might expect: that our conscious experience consists of organizations of the surface of our sensory experience, whether conjured up through perception, imagination or memory. We have no subjective experience of 'deep' concepts of mathematics, the inner workings of our minds, or, indeed, consciousness itself. We can talk and write about these things; we can express them in symbols and sketches. But we are conscious only of the perceptual properties of these words, symbols and pictures, not of the supposedly shadowy abstract realms themselves. In short, we consciously experience the sensory information, broadly construed (including images generated by our own minds; sensations from inside our bodies, such as pain, feelings of exhaustion or hunger; and crucially from inner speech). But there is nothing more.

RETHINKING THE BOUNDARY OF CONSCIOUSNESS

It is tempting to imagine that thoughts can be divided in two as the waterline splits an iceberg: the visible conscious tip and the submerged bulk of the unconscious, vast, hidden and dangerous. Freud and later psychoanalysts saw the unconscious as the hidden force behind the frail and self-deluded conscious mind. Psychologists, psychotherapists and psychiatrists have often suspected there may be two (or more) different types of mental system fighting for control of our behaviour: one or perhaps many unconscious mental systems that are fast, reflexive and automatic; and a deliberative system that is conscious, reflective and slow.[9] Neuroscientists have suggested there may be multiple decision-making systems in the brain, at most one of which operates consciously, and which can generate conflicting recommendations concerning how we should think and act.[10]

But the vision of the iceberg, with its vast dark mass hidden below the water, hides an important but entirely flawed assumption. In an iceberg, the material that is above and below the waterline is precisely the same – ice is ice, whether deep beneath the waves or sparkling in the sunlight. And, for this reason, it seems only natural that what is hidden can be made visible and what is visible can be made hidden – it is still the same ice whether we lift it from the waters or plunge it into the depths. The metaphor suggests that the very same thought could be either conscious or unconscious – and could jump between the two states. Accordingly, a thought that was previously unconscious might be brought into the light of consciousness (whether through casual introspection, intense soul-searching or years of psychoanalysis). And a thought that was once conscious could sink into our unconscious (through sheer forgetfulness, or perhaps some mysterious psychic process of active repression). To continue the iceberg metaphor, the same story applies not just to individual thoughts but to our thought processes as a whole. Our conscious trains of thought are presumed to be paralleled by shadowy unconscious musings, torments and symbolic interpretations. This unconscious mental activity is supposed to be the same 'stuff' as conscious thought – the only difference being that it is submerged below the level of conscious awareness.

From the point of view of the cycle of thought, the iceberg metaphor could scarcely be more misleading. Remember that we have already concluded that we are *always* conscious of the results of our interpretation of sensory information, and we are *never* conscious of the process by which these interpretations are created. The division between the conscious and the unconscious does not distinguish between different types of thought. Instead, it is a division within individual thoughts themselves: between the conscious result of our thinking and the unconscious processes that create it.

There are no conscious thoughts and unconscious thoughts; and there are certainly no thoughts slipping in and out of consciousness. There is just one type of thought, and each such thought has two aspects: a conscious read-out, and unconscious processes generating the read-out. And we can have no more conscious access to these brain processes than we can have conscious awareness of the chemistry of digestion or the biophysics of our muscles.

THE UNCONSCIOUS MIND THAT ISN'T

Unconscious thought is a seductive and powerful myth. But the very possibility of unconscious thought clashes with the basic operating principles of the brain: the cooperative computation across billions of neurons, harnessed only to the challenge of the moment.

Prior to Freud, such a conclusion would have seemed natural enough – and the very idea of unconscious thought would have seemed rather paradoxical, because the very idea of thought was tied up with conscious experience. Since Freud, though, we have become so familiar with the idea of the 'Unconscious' that we feel an undue attachment to it – any and every unexpected, paradoxical, insightful or self-defeating aspect of thought and behaviour can be attributed to mysterious subterranean forces intruding upon our frail and perhaps slightly foolish conscious selves. If the present argument is correct, there can't be another mind, system or mode of thought operating under the radar of conscious mental processing – the brain (or, at least, a given network of neurons) can only do one thing at a time.

As we've seen, the operation of this cycle of thought is by no means transparent to us: we are only ever conscious of its outputs – the meaningful organizations of sensory information. The flow of conscious experience is a sequence of 'meanings', but the processes generating those meanings (and the sensory data and the memories upon which they work) are never directly available to us. And this is not, perhaps, surprising: we can't introspect how our lungs or stomachs work – why should it be any different for the brain? So rather than imagining that there may be two systems of thought vying for control of our thoughts and actions, we see that there is just *one system*, striving cycle by cycle to impose meaning on sensory input. The meaningful interpretations are conscious – yielding a world of patterns, objects, colours, voices, words, letters, faces and more; the brain processes through which these interpretations are achieved are no more conscious than any other physiological process.[11] Novelists exploit the chatter and imagery running through our heads – but notice that the stream of consciousness of Virginia Woolf's *To the Lighthouse* or James Joyce's *Ulysses* is hardly an exploration of the innermost workings of the mind. Quite the reverse: the technique displays, at best, a sequence of partial results, workings, intermediate steps – the outputs of successful cycles of thought. These partial steps may sometimes offer useful clues – indeed, the Nobel Prize-winning psychologist, computer scientist, economist and social scientist Herbert Simon (1916–2001) put great stress on the value of analysing 'think aloud' data, obtained while people were reasoning or solving problems.[12] But they are no more than clues: the process by which the cycle of thought generates ideas, crossword solutions and chess moves – and hence the question of why some ideas 'pop' into our minds and others don't – remains entirely outside the realm of consciousness. After all, we only see the results of our perceptual experience – that is, we see objects, colours and movement, but we have no insight whatever into the calculations the brain went through to present the world to us in this particular way.

It seems, then, that we can at least say something about what flits across our own 'stream of consciousness', moment by moment – we engage in introspection to a limited degree, not about the operation of the cycle of thought, but about its successive outputs. Yet reporting even these conscious states can be a hazardous business. The philosopher John Stuart Mill (1806–73) famously remarked: 'Ask yourself whether you are happy, and you cease to be so.'[13] And there is a parallel danger for introspection: 'Ask yourself what you are thinking, and you cease to think it.'

FROM SPIKY SPHERES TO THE MEANING OF LIFE

Our brain is perpetually struggling to organize and make sense of the sensory information to which we are currently attending. We find meaning in Idesawa's wonderful demonstration (Figure 36) by creating a 'spiky sphere' to explain the arrangement of black and white patterns. And that very same drive to find meaning applies, of course, when we are trying to make sense of snippets of conversation, paragraphs of text, or entire plays and novels. Of course, our attempt to make sense of a movie or symphony will proceed in many sequential steps, following the flow of dramatic or musical events as they occur, but also stepping back to ponder their interrelationships and significance.

It is interesting to ponder what is happening when we are in this type of reflective mode, exploring and critically analysing. Looking back on a film, for example, we try to make sense of the plot, and point out real or apparent flaws ('if she had the key then, why did she need to break in the first time?'); we try to get a grip on the thoughts and motivations of the characters ('Romeo and Juliet can't have had more than a romantic infatuation – they hardly knew each other!'); we may connect the setting and action of the film with other films or books (e.g. 'that scene was straight out of *Casablanca*') or real life ('that's a total violation of police procedure!' or 'a wonderful evocation of 1950s Spain').

We can draw back further, arguing about whether a particular analysis or critique itself makes sense ('that's totally unrealistic', 'it's supposed to be a whodunnit, not a police training film'); and the chatter of analysis and re-analysis, evaluation and re-evaluation, can continue indefinitely. After all, the *Mahabharata*, and the works Homer, Dante and Shakespeare are probably subject to as much critical analysis today as at any time in history. And, in the broadest sense, such discussion concerns what works of literature and art *mean*: their internal structure, their relation to other pieces of literature and art, to history and society, and to us, living in the twenty-first-century.

I suspect that the way we project meaning onto works of literature and art has a lot in common with how we understand events, stories and relationships in our daily lives. As our lives unfold, we continually attempt to make sense of what is happening to us: why we, and the people around us, act as we do; we compare our lives with other lives and, indeed, with lives in art, literature and the movies. And, from time to time, we step back and try to make sense of how the different pieces of our lives fit together (or don't); and we do the same for other people's lives, our relationships, the groups we are part of, the projects we are engaged in, and so on. We can debate endlessly and reconsider not just our own lives, but our analysis and evaluations of our lives.

As with art and literature, such evaluations are about *meaning*: how best to make sense of our lives, and how to make our lives more meaningful in the future. Meaning, in this broad sense, is about fitting together, finding patterns, seeking coherence. We do not merely live our lives, but frequently step back to comment on what happens and why; and we also wonder about the validity of our commentary, and so on, without any definite limit. But at each of these moments, the cycle of thought has a single task: to lock onto sensory (including, crucially, linguistic) information and organize and interpret that information as far as possible.

Each process of interpretation is local and piecemeal – we can't 'zoom out' to consider the meaning of an entire literary work, a whole symphony or an entire relationship. Imagining that we can, of course, would be to fall for yet another variation of the grand illusion: thinking that we can load up, simultaneously, a complex whole in its entirety, when in reality our minds dash from one fragment of experience, commentary or argument to the next. We can, of course, debate art, literature and life endlessly – and each turn of the cycle of thought attempts to impose meaning on those fragments that have gone before.

Our ability to create 'meaning' from nothing is beautifully exemplified in games and sports. How could kicking a ball towards one rectangular frame and away from another possibly be a 'meaningful' activity? Or knocking a small white ball into a hole in the ground, with as few blows as possible from specially designed sticks? Or propelling a bouncy greenish yellow ball backwards and forwards over a horizontal net, using a stringed bat? Yet football, golf, tennis and many more games and sports are, perhaps, among the most meaningful ways in which millions of people choose to spend their time – the actions, tasks, challenges involved achieve no higher purpose, but fit together delightfully (everything just 'works') when things are going well (each shot sets up the next shot), and horribly badly (each action foils the next action) when we are playing poorly.

It is tempting to think, though, that meaning-as-coherence is not enough: that our lives should be guided by some ultimate purpose – something beyond our everyday understanding, or perhaps deep inside our innermost core. Or we may conclude that no such transcendental meaning exists and that human life is no more than a brief, purposeless biochemical agitation at one edge of a vast and lifeless cosmos. I think that this temptation, and its tendency to lead both to hope and to despair, is based on a misunderstanding.

The search for meaning is the object of each cycle of thought; and meaning is about organizing, arranging, creating patterns in and making sense of thoughts, actions, stories, works of art, games and sports. In short, finding meaning is about finding coherence. And coherence is created step by step, one thought at a time; it is never complete, but is continually open to challenge and debate. And this is how it should be: surely no novel, poem or painting, however profound, can be as rich, complex, challenging and as endlessly open to re-evaluation and reinterpretation as an individual human life.

11

Precedents not Principles

THE STRANGE CASE OF CHESS

In 1922, the reigning world chess champion, the Cuban José Raúl Capablanca, simultaneously took on 103 opponents in Cleveland, Ohio. After seven hours, he had won 102 games and drawn one. But with so little time to calculate, how could this be possible?

It is all too natural to imagine that Capablanca must have been playing lightning chess with a lightning brain; that he must have been able to race through the forking paths of move and counter-move faster than his bemused opponents. If this was indeed his secret, then it would imply that Capablanca could calculate a hundred times faster than his hundred opponents, just to get a hundred draws (after all, Capablanca has just one hundredth of the time each of them has to think through the next move). Not only that, Capablanca – unlike his opponents – would have to spend a great deal of time moving from board to board (whereas his opponents would be able to focus relentlessly on a single game). Over the entire seven-hour period, he made, on average, about ten moves per minute: this pace is consistent with sidling up to a board, taking a quick look, making a move, and then shifting onto the next game And, of course, if Capablanca's forte was lightning calculation, then he would need not just to match the calculation of his opponents, but to exceed it very considerably – after all, his opposition was comprehensively flattened. So, in short, one might suspect that, if Capablanca's magic trick was lightning-fast calculation, then he must have been able to calculate several hundred times faster than anyone else – a sort of human supercomputer.

Now this story would, indeed, be a pretty good model for

computer chess. Of course, the chess-playing ability of a computer program depends a great deal on how cleverly the program is designed. But a decisive factor in the dramatic rise in the quality of computer chess over the past few decades has been the equally dramatic increase in the raw speed of computer processing. Contemporary computer chess programs really do calculate at lightning speed – evaluating many millions of possible board positions per second. So a super-fast computer chess program could, indeed, simultaneously crush one hundred more sluggish chess programs, if it could calculate, say, 500 or 1,000 times faster. The super-fast computer would simply be able to look further into the forking tree of possible moves and counter-moves that its ponderous opponents could make.

Yet Capablanca did not have the brain of a lightning calculating machine – and he did not need it. A glance at the board would instead call up past games, and past good (and bad) moves – one clue is that experimental tests show that chess grandmasters have a phenomenal ability to remember chess positions from real chess games of the past. After five seconds, a top chess player is able to 'read' the structure of a chess position – searching out which pieces are threatening which others, noting familiar patterns of pieces (e.g. a castled king and rook behind a row of pawns; advanced central pawns defended by knights, and so on), finding, in short, what the position *means*. And this is usually enough, not just to decide on a high-quality next move, but to commit the position, aside from a few incidental details, completely to memory – indeed, a grandmaster may be able to recall that very position many minutes or even hours later. To the inexpert chess player, this astonishing feat suggests that grandmasters supplement fantastic calculating ability with stupendous powers of memory. But the feat is no more remarkable than our ability to commit to memory an enormously long string of letters, simply because they are arranged meaningfully, as in this sentence. Someone unfamiliar with the English language, or even the Roman alphabet, would find this ability equally astounding – precisely because they could impose no meaning upon it (consider your own ability to remember strings of characters in a distant language in an unfamiliar script). Or consider a skilled musician's ability to reproduce a lengthy stream of musical notation, because it can be turned into a meaningful tune (while, to the rest of us, the pattern of notes on a stave is mere gobbledygook). In each case, memory is the by-product of understanding: what we cannot interpret, we cannot remember.

It seems, then, that grandmasters are special not because of their unusual mental powers, but because, through long experience, they have learned to find meaning in chess positions with particular fluency; and they can do this because they can link the current board position with their memory traces of past board positions, acquired through thousands of hours of chess-playing.

Two further observations reinforce this picture. The first concerns the nature of the memory mistakes that grandmasters make. They recall, more or less unfailingly, the pieces that matter to the progress of the game, but where some peripheral piece plays no active role its precise location need not be encoded exactly. By contrast, non-chess players make mistakes of all and every kind – to them, of course, the board is a mere jumble of pieces, not a subtly interlocking set of threats, counter-threats and defences.

The second observation is that grandmasters are no better than the rest of us at remembering random board positions – their superior memory skills evaporate as soon as they are faced with arbitrary chess positions, because they can impose no meaningful interpretation on these positions in relation to their huge repertoire of past chess experience.[1] In the same way, readers of English will struggle to learn random sequences of letters, just as expert musicians will have no special ability to recall arbitrary forests of musical notation.

The ability to make sense of current chess positions, by linking them with the vast library of past positions, greatly simplifies the problem of choosing the right move (just as familiarity with English makes continuing an English sentence relatively straightforward, and musical expertise makes it possible to write out a plausible next bar or two of a simple tune). In chess, of course, the number of possible continuations explodes as we attempt to see further ahead in the game – but almost all of these moves are wildly implausible and can safely be ignored.

Grandmasters do not reach such impressive levels of performance by out-calculating their bemused opponents and seeing many more moves ahead. Instead, they look only a little further ahead than amateur chess-players, but their memory bank of past experience and, in particular, their library of meaningful analyses of chess positions, allows them to focus on only the best moves, and to ignore the rest.

Notice, too, that Capablanca had no 'theory' of chess, beyond his vast fund of experience. He wrote a number of celebrated chess books, one promisingly entitled *Chess Fundamentals*, with lists of 'principles' to guide the aspiring player.[2] Yet these principles are, in reality, a series of helpful examples illustrating useful rules of thumb – there is no chess equivalent of Newton's Laws! Tellingly, Capablanca is attempting to distil some of his knowledge not into *principles*, but into particularly helpful *illustrations*.

To learn to play chess is to learn to impose meaning on each board; and each board makes more sense in the light of the meaning imposed on previous boards. Perhaps expertise in any domain, however remarkable, is not based on superior mental calculating power, but on richer and deeper experience: Capablanca could play new chess position because he had a vast library of *precedents* from imposing meaning on prior chess positions – and could use those precedents more creatively and effectively than anyone else. And perhaps that is how skills, learning, memory and knowledge always work. We layer each momentary thought on top of past momentary thoughts, tracing an ever-richer web of connections across our mental surface.

PERCEPTION–MEMORY RESONANCE

The interpretation of each new chess position depends on a vast battery of interpretations of prior chess positions; and, in the same way, the interpretation of each everyday scene depends on a vast hoard of past interpretations of everyday scenes. Indeed, perception works by relating, often in the most flexible and creative fashion, our sensory input with our memory of past experience. We do not interpret every sensory impression afresh, but in terms of the memory traces of past sensory impressions. Consider the rather delightful 'found faces' in Figure 37. In terms of superficial shapes and colours, these items – variously a leather bag, cheese-grater, a block of wood and the detail

Figure 37. Found faces.[3]

of a wash basin – are about as distant as possible from human form. Yet we see them, more or less immediately, not merely as faces, but as faces with personalities, expressions and even a measure of pathos that seems particularly incongruous given that each of these objects is patently inanimate.

The cycle of thought should, then, create an organization of the sensory input that depends not just on the input itself, but on 'resonance' with memory traces of past inputs (Figure 38) – for example, previous faces that we have encountered. The brain interprets one word, face or pattern at a time, but in doing so it simultaneously explores possible links between the current stimulus and a vast array of memories of interpretations of past stimuli. 'Resonances' between current and past stimuli are not defined by superficial similarity – otherwise the brain could only interpret a cheese-grater in terms of past silver metallic box-like objects, and never as a face. Yet the brain rapidly sees the 'eyes and mouth' pattern in this otherwise incredibly un-face-like object. The 'found faces' of Figure 37 are illustrations of just how flexibly the brain can map past memory traces (of human faces) to impose meaning on the current input.

The resonance between perception and memory must occur 'in parallel', however. Given our sluggish neurons, matching the current perceptual input with each of our vast repertoire of memory traces one at a time would be unfeasibly slow. And, when interpreting a new stimulus, the brain may have little idea which memories it needs to search – indeed, it seems able to draw on its entire stock of memory traces equally easily. Before the interpretation has been made, the brain can't know which memories will be relevant – so it has to search them all.[4]

Notice that, from this viewpoint, each new perceptual interpretation is based on memories of past interpretations. We *never* see the world 'with fresh eyes'. Each new interpretation is an amalgam and transformation of past interpretations. Consider what happens when you read a word, or 'read' a face, or a chessboard – those perceptual interpretations depend on years of past experience of our language and writing system, of our long history of interactions with other people, and the nature of past experience (if any) with the game of chess. As usual, of course, we have awareness only of the *output* of thought – the result of our current interpretation; all other mental processes leading to that output are never conscious. Thus we have no awareness of the memories activated, or how they were transformed and combined to interpret the current stimulus. Listening to our own native language, we 'hear' the speech sounds, words and pauses as if they are plainly observable aspects of the speech signal. But listening to an entirely unfamiliar language, we are confronted with a baffling, uncategorized and apparently chaotic flow of sound. The difference is that, for our own language, we can map new streams of sounds to a vast range of previously interpreted speech sounds, words, phrases and more. We can interpret new speech input in terms of a vast repertoire of memory traces from our past interpretations of past speech input. As with learning any other skill, we break down the code of our language piece by piece, over many months and years; and, as with any other skill, we are aware only of the results of our current competence, oblivious to the myriad of memory traces on which that competence depends.[5]

What are memory traces like? What information do they contain? The most natural answer is that they are nothing more than the remnants of past interpretations of past perceptual inputs. As far as we know, these remnants are not later reorganized, filtered, corrected or generally tidied up; and there is no internal librarian to carefully file and index each memory trace into a coherent archive. The remnants of each individual episode of perceptual processing lie, as it were, where they fall; the brain is immediately busy with the next cycle of thought, and the next.

The brain is therefore not a theorist trying to distil deep abstract principles from experience – it is, instead, focused on coping with the present, as far as possible, *by relating the present to amalgams and transformations of the past*. According to this viewpoint, then, memory traces are fragments of past processing – so that it is past *interpretations* that are stored in memory, rather than raw, disorganized sensory input. So, for example, if we see a cheese-grater as a face in one situation, then that interpretation will be stored in memory. When we next encounter a similar cheese-grater, we are more likely to see that grater, too, as a smiley face – we remember the interpretation.

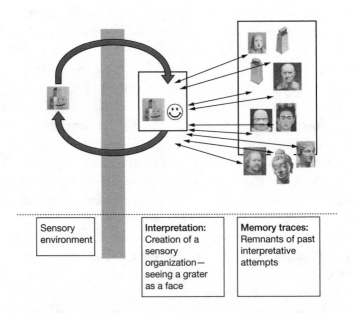

| Sensory environment | Interpretation: Creation of a sensory organization— seeing a grater as a face | Memory traces: Remnants of past interpretative attempts |

Figure 38. Perception–memory resonance. *Left*: Our senses provide us with highly ambiguous information (here, the face-like image of a cheese-grater in Figure 37). *Middle*: we interpret the cheese-grater as a rather foolish grinning face (this interpretation is depicted by the addition of a smiley face). *Right*: but, of course, the interpretation of the image as a cheese-grater, or as a face, depends on transformations of previous experiences of cheese-graters and faces (a selection of images of past cheese-graters and faces are shown) – interpretation involves the transformation of past memory traces.

Conversely, uninterpreted aspects of the sensory world will be forgotten: a piece of handwriting that is too difficult for us to read, a fragment of a language we don't understand, or the outlines of a distant figure in the trees that we fail to notice, will not, by this account, be filed away in our memory to be subject to future analysis, or to shape later perceptions. They will be lost for ever. (In passing, note that this is reassuring news for those worried about subliminal messages that might be planted by advertisers or nefarious forces wishing to control our minds by stealth.)

Perception and memory are therefore intricately entwined. Recognizing a friend, a word or a tune requires not merely linking together different aspects of the perceptual input, but connecting these fragments to stored memories of faces, words and melodies. So, for example, a recognized face typically does not merely feel vaguely familiar: we can also access information about the corresponding person. The string of letters making up a word is typically also linked to its meaning, its sound, and much more; and recognizing a tune may conjure up the associated lyrics, singer, era in which we first heard it, and more. So the interpretation of the information flowing through our senses depends on a huge body of remembered information, but this information is, of course, nothing more than the memory of past interpretations of previous sensory information. Today's memories are yesterday's perceptual interpretations.

Successful perception, then, requires almost instant conjuring up, and deploying, of the 'right' memory traces to make sense of the current sensory input, just when we need them. This is remarkable in the light of the sheer number of such traces, accumulated over a lifetime. It is more remarkable still, given that the right memories can be very indirectly related to the perceptual fragments: that images ostensibly of handbags, cheese-graters, blocks of wood or hand basins can trigger memories of faces (see Figure 37); that a few scratches of ink on a sheet of paper can conjure the human figure in a landscape (Figure 39b); that the rearrangement of the same few geometric shapes can remind us of a rocket, a kneeling person, a rabbit and many other images (Figure 39a). And the same spectacular flexibility of thought arises of course throughout the metaphors that pervade our language and our thoughts – memories of one thing are fluidly and

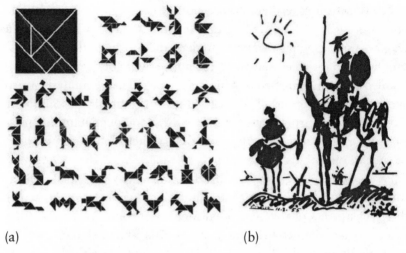

(a)   (b)

Figure 39. The interaction of memory and perception. (a) Tangrams are seven simple geometric shapes made from dissecting a square (*top left*), but can be made to resemble an almost infinite variety of people, animals and objects.[6] (b) Picasso's famous sketch of Don Quixote, Sancho Panza and a background of distant windmills is remarkably underspecified, yet sufficient to conjure up these literary characters, the burning sun and the bare Spanish landscape.

naturally linked to our memories of another thing. So, for example, we can 'see' our boss variously as a conductor, a general, a robot or a shark.

A helpful way to view how perceptual or memory information is analysed is to regard the given information (the clues from memory and perception) as providing parts of a pattern, with the brain's task being to 'fill in' the gaps in the pattern. But this image underplays the spectacular flexibility of the brain in transferring knowledge from one domain to some apparently entirely unrelated topic. So, for example, taking some fragments of visual information about a hand-bag, the brain may indeed fill in various other details (inferring, perhaps, that the sealed container – the handbag – has an opening only at the top, or that it comes from a specific period or country, or that it has a certain monetary value), but equally the brain may well interpret it as an alarming, if slightly comical, snarl. The brain operates by the routine exercise of an astonishingly exuberant imagination.

Very much the same story applies when we consider consulting not the contents of the visual world (handbags, cheese-graters, actual human faces), but our own memories. We can have the feeling of immediate and simultaneous access to a vast repository of general knowledge, autobiography, likes and dislikes, moral and religious convictions, and more. But in truth we impose meaning on one set of memory traces at a time. And when we do lock onto those memory traces, we impose meaning on them with the same flexibility and urgency that applies in perception. The memories themselves are not thoughts: they are not, for example, beliefs, choices or preferences. And we cannot merely 'read off' their contents to know what we think, what we like, or what sort of person we are. Instead, they consist of mere fragments of past thoughts, to be reused, reconstituted and transformed by the cycle of thought.

PEOPLE AS TRADITIONS

What makes me, me? What makes you, you? Tempted, as ever, to peer into the darkness of our mental depths, we search for the attributes of character: bravery, stoicism, anxiousness, kindness or cruelty. What are we really like, deep down? It seems hard to be sure of our own nature – each of us is, of course, a mixture of momentary thoughts and feelings, at one moment brave, at another timorous; sometimes stoical, at other times anxious. But it is a seductive idea that our confusions and contradictions are merely the stuff of our turbulent surface, the vagaries of the moment pushing us here and there. Deep down, perhaps too deep for us to fathom, lies our inner self, replete with the virtues and vices of our true character. But mental depth is, we have seen, an illusion; there is no inner core, virtuous or venal.

Yet if the mind is an engine of precedent, continually reshaping past thoughts and actions to deal with the present, then each of us is not just a bundle of character traits, but a rich store of distinctive past experience: we are like corals layered, polyp by polyp, into infinitely diverse forms. What makes each of us unique is our individual and particular history – our own specific trail of precedents in thought and action. We are each unique, in short, because of the endless variety of our layered history of thoughts and actions.

This viewpoint might seem to imply that we are nothing more than 'creatures of habit'. Not at all. As we shall see in the next and final chapter, it is our remarkable ability to make imaginative leaps, both large and small, that breaks us free of blind repetition. We can project our experience of everyday human faces onto the 'found faces' in handbags and sinks (remember Figure 37). The subtle and measured application of past precedents, not merely the sheer number of chess-playing hours, surely distinguishes the brilliance of great champions like José Raúl Capablanca, Bobby Fischer or Magnus Carlsen from the everyday run of Masters and Grandmasters. Or consider our ability to improvise dance, create songs, paint and draw, spin stories, or invent imaginary worlds – not from scratch, but rather through the reinterpretation and reconfiguration of the elements of the world we know.

Each of us is a tradition, guided and shaped by our past. Like traditions in music, art, literature, language or the law, we are capable of refinement, adjustment, reinterpretation and whole-sale reinvention. Our mental present is built out of our mental past, but our imagination need not be trapped in cells we constructed long ago; we continually build and rebuild ourselves. Re-routing our minds is always slow and difficult. But where we can purposefully shift our present, there is hope of reshaping our future.

PRECEDENTS NOT PRINCIPLES

Each turn of the cycle of thought leaves a trace, and that trace may shape future turns in the cycle. Thoughts are like water droplets finding their way from high ground to the sea, following the channels in the landscape, whether gullies, streams or river valleys. And, in its passing, each droplet cut those channels just a little more deeply. The landscape, then, is partly a history of past water flow, as well as a guide for how water will flow in the future. In the same way, our mental life follows channels carved by our previous thoughts, and traces of our present thoughts and actions will shape how we think and act in the future.

Droplets of water make their way downhill by the steepest available path, each heedless of the incalculable number of droplets that have created the landscape through which it runs, and heedless, too, of how its own imperceptible corrosive force may alter, ever so slightly, the path of the next droplet, and the next. Similarly, each cycle of thought lays down memory traces that may smooth, or obstruct, future cycles. Each momentary interpretation draws on and adapts our previous attempts to understand the world. So each cycle of thought maybe viewed as creating, over time, mental channels along which our thoughts most easily flow; and, indeed, each cycle of thought attempts, as far as possible, to make our interpretation of current sensory information cohere with our interpretations of prior sensory information.

Over a lifetime, the flow of thought shapes, and is shaped into, complex patterns: our habits of mind, our mental repertoire. These past patterns of thought, and their traces in memory, underpin our remarkable mental abilities, shape how we behave and make each of us unique. So, in a sense, we do, after all, possess some inner mental landscape. But this is not an inner copy of the outer world or, for that matter, a library of beliefs, motives, hopes or fears; it is, instead, a record of the impact of past cycles of thought – rather than, as it were, any mysterious subterranean geological forces.

The brain operates by precedents not principles. Each new cycle of thought makes sense of the information to which we are currently attending, by reworking and transforming remnants of past related thoughts. And the result of each cycle of thought becomes, itself, raw material for future thoughts.

So the failure of early artificial intelligence to discover the principles that underlie our knowledge of the physical and social worlds; the failure of linguistics to uncover the grammatical principles that generate language; and the failure of philosophy to articulate the principles underlying the true significance of truth, goodness and the nature of mind – all have a common source. The system of precedents underpinning human intelligence can be contradictory, highly flexible and open-ended – especially in relation to cases for which no nearby precedent has yet been set. But this very open-endedness is precisely what is required when dealing with a world that is still far too complex for us fully to understand.[7]

12

The Secret of Intelligence

In the 1950s, Canadian psychologist Craig Mooney created a remarkable array of black and white images (Figure 40). The faces were created for a rather narrow purpose, as a test of the development of face perception in childhood.[1] Yet thinking about these faces, and how our brain understands them, provides an opportunity to encapsulate some of the key themes we have explored in this book – and provides a starting point for investigating the 'secret' of intelligence.

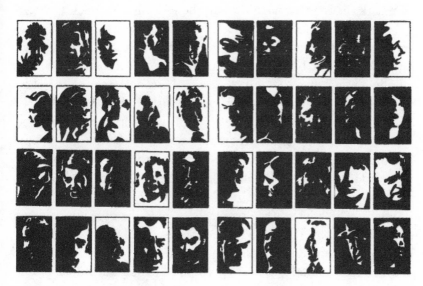

Figure 40. Craig Mooney's black and white faces. Many of these images are, on first inspection, pretty baffling. But look more closely, and we see not just faces, but glimpses of full, rounded, psychologically rich, individual people.[2]

Initially, the display is rather mystifying, but spend a minute or two looking at these strange black and white patterns and the experience becomes more interesting. Somewhat miraculously, the initially inchoate patterns start to make sense. To my eye at least, each face creates a vivid sense of a particular person caught in a particular mood, with a specific expression, gender, age, personality, and perhaps even a historical period. Some of these simple arrangements of black and white patches seem to have as much life, pathos and a sense of human drama as the most detailed photographic image. They are also rather beautiful.

Some faces jump out at us almost right away; others remain enigmatic until, mysteriously, the baffling bumps, curves and blobs resolve into a portrait of a human being. You may not be able to see all the patterns as faces – indeed, there are still a few of these images that I can't make sense of, having looked at them countless times over the years. But if you see even a few, you are still far ahead of any computer vision technology yet invented.

On reflection, finding faces in these incredibly simplified and stylized patterns is an astonishing feat: these strange 'woodcut' patterns are so utterly unlike the colourful, three-dimensional, moving people we see around us. Where are the eyes, nose and mouth that we might be expecting our brain to pick up on? These features appear to be wholly absent, at least until we crack the code revealing the entire face. The components of the image are just jumbled bumps, curves and blobs, until, of course, the delightful moment that a human face breaks through to us from the darkness. Once the 'insight' occurs, our interpretation of that image is permanently or near-permanently recorded in memory – a jumble has become a face, and will now be a face for ever.[3]

To make life more difficult still, try turning the page upside down. A few of the faces you initially identified will still make sense. Many, though, will return to seeming no more than abstract patterns. Give yourself time, though; look back at the face the right way up. Gradually, more and more images will snap into coherence.

There are several interesting conclusions to draw from looking at Mooney's faces, both the right way up and upside down. Seeing the images upside down gives us a sense of how truly chaotic they are – that there are, indeed, no eyes, noses, mouths or ears that can be identified in isolation. When the faces are the right way up, some of these features can, sometimes sharply and sometimes only dimly, be discerned – we see the parts only when we are able to grasp the whole. The holistic way we perceive Mooney faces (i.e. the interdependence of perceiving a whole pattern and its component parts) reflects the general operation of the brain. Reading scrawled handwriting, we recognize the letters in tandem with understanding the whole word. We recognize speech sounds, word-breaks and so on at the same time as we decode the message that a person is attempting to convey (and recall that speech in an unfamiliar language is little more than a blur of sound). And we interpret a small wooden object being slid from a white square to an adjacent black square as advancing a pawn, threatening the opponent's knight, or leading to checkmate in three moves, by interpreting a physical aspect of the world in terms of the rules of chess. Further, as we saw in Chapter 5, Lev Kuleshov demonstrated how the same facial expression can be interpreted as subtly conveying sorrow, hunger or lust; and Schachter and Singer showed that the way we interpret our own bodily states (rushes of adrenaline, racing heart) as anger or elation depends on our interpretation of the social interaction we are engaged in (e.g. whether the person we are interacting with is being annoying or amusing).

Note, too, that our sense of the entire face is remarkably rich, even if those individual features are difficult to discern; I suspect you feel, as I do, that you might be able to pick out some of these people if they appeared in a police line-up. The leap from a stark, black-and-white image to a three-dimensional real person is, of course, vast – the fact that we can make such remarkable perceptual leaps is a reminder of the astonishing flexibility and, one might even say, creativity of the perceptual system.

The human brain is wonderfully attuned to faces – so that we can detect and reconstruct them on the flimsiest of evidence, as the Mooney faces attest. And, indeed, we can see faces when the evidence is flimsier still. Recall the 'found faces' we saw in Figure 37. The snarling handbag at the extreme left looks, to my eye, at once angry and supercilious; the cheese-grater is youthful, eager to please, and perhaps a little anxious; the block of wood has a relaxed but slightly drunken look; while the taps and sink on the extreme right seems preoccupied with its own thoughts, and riddled with anxiety. Yet what is really remarkable about this array of faces is that we can see them at all. Each image is incredibly distant from any real human (or indeed animal) face we have ever encountered. Yet they not only seem face-like, but, like the Mooney faces, they convey emotional expressions and even, to a degree, personalities. The imaginative leap required to distort and stretch these everyday objects onto the templates of a prototypical human face is very great; our brain makes such leaps so rapidly and so naturally that we think of it, if we consider it at all, as entirely unremarkable.

These imaginative jumps are, I believe, at the very core of human intelligence. The ability to select, recombine and modify past precedents to deal with present experience is what allows us to be able to cope with an open-ended world we scarcely understand. The cycle of thought does not merely refer passively to past precedents – we imaginatively create the present using the raw materials of the past.

THE UBIQUITY OF METAPHOR

The wild inventiveness of the human brain is perhaps best exemplified by the ubiquity and centrality of metaphor in our thoughts. Beyond seeing cheese-graters as grinning stupidly and hand basins looking diffident, we are forever seeing one thing in terms of something else completely. We portray each other as bursting with (or just full of) emotion, letting off steam, feeling down or depressed, or on top of the world; being weighed down or buoyed up, feeling flat or bouncy. We can be mixed up, messed up, straightened out, put straight; thoughts can be crowding in on us, we can be teeming with ideas, or our mind can be blank, empty, a void; we can be light-hearted or our thoughts can turn dark or even black. Our ideas can be sharp, penetrating, incisive, sparky, sparkling, fizzing, bright, brilliant, illuminating, or simply dull and blunted; and our words can be cutting, barbed or pointed, or perhaps smooth, silky, silvery or even oily. Or consider our physical condition, which can be in shape, out of shape, full of – or drained of – energy, broken down or patched up, out of gas, or having a second wind. And, of course, the very idea of *seeing* one thing as another is itself a metaphor, using visual perception as a proxy for thought. Our language is thoroughly soaked in metaphor.

Metaphors also thoroughly permeate our thoughts. Consider the illusion of mental depth that we discussed in Part One. Once we begin to see how thoughts are 'hidden' below a mental 'surface', it seems only natural to try to 'uncover' them, 'bring them to the surface'; to suspect that some people's thoughts run deep, while others are shallow. And the very idea that the mind is flat is, of course, just one more metaphor, albeit, I hope, a helpful antidote to our standard repertoire. And, needless to say, *antidote* and *repertoire* are metaphors too![4]

Just like faces, metaphors are everywhere, when we stop to notice them. And, indeed, it is hard to imagine how we could talk, or think, without them. If you have your doubts, try rewriting a few sentences of this book with the metaphors taken out, stripped away, removed, excised, deleted, cut out, missing, absent or eliminated, or whatever would be the appropriate, completely literal, phrasing, if one exists.

Some metaphors can of course become fossilized in the language (to deploy yet another metaphor), divorced (help, another one!) from any original meaning, and sometimes continue to be used where their origin is entirely forgotten. Presumably, *riding* a bicycle was once a metaphorical extension of riding a horse, but in a world in which bicycles are plentiful and horses are few, any such link has been lost. Indeed, our entire language (including this very sentence) is a graveyard of dead or half-dead metaphors.

Found faces and metaphors have a lot in common. Like found faces, metaphors embody three characteristics. First, a metaphor requires non-obvious, lateral thinking (another metaphor, of course), to link together two apparently unrelated domains (cheese-graters versus faces; real objects being hidden, buried, brought to the surface, and thoughts being 'hidden', 'buried', or 'brought to the surface'). Second, metaphor, by its very nature, requires the *transformation* of past experience into present experience: between, say, resolving outstanding issues in a project and 'tying up loose ends' of string or rope.

We can only see an unthreatening shark as a teddy bear if we have some experience or knowledge of teddy bears. And we can only see a person as a shark if we have some experience of, or at least some prior knowledge of, sharks. And, third, metaphors are just as apt to *mislead* as they are to inform. Just as a cheese-grater doesn't really feel eager to please and a block of wood can't get slightly inebriated, our inventive metaphorical leaps can be wildly off-target. For example, if the intricate mechanism of Nature is like the workings of a watch, as the eighteenth-century clergyman and theologian William Paley famously suggested, then it is easy to leap to the conclusion that it must have a designer, and one far more skilled and intelligent than any watchmaker. Evolutionary biology, of course, tells a very different story.

Battles of ideas are often fought over which metaphor is appropriate: is light made up of particles or waves? Are humans 'risen' apes or fallen gods? Is nature a harmonious society or a brutal war of all against all? Such metaphors are not marginal to thought, but its very essence. Our continual search for meaning is the struggle to find patterns in our present experience, in the light of the past. And so we see one thing in terms of another: a wash basin as a face; a mind as a container, a sea, or an inner world. Metaphors, too, are also employed to impose *meaning* upon one aspect of the world, by drawing on an understanding of another. We have lots of everyday experience with water waves (whether in puddles, ponds or the sea); and this helps us understand what it might mean for sound, light or even gravitation to be a type of wave (interfering, refracting, diffracting and so on). Or we can take our intuitions about water flow to help us understand the flow of heat or electricity.

Or, to consider a final, more whimsical, example, consider the game of charades. The title of a book, song or film is whispered in your ear; and you must communicate its identity to other members of your team with a sequence of improvised gestures and movements. One moment we may be transformed into a ravening dog for *The Hound of the Baskervilles*; the next we may desperately attempt to indicate the form of a rose flower, closing into mere bud, or, failing that, to stagger about with an imaginary stick, in an attempt to convey *Citizen Kane*. What is astonishing about charades is that we can play it at all: that a person can take on enough of the movement and gnashing teeth of a dog to convey the famous Hound; that a mime with the hands can imply the stalks, thorns, flower and even bud of a rose; and that we can walk *as if* supported by a stick, when the stick is patently absent. And we can do this naturally and spontaneously, and without years of dedicated preparation or rehearsal.

The team-mates attempting to decode our movements face a challenge somewhat akin to seeing found faces: they need to find some aspects of the communicator's demeanour and actions which suggest, however remotely, the target idea (and they will, of course, have additional clues from what they know about the communicator, their shared cultural knowledge, and so on). The communicator has to go in a reverse direction, creating something akin to the 'found hound', 'found rose' or 'found stick' sensory input for her team-mates – and to do so on the spot.

The search for interpretation is centre-stage again: we are able to create and decode inventive *transformations of past experience* – all the way from the book, to a hound, to a hound engaged in a violent raging attack (we don't attempt to portray the hound sleeping peacefully, or drinking from a bowl of water) – then map the imagined hound's body movements onto our own pantomime actions. And all of this requires the ingenious transformation of a wealth of knowledge – of the book and its central theme, and some crude grasp of the motifs of a canine attack, and how this can map onto the human body (so that, for example, arms become front legs, and fingers become claws). Such coding and decoding is all too imperfect, as players of charades will be aware. A mime intended to portray the flailing claws and gnashing teeth of the famous hound can so easily be read as *Jurassic Park*.

IMAGINATION AND INTELLIGENCE

The whimsical imagination which creates faces from handbags or from apparently meaningless black and white patterns, which plays with metaphors and invents stories, and which creates and perceives songs and art, might seem charming but impractical. Such exuberant mental leaps may appear primarily to be the province of the arts. After all, the worlds of painting and sculpture are replete with incredibly sketchy, incomplete and distorted representations of the human face, or indeed of many other things; and literature is full of metaphors, one character or story representing some other character or story, and relies on our brains turning a text, a stage, or the movements of a TV or film screen into the semblance of an entire world.

Why has our species developed such rich imaginative powers? Survival and reproduction surely don't depend on seeing faces in inanimate objects, viewing moods as spatial locations (up or down) or personalities as light sources (brilliant, sparkling, dazzling, bright on the one hand, or dull and dim on the other), or generating a continual stream of stories, whether credible or completely fantastical, to explain the world around us. Why, indeed, hasn't the iron logic of evolution by natural selection eliminated such playfulness in favour of a relentless focus on, say, commando-style survival skills? And how could the infinite imaginative landscape of romance and love arise in a species shaped, one might think, to have a one-dimensional focus on sex for reproduction?

Putting evolution to one side, and simply considering the demands of modern life, one might also suspect that capricious flights of fancy, while perhaps entertaining and enriching, must be secondary to the core practical business of the mind: understanding the world around us, making decisions and planning actions, and sending precise instructions and observations to others. Years of formal education, and the experience of working, as most of us do, somewhere in the middle of a complex web of bureaucratic processes, might reinforce such suspicions. Isn't the essence of thought discipline and control, rather than whimsical and wild connections? It is tempting to see imagination as no more than a mental 'bauble': conspicuous but entirely dispensable.

But we have seen that the opposite is true: imaginative leaps are essential for perceiving the world and making sense of each other. Such leaps allow us to project our past experiences onto an open-ended and continually surprising world. Any discipline of thought (learning to programme computers, play in an orchestra, prove

mathematical theorems) restricts the direction in which our imaginations take us; and the ability to work within these restrictions is
learned painfully and effortfully. Indeed, I suggest such discipline is
difficult precisely because it requires taming and trammelling our
sometimes unruly imagination. Our natural 'mode' of thinking is
wildly flexible – we only think of discipline and control as the essence
of thought because these require our conscious and careful attention.
The sheer ubiquity of our imaginative flexibility renders it invisible.

Leaps of the imagination are, on reflection, evident even when
solving what we might think of as 'logical' puzzles, which are central
to intelligence. Spend a few minutes on the perhaps familiar IQ
puzzles below:

(1) *Space* is to *ruler* as *time* is to: A: Metronome

                                                        B: Chronometer

                                                        C: Clock

                                                        D: Stopwatch

(2) *Sound* is to *echo* as *light* is to   A: Shadow

                                                        B: Reflection

                                                        C: Refraction

                                                        D: Mirror

(3) *Replicate* is to *duplicate* as *divide* is to   A: Split

                                                        B: Segment

                                                        C: Fractionate

                                                        D: Halve

IQ questions of this type are tests of mental elasticity – but also precision. Considering (1), for example, we need to map between time
and space. A ruler measures the distance between two points in space.
So what measures the distance between two points in time? Aha! – a
stopwatch (a clock – which is a good second choice – measures the

time, not the difference between times). But finding this mapping is not easy (and not entirely uncontroversial, perhaps).

Or consider (2): when *sound* bounces back off a surface (e.g. the walls of a ravine or the roof of a cave) we sometimes hear a copy of the original sound: an *echo*. When *light* from an object bounces off a surface (e.g. a mirror, or the surface of a still pond), we sometimes see a copy of that object: a *reflection*. This line of thinking suggests that B is the right answer.

Finally, in (3), when we make one or many copies of a gene, a computer file or a sheet of music (perhaps many times), we *replicate* it. When we create precisely one copy, we *duplicate* the original: we end up with precisely two versions of our gene, file or sheet of music. When we divide a number, we break it into several equal-sized pieces; when we divide it to create precisely two equal sized pieces, we halve it. This line of thinking suggests that D is the right answer.

Notice that solving these puzzles is very different from solving Sudoku or squaring a large number. In open-ended IQ problems, imagination is required even to make the problem meaningful at all. What, after all, is the relationship between the words *space* and *ruler*? A ruler takes up space? A ruler measures spaces? Space has no ruler – i.e. it is not ruled by anyone? Rulers typically have lots of space to live in? These fairly daft possibilities didn't even cross your mind, I suspect. One clue that they would be on the wrong track comes from the fact that we need to find a link between *space* and *time*. So presumably *space* and *time* must be considered quite abstractly. And then we might think of a ruler as a measure of space, but then several of the available options (*chronometer, clock, stopwatch*) are measures of time – so this doesn't give us a unique answer. A bit more thought might lead to the idea that both rulers and stopwatches measure intervals (in space or time), whereas clocks just give an absolute value. At least this interpretation picks out a unique answer, *stopwatch*, to be paired with *time*. Of course there are endless other ways of picking out a unique answer – though some seem more natural than others.

Suppose, for example, that we reason: a ruler can be used to divide space into equal intervals – and a metronome can be used to divide time into equal intervals – and hence we plump for option A. This seems a bit of a stretch (another metaphor), because rulers can do many other things than divide space into equal intervals (in particular, a ruler has a measuring scale, which has no analogue in the metronome).

Or, even less convincingly, we notice that the first letters of *space* and *ruler* are consecutive letters in the alphabet: *r* is the letter before *s*. Now time begins with a *t*, so perhaps the related word should begin with the letter of the alphabet before *t*, namely *s*. And indeed, there is a unique option beginning with an *s*, namely *stopwatch*. So we get the same 'right' answer – but using rather tenuous and forced reasoning. After all, the fact that the words are all about time, space and measurement is purely coincidental.

So, unlike Sudoku or arithmetical calculations, for which a solution is precisely defined (and there are, indeed, methods for systematically finding such solutions), these IQ test problems are actually remarkably open-ended. They are capturing our ability to search in the vast space of possible metaphorical links between words (or the ideas they bring to mind), and judging our ability to find natural, sensible mappings rather than perverse and tortured links.

But what, precisely, *counts* as the right answer in analogy problems like these? It is not entirely clear what the right criterion is, but surely the best answer is something like the consensus answer – not the one most of us think of, perhaps, but the one that most of us think is the best, when it is pointed out.[5]

This is not so different from the problem of interpreting faces in found objects. These ambiguous images *could* be given all sorts of interpretations, at a stretch. The handbag in Figure 37 looks like a snarling face to most of us, but could also vaguely remind one of an owl, a rubbish bin, the mouth of a fish, or a beetle. But all interpretations are not equal – again, there is a clear consensus; indeed, once we've seen our 'found faces' *as faces*, it is difficult to see them any other way. Imagination – our ability to construct rich interpretations in complex, open-ended problems – seems to be just what many IQ tests are measuring. Thus the secret of intelligence is imaginative interpretation, rather than 'cold logic'.

But intelligence requires us to harness our imagination in a disciplined way – intelligence requires more than merely blurting out the first interpretation or metaphor that comes to mind. It turns out to be highly productive to think of gases as consisting of clouds of tiny frictionless billiard balls continually bumping into each other in three dimensions – indeed, this is the standard model in physics. This insight proves to be crucial in understanding how the microscopic properties of trillions of molecules can lead to 'macroscopic' observations of pressure, temperature, volume and so on. Suppose, for example, sticking to two dimensions for a moment, we imagine expanding our billiard table dramatically – the billiard balls will continue to race about and bounce into each other as before, but now they will be much sparser – and hence far fewer balls will thump into the sides of the billiard table at any moment. And the reduced pummelling of the sides of the billiard table corresponds to lower pressure. Or suppose that we have two adjacent billiard tables, one in which a rather sparse set of balls is hurtling around at tremendous speed; and another where a much denser cloud of balls is moving about, on average, much more slowly. If we remove the partition between the two tables, then the density, and the average speeds, of the balls will gradually even out. The speed of the balls corresponds to temperature in the billiard-ball model of gas – so this means that the temperature in the two initially separate 'gases' will gradually become equal as they are joined together; and their density (i.e. the crowdedness of the billiard balls) and pressure (pummelling of the sides of the billiard tables) will reduce to an equilibrium as well.

The billiard-ball model of gases turned out to be incredibly useful, and now serves as the basis for capturing all sorts of aspects of known gas behaviour. It produces a beautiful link between the microscopic behaviour of, not billiard balls, but tiny gas molecules, whizzing about roughly according to Newton's laws of motion (the very same laws we use for projectiles and planets), and the way gases work. Developing and utilizing an analogy like the billiard-ball model of gases requires great care and subtlety. The goal is to create a rigorous, mathematically precise model – not merely a fanciful metaphor – and to test it in experiments to see where it works, and where it fails. Such carefully developed analogies are the foundation of many areas of science.

But to do this, I suggest, doesn't require switching to some entirely different style of thought – some imagined cold logic with which the products of our imagination can be soberly assessed. Instead, we need to direct successive thoughts to search for alternative interpretations, check that those interpretations make sense, and so on, by 'locking onto' different aspects of the information in the problem. Figuring out unexpected predictions from our analogy, deciding how to map them into known mathematics, and establishing which key experiments we need to conduct, all require ingenuity and inspiration, not mere handle-cranking. Both intelligence and analogy-making, even in science, are driven by our wonderfully elastic imagination, properly harnessed and directed.

THE DISTANT PROSPECT OF INTELLIGENT MACHINES

If our spectacular mental elasticity – our ability to imaginatively interpret complex, open-ended information into rich and varied patterns – is the secret of *human* intelligence, what does this imply for the possibility of *artificial* intelligence (which we began to examine in Chapter 1)?

My suspicion is that the implications are far-reaching. As we saw, the early attempts to extract and codify human 'reasoning' and knowledge into a computer database failed comprehensively. The hoped-for hidden inner principles from which our thoughts and behaviour supposedly flow turned out to be illusory. Instead, human intelligence is based on precedents – and the ability to stretch, mash together and re-engineer such precedents to deal with an open-ended and novel world. The secret of intelligence is the astonishing flexibility and cleverness by which the old is re-engineered to deal with the new. Yet the secret of how this is done has yet to be cracked.

The spectacular progress in computational intelligence over the last half-century has not been achieved by replicating the elasticity of the human imagination, which allows us to see, for instance, in a game of charades, a middle-aged man beating his chest and swatting the air with his fists as a representation of the film *King Kong*, or read rich emotion and humanity into Mooney's black and white patches, or see the world through an endlessly shifting blizzard of metaphors. Computational intelligence has instead taken a very different tack: focusing on problems, like chess or arithmetic, that require no free interpretation at all, but which can be reduced to vast sequences of calculations, performed at lightning speed. In addition it has proved to be invaluable for things like speech recognition, machine translation and general knowledge tests, hoovering up solutions to almost unimaginably vast quantities of past problems to enable the machine to solve new problems, which are only a little different.[6]

Yet what is astonishing about human intelligence, and perhaps biological intelligence more broadly, is its spectacular flexibility. To us, it is unremarkable that our brains can map J. M. W. Turner's smudges of paint, or Debussy's sinuous orchestration in *La Mer* into a turbulent or calm seascape; that we can interpret the movements of cartoon characters, shadow puppets or ballet dancers as playing out human dramas; that we make instant mental leaps from properties of tensile materials to states of mind (being under strain, stretched, over/under-stretched, pulled in too many directions, spread too thinly, taut, tense, likely to snap, at breaking point, (in)flexible, rigid, stiff, fragile, shattered); that our brains are able to discern links between ripples on water, sound, light, radio, vibrations, the wriggling of a rope and perhaps even the force of gravity itself.

But my suspicion is that it is our mental elasticity that is one of the keys to what makes human intelligence so remarkable and so distinctive.[7] The creative and often wildly metaphorical interpretations that we impose on the world are far removed from anything we have yet been able to replicate by machine.

To those who, like me, are fascinated by the possibilities of artificial intelligence, the moral is that we should expect further automation of those mental activities that can be solved by 'brute force' rather than mental elasticity – the routine, the repetitive, the well defined. This is part of a trend that started with the development of stone tools in the Olduvai Gorge in present-day Tanzania, more than two and a half million years ago and accelerated spectacularly in the Industrial Revolution: people and technology can achieve far more than people alone. It is a continual source of amazement to us that tasks that seemed to require the full power of human ingenuity can be solved, often far more efficiently, by processes of standardization and mechanization: the flexibility and dexterity of human hand-weaving could, in many cases, be replaced by the precision achieved by the hand-loom, and then the steam-driven Jacquard loom, controlled by punched cards around 1800, and on to the phenomenal productivity of the computerized power looms of today. At each step, the environment is made more precise and more standardized; and more of the task can be handed over to machines.

In the same way, the rise of digitization and big data can create an ever more frictionless and more precisely defined world in which computers can operate far better than we can. But the secret of human intelligence is the ability to find patterns in the least structured, most unexpected, hugely variable of streams of information – to lock onto a handbag and see a snarling face; to lock onto a set of black-and-white patches and discern a distinctive, emotion-laden, human being; to find mappings and metaphors through the complexity and chaos of the physical and psychological worlds. All this is far beyond the reach of modern artificial intelligence.

It is our wild imposition of meaning upon the world by the appropriation and transformation of past experience that is the essence of human thought, from which our more sober reflections can, with difficulty, be constructed. Watching the mind at play is our best guide to its natural mode of operation. This reveals the search for interpretation that drives us – the effort to find meaning that is channelled by, rather than replaced with, step-by-step conscious deliberation.

To those who fear the march of the machines, this should be of some comfort. If imagination and metaphor is the secret of our intelligence, then that secret may, perhaps, be safely locked away in the human brain for centuries and perhaps for ever.

Epilogue: Reinventing Ourselves

We have all been victims of a hoax, perpetrated on us by our own brains. Our brains are spectacular engines of improvisation that can, in the moment, generate a colour, an object, a memory, a belief or a preference, spin a story, or reel off a justification. And it is such a compelling storyteller that we are fooled into thinking that it is not inventing our thoughts 'in the moment' at all, but fishing them from some deep inner sea of pre-formed colours, objects, memories, beliefs or preferences, of which our conscious thoughts are merely the shimmering surface. But our mental depths are a confabulation – a fiction created in the moment by our own brain. There are no pre-formed beliefs, desires, preferences, attitudes, even memories, hidden in the deep recesses of the mind; indeed, the mind has no deep recesses in which anything can hide. The mind is flat: the surface is all there is.

Our brains are, then, relentless and compelling improvisers, creating the mind, moment by moment. But, as with any improvisation – in dance, music or storytelling – each fresh thought is not created out of nothing. Each fresh improvisation is built from the fragments of past improvisations – so each of us is a unique history, together with a wonderfully creative machine for redeploying that history to create new perceptions, thoughts, emotions and stories. The layering of that history makes some patterns of thought natural for us, others awkward or uncomfortable. But while drawing on our past, we are, none the less, continually reinventing ourselves; and by directing that re-invention, we can shape who we are, and who we will become.

So we are not driven by hidden, inexorable forces from a dark and subterranean mental world. Instead, our thoughts and actions are transformations of past thoughts and actions, and we often have considerable latitude, and a certain judicial discretion, regarding which precedents we consider, which transformations we allow. As today's thought or action is tomorrow's precedent, we are, quite literally, reshaping and reinventing ourselves thought by thought.

This is not a familiar story. It is not an intuitive story. It is a story that shakes our faith in everything we think we know about how our minds work – including what we 'see' and 'feel', the nature of memory, decision-making and personality. It is a story in which we cannot find ourselves, because there are no selves to find. So yes, it is a story of a hoax, a conspiracy, an illusion, which enfolds us so completely that we cannot see behind its veil – or even notice that there is a veil we might wish to lift. But it is also a story of how more than a century of scientific investigation of the mind has, step by step, allowed the hoax to be uncovered. Once the spell of the inner worlds, true selves, mental depths and unconscious mental forces is broken, we can see ourselves in a clearer light: we are astonishingly inventive ad hoc reasoners, creative metaphor-machines, continually welding together scattered scraps of information into momentarily coherent wholes. We are very different from the image we create for ourselves, and much more remarkable.

This is all very well, you may say. But surely we need beliefs and motives to explain why our thoughts and behaviour make sense, rather than being a completely incoherent jumble. Surely there are crucial inner facts about us, large and small, that set the course of our actions: the things we value, the ideals we believe in, the passions that move us. But if the mind is flat, despite the stories we tell about ourselves and each other, beliefs and motives cannot, in reality, be driving our behaviour – because there are no inner beliefs, and motives are a projection rather than a reality.

On the other hand, layers of precedents – the successive adaptation and transformation of previous thoughts and actions to create new thoughts and actions – can provide a very different, and more convincing, explanation for the orderly (and, on occasions, the disorderly) nature of thought. Moreover, moving from individual minds to society as a whole, our culture can be viewed as a shared canon of precedents – things we do, want, say or think – which create order in society as well as within each individual. By laying down new precedents, we incrementally and collectively create our culture. But our new precedents are based on old, shared precedents, so that our culture also creates us. Considered in isolation, our 'selves' turn out to be partial, fragmentary and alarmingly fragile; we are only the most lightly sketched of literary creations. Yet collectively we can construct lives, organizations and societies which can be remarkably stable and coherent.

The idea of continuous reinvention is particularly vertigo-inducing when we realize that, once the hoax is uncovered, the very idea of an objective, and external, yardstick against which to judge our behaviour as individuals, and as a society, is not just impractical, but also wholly unsustainable. There is, after all, no solid foundation upon which we can build. New thoughts, values and actions can only be justified or criticized from within a tradition of past precedents. Of course, which precedents should be applied, and which should dominate, may be matters of dispute, just as they are in the law. This does not mean that anything goes – but it does mean that the construction of our lives and our society is an inherently open-ended, creative process, and that the standards by which we judge our decisions and actions are part of that same creative process. In short, life is a game in which we play, invent the rules and keep the score ourselves.

This perspective might appear to be a recipe for a relativist nightmare: that any point of view is equally valid or equally dubious. But the reverse is true. If there are no ultimate foundations on which the good life, or the good society, is based, then the challenge in our own lives and societies is to explore and resolve conflicts in thought, whether within ourselves or between individuals. While holding onto old precedents can be seen as a conservative political impulse, the aim of bringing distinct traditions into contact, and ultimately perhaps into alignment, is the impulse behind the liberal political tradition. For example, the principle of freedom of speech is designed to allow public debate to link together momentary beliefs across time, individuals and communities; and such debate may be codified by mathematical and scientific methods. Free markets, money, trade and the modern economic system connect together our preferences by means of the exchange of goods, services and money. Democratic politics and the rule of law can resolve potential clashes between our actions (where a decision at one moment may encroach on a decision at some future moment, by the same person or another). In a liberal society, then, we do not merely dream our own individual dream or write our own particular story; rather, we continually strive to link our stories together into a single cohesive whole.

Yet, even in a liberal society in which preferences, beliefs and actions can be connected, precedent-based thinking appears inherently conservative. How, then, are perceptual reorganizations, sudden insights, religious conversions and conceptual and political revolutions possible? One answer is that memory is fragile; so that we can often end up starting again from scratch, and coming up with a different answer. We forget the old 'story' and create a new one.

But there is another possibility: that changing *part* of the story can lead to a cascade of far-reaching consequences. For all its focus on the authority of the past, we should remember that successions of precedents can, step by step, lead to remarkable metamorphoses. Legal and political systems can transform themselves over the generations, though at each step guided by the interpretation and reinterpretation of what went before. A mathematician may use past precedents in methods of reasoning in order to show that an entire theory is inconsistent – and may even conclude that a great swathe of apparent precedents (previous 'results' from that theory) must be abandoned. Individuals may gradually begin, or cease, to trust a cult leader, or a religious or political text; they may take up, or abandon, a cause, a project, a relationship – or in a million other ways transform their lives So what counts as a precedent can itself shift – and shift again. We hope to stumble towards better and better 'stories' – but we can only create new stories by starting with the stories we have.

We should, moreover, never assume that achieving greater coherence necessarily implies cultural or intellectual progress. And we must be ever-vigilant against allowing ourselves or our societies to ossify into coherent, but crushing systems of precedent. But we should also remember that we are not hemmed in by occult psychic forces within us: any 'prisons' of thought are of our own invention, and can be dismantled just as they have been constructed. If the mind is flat – if we imagine our minds, our lives and our culture – we have the power to imagine an inspiring future, and to make it real.

Notes

PROLOGUE: LITERARY DEPTH, MENTAL SHALLOWS

1 D. Dennett, *Consciousness Explained* (London: Penguin, 1993), p. 68.
2 There are many different versions of this metaphor of introspection as perception of an inner world. We examine our consciences; find (or lose) ourselves; try to learn who we really are, what we really believe or stand for.
3 Those sceptical of common-sense explanations of the mind who have particularly influenced my thinking include Daniel Dennett, Paul Churchland, Patricia Churchland, Gilbert Ryle, Hugo Mercier, James A. Russell, Dan Sperber, among many others. A particularly influential study that cast doubt on the psychological coherence of common-sense explanations of all kinds is: L. Rozenblit and F. Keil (2002), 'The misunderstood limits of folk science: An illusion of explanatory depth', *Cognitive Science*, 26(5): 521–62.
4 Experimental methods relying on introspection, for example those in which people describe their experiences of different perceptual stimuli, were a focus of the very first psychological laboratory, set up in Leipzig by Wilhelm Wundt in 1879. Philosophy and psychology continue to contain strands of phenomenology – where the goal is to try to understand and explore our minds and experience 'from the inside'. These methods have been, in my view, notably unproductive – phenomenology draws us into the illusion of mental depth, rather than uncovering its existence.
5 Sceptics include behaviourists such as Gilbert Ryle and B. F. Skinner, theorists of direct perception such as J. J. Gibson and Michael Turvey, and philosophers influenced by phenomenology (Hubert Dreyfus). Paul and Patricia Churchland have long argued that everyday 'folk' psychology is no more scientifically viable than 'folk' physics or biology. Over the years I have argued both in favour of this view (see N. Chater and M. Oaksford (1996), 'The falsity of folk theories: Implications for

psychology and philosophy', in W. O'Donaghue and R. F. Kitchener (eds),*The Philosophy of Psychology* (London: Sage), pp. 244–56) and (wrongly, I now feel) against it (see, for example, N. Chater (2000), 'Contrary views: A review of "On the contrary" by Paul and Patricia Churchland', *Studies in History and Philosophy of Biological and Biomedical Sciences*, 31: 615–27). The ideas in this book owe a lot to the philosopher Daniel Dennett and his discussion of an 'instrumentalist' view of everyday psychological explanation and the nature of conscious experience (D. C. Dennett, *The Intentional Stance* (Cambridge, MA: MIT Press, 1989) and D. C. Dennett, *Consciousness Explained* (London: Penguin, 1993)).

6 Some of the ideas in Part Two of this book have close links to joint work with my close friend and colleague Morten Christiansen of Cornell University on how we use and learn language (e.g. Morten H. Christiansen and N. Chater, *Creating Language: Integrating Evolution, Acquisition, and Processing* (Cambridge, MA: MIT Press, 2016); Morten H. Christiansen and N. Chater (2016), 'The now-or-never bottleneck: A fundamental constraint on language', *Behavioral and Brain Sciences*, 39, e62).

1. THE POWER OF INVENTION

1 After all, given that humans have a common ancestor, we are all Elvis's *n*th cousins *m* times removed, for some numbers *n* and *m*. As all life has a common ancestor, we are also rather more distant cousins of pond algae.

2 Mendelsund gives this and many other compelling examples of the astonishingly sketchiness of fiction and the vagueness of the imagery that we conjure up when reading. We can, none the less, have the subjective sense of being immersed in another 'world' full of sensory richness. P. Mendelsund, *What We See When We Read* (New York: Vintage Books, 2014).

3 We could, of course, make a parallel, and equally strong, argument for any scientific or mathematical topic, from chemistry, biology, economics and psychology to mathematics and logic.

4 Two particularly sophisticated and influential papers were: J. McCarthy and P. J. Hayes (1969), 'Some philosophical problems from the standpoint of artificial intelligence', in B. Meltzer and D. Michie (eds), *Machine Intelligence 4* (Edinburgh: Edinburgh University Press, 1969); and P. J. Hayes, 'The naive physics manifesto', in D. Michie (ed.), *Expert Systems in the Micro-Electronic Age* (Edinburgh: Edinburgh

University Press, 1979). It is important to stress that artificial intelligence has proceeded primarily not by solving the deep problems of understanding human knowledge, but by strategically skirting around them. The challenges raised by early artificial intelligence remain both hugely important and largely unresolved.

5 My friend and colleague Mike Oaksford and I have called this the fractal nature of common-sense knowledge – each step in a chain of reasoning seems to be just as complex as the whole chain. M. Oaksford and N. Chater, *Rationality in an Uncertain World: Essays on the Cognitive Science of Human Reasoning* (Abingdon: Psychology Press/Erlbaum (UK), Taylor & Francis, 1998).

6 L. Rozenblit and F. Keil (2002), 'The misunderstood limits of folk science: An illusion of explanatory depth', *Cognitive Science*, 26(5): 521–62. We have the same shallow understanding of complex political issues. Perhaps not entirely surprisingly, people with extreme political views appear to have a particularly shallow understanding: P. M. Fernbach, T. Rogers, C. R. Fox and S. A. Sloman (2013), 'Political extremism is supported by an illusion of understanding', *Psychological Science*, 24(6): 939–46.

7 An aside: where philosophy has mutated into theory – including psychology, probability, logic, decision theory, game theory, and so on – it becomes, like physics, drastically disconnected from its intuitive foundations. The theory will have all sorts of implications that are wildly counter-intuitive, but this is inevitable, because our intuitions are inconsistent. To my mind, one of the spectacular successes of philosophy has been its propensity to 'spin-out' theories that ultimately transcend mere 'intuition-matching' and which, like physics, come to have a life of their own.

8 The project of generative grammar still struggles on. But the prospect of anyone writing down a generative grammar of, say, English, seems ever more remote – and indeed, Chomsky and his followers have drifted ever further from practical engagement with the project, and have resorted to abstract theory and philosophical speculation. In the last couple of decades, a new movement in linguistics – construction grammar (A. E. Goldberg, *Constructions at Work* (New York: Oxford University Press, 2006); P. W. Culicover and R. Jackendoff, *Simpler Syntax* (New York: Oxford University Press, 2005)) – has abandoned the 'grammar-as-theory' point of view and embraced the piecemeal nature of language wholeheartedly. This viewpoint also fits well with the fact that language is learned, and languages change over time, incrementally 'piece-by-piece' rather than undergoing system-wide

reorganizations (M. H. Christiansen and N. Chater (2016), 'The now-or-never bottleneck: A fundamental constraint on language', *Behavioral and Brain Sciences*, 39, e62; M. H. Christiansen and N. Chater, *Creating Language* (Cambridge, MA: MIT Press, 2016).

9 Multiple systems views have been prevalent, from early psychoanalysis (e.g. Sigmund Freud, *Das Ich und das Es*, (Leipzig, Vienna and Zurich: Internationaler Psycho-analytischer Verlag, 1923); English translation, *The Ego and the Id*, Joan Riviere (trans.) (London: Hogarth Press and Institute of Psycho-analysis, 1927)) to modern cognitive science (e.g. S. A. Sloman (1996), 'The empirical case for two systems of reasoning', *Psychological Bulletin* 119: 3–22; J. S. B. Evans (2003), 'In two minds: Dual-process accounts of reasoning', *Trends in Cognitive Sciences*, 7(10): 454–9).

2. THE FEELING OF REALITY

1 A close variant of the triangle on the left-hand side of Figure 1 was later independently discovered by the father and son team of Lionel and Roger Penrose (L. S. Penrose and R. Penrose (1958), 'Impossible objects: A special type of visual illusion', *British Journal of Psychology*, 49(1): 31–3) and their very elegant version is known as the Penrose triangle. Reutersvärd worked entirely intuitively and had no background in geometry, discovering his famous triangle while still at school. The Penroses were both distinguished academics; indeed, Roger Penrose went on to apply geometry with spectacular results in mathematical physics. It strikes me as remarkable that the same astonishing figure could independently be created from such different starting points.

2 The philosopher Richard Rorty famously argued that the 'mirror of nature' metaphor marks a fundamental wrong turn in Western thought (R. Rorty, *Philosophy and the Mirror of Nature* (Princeton, NJ: Princeton University Press, 1979)). Whether or not this is right, viewing the mind as a mirror of nature, creating an internal copy of the outer world, is certainly a wrong turn in understanding perception.

3 Strictly speaking, there are 3D interpretations of the 2D patterns we view as 'impossible' objects, but they are bizarre geometric arrangements, which are incompatible with the natural interpretations of parts of the image.

4 http://www.webexhibits.org/causesofcolor/1G.html.

5 http://www.scholarpedia.org/article/File:Resolution.jpg.

6 http://www.bbc.co.uk/news/science-environment-37337778.

7 J. Ninio and K. A. Stevens (2000), 'Variations on the Hermann grid: an extinction illusion', *Perception*, 29(10): 1209–17.

8 K. Rayner and J. H. Bertera (1979), 'Reading without a fovea', *Science*, 206: 468–9; K. Rayner, A. W. Inhoff, R. E. Morrison, M. L. Slowiaczek and J. H. Bertera (1981), 'Masking of foveal and parafoveal vision during eye fixations in reading', *Journal of Experimental Psychology: Human Perception and Performance*, 7(1): 167–79.

9 A. Pollatsek, S. Bolozky, A. D. Well and K. Rayner (1981), 'Asymmetries in the perceptual span for Israeli readers', *Brain and Language*, 14(1): 174–80.

10 G. W. McConkie and K. Rayner (1975), 'The span of the effective stimulus during a fixation in reading', *Perception & Psychophysics*, 17(6), 578–86.

11 E. R. Schotter, B. Angele and K. Rayner (2012), 'Parafoveal processing in reading', *Attention, Perception, & Psychophysics*, 74(1): 5–35; A. Pollatsek, G. E. Raney, L. LaGasse and K. Rayner (1993), 'The use of information below fixation in reading and visual search', *Canadian Journal of Experimental Psychology*, 47(2): 179–200.

12 E. D. Reichle, K. Rayner and A. Pollatsek (2003), 'The E–Z Reader model of eye-movement control in reading: Comparisons to other models', *Behavioral and Brain Sciences*, 26(4): 445–76.

13 By stabilizing the retinal image, so that the eye can no longer scan from place to place, we are drastically reducing our ability to make sense of different parts of the image. However, we can, to a limited degree, shift our attention, even without moving our eyes, so that retinal stabilization dramatically reduces, but doesn't entirely eliminate, our ability to change which pieces of visual information we lock onto.

14 R. M. Pritchard (1961), 'Stabilized images on the retina', *Scientific American*, 204: 72–8.

15 Here, I'm picking out some highlights from research on stabilized images, and not, of course, attempting to be comprehensive. One still controversial issue is whether the image necessarily fades completely and irretrievably, if it is perfectly stabilized – it is difficult to completely eliminate any 'wobble' which might be sufficient for the eye to register change (H. B. Barlow (1963), 'Slippage of contact lenses and other artefacts in relation to fading and regeneration of supposedly stable retinal images', *Quarterly Journal of Experimental Psychology*, 15(1): 36–51; L. E. Arend and G. T. Timberlake (1986), 'What is psychophysically perfect image stabilization? Do perfectly stabilized images always disappear?', *Journal of the Optical Society of America A*, 3(2): 235–41).

16 A. Noë (2002), 'Is the visual world a grand illusion?', *Journal of Consciousness Studies*, 9(5–6): 1–12; D. C. Dennett, ' "Filling in" versus finding

out: A ubiquitous confusion in cognitive science', in H. L. Pick, Jr, P. van den Broek and D. C. Knill (eds), *Cognition: Conceptual and Methodological Issues* (Washington DC: American Psychological Association, 1992); D. C. Dennett, *Consciousness Explained* (London: Penguin Books, 1993).

3. ANATOMY OF A HOAX

1 Image (a) from A. L. Yarbus (1967), *Eye Movements and Vision* (New York: Plenum Press), reprinted by permission; image (b) from Keith Rayner and Monica Castelhano (2007), 'Eye movements', *Scholarpedia*, 2(10): 3649, http://www.scholarpedia.org/article/Eye_movements.

2 J. K. O'Regan and A. Noë (2001), 'A sensorimotor account of vision and visual consciousness', *Behavioral and Brain Sciences*, 24(5): 939–73; R. A. Rensink (2000), 'Seeing, sensing, and scrutinizing', *Vision Research*, 40(10): 1469–87.

3 Reprinted from Brian A. Wandell, *Foundations of Vision* (Stanford University): https://foundationsofvision.stanford.edu.

4 L. Huang and H. Pashler (2007), 'A Boolean map theory of visual attention', *Psychological Review*, 114(3): 599, Figure 8.

5 If so, then we might expect some interesting effects of the colour grids stabilized on the retina, e.g. that patterns corresponding to individual colours might be seen, with the rest of the grid entirely invisible. This has not, to my knowledge, been attempted, but it would be a fascinating experiment.

6 Patterns can also be 'shrink-wrapped' by sharing properties other than colour – for example, being lines with the same slant, or items which are all moving in synchrony (like a flock of birds).

7 J. Duncan (1980), 'The locus of interference in the perception of simultaneous stimuli', *Psychological Review*, 87(3): 272–300.

8 Huang and Pashler (2007), 'A Boolean map theory of visual attention', Figure 10.

9 Note, though, that the perception of the colour of each patch will be influenced by neighbouring patches; indeed, the perceived colour of any individual patch on the image is determined by the comparison of that specific patch with neighbouring patches in a very complex and subtle way (for an early and influential theory, see E. H. Land and J. J. McCann (1971), 'Lightness and retinex theory', *Journal of the Optical Society of America*, 61(1): 1–11). The key, and remarkable, point is that, none the less, the output of this interactive process is sequential: we can only see one colour at a time.

10 D. G. Watson, E. A. Maylor and L. A. Bruce (2005), 'The efficiency of feature-based subitization and counting', *Journal of Experimental Psychology: Human Perception and Performance*, 31(6): 1449.

11 Masud Husain (2008), 'Hemineglect', *Scholarpedia*, 3(2): 3681, http://www.scholarpedia.org/article/Hemineglect.

12 Nigel J. T. Thomas, 'Mental Imagery', in the *Stanford Encyclopedia of Philosophy*, Edward N. Zalta (ed.): http://plato.stanford.edu/archives/fall2014/entries/mental-imagery/.

13 The remarkable video of this interaction can be found online at <https://www.youtube.com/watch?v=4odhSq46vtU>.

4. THE INCONSTANT IMAGINATION

1 This is the so-called Cathode Ray Tube theory of imagery (see S. M. Kosslyn, *Image and Mind* (Cambridge, MA: Harvard University Press, 1980)).

2 The illusion that the mind is the stage of an inner theatre is explored by philosopher Daniel Dennett in his book *Consciousness Explained*. My thinking has been heavily influenced by Zenon Pylyshyn's long-standing critique of pictorial theories of imagery (Z. W. Pylyshyn (1981), 'The imagery debate: Analogue media versus tacit knowledge', *Psychological Review*, 88(1): 16).

3 G. Hinton (1979), 'Some demonstrations of the effects of structural descriptions in mental imagery', *Cognitive Science*, 3(3): 231–50.

4 J. Wolpe and S. Rachman (1960), 'Psychoanalytic "evidence": A critique based on Freud's case of little Hans', *Journal of Nervous and Mental Disease*, 131(2): 135–48.

5 Wolpe and Rachman (1960), 'Psychoanalytic "evidence": A critique based on Freud's case of little Hans'.

6 S. Freud, 'Analysis of a phobia in a five-year-old boy 'Little Hans' (1909), *Case Histories I*, Vol. 8, Penguin Freud Library (London: Penguin Books,1977).

7 Wolpe and Rachman (1960), 'Psychoanalytic "evidence": A critique based on Freud's case of little Hans', quoting Freud.

5. INVENTING FEELINGS

1 http://www.elementsofcinema.com/editing/kuleshov-effect.html.

2 See online at <http://www.imdb.com/name/nm0474487/bio>;

3 See online at <https://www.youtube.com/watch?v=DGA6rCOyTh4>;
4 L. F. Barrett, K. A. Lindquist and M. Gendron (2007), 'Language as context for the perception of emotion', *Trends in Cognitive Sciences*, 11(8): 327–32. Reprinted by permission; original photo Doug Mills/ New York Times/Redux.
5 http://plato.stanford.edu/entries/relativism/supplement1.html.
6 W. James, *The Principles of Psychology* (1890), 2 vols (New York: Dover Publications, 1950).
7 J. A. Russell (2003), 'Core affect and the psychological construction of emotion', *Psychological Review*, 110(1): 145; J. A. Russell (1980), 'A circumplex model of affect', *Journal of Personality and Social Psychology*, 39(6): 1161.
8 P. Briñol and R. E. Petty (2003), 'Overt head movements and persuasion: A self-validation analysis', *Journal of Personality and Social Psychology*, 84(6): 1123–39.
9 Briñol and Petty (2003) explain their results using a different account, which they call self-validation theory. They interpret the nodding as 'validating' one's own thoughts (i.e. one's internal monologue of 'this is nonsense, total nonsense!' when given the unpersuasive message), rather than affirming the message itself. Experimentally splitting apart these approaches is an interesting challenge.
10 D. G. Dutton and A. P. Aron (1974), 'Some evidence for heightened sexual attraction under conditions of high anxiety', *Journal of Personality and Social Psychology*, 30(4): 510.
11 B. Russell, *The Autobiography of Bertrand Russell* (Boston, MA: Little, Brown & Co., 1951), p. 222.

6. MANUFACTURING CHOICE

1 Wikipedia: http://upload.wikimedia.org/wikipedia/commons/6/60/Corpus_callosum.png.
2 M. S. Gazzaniga (2000), 'Cerebral specialization and interhemispheric communication: Does the corpus callosum enable the human condition?', *Brain*, 123(7): 1293–326.
3 L. Hall, T. Strandberg, P. Pärnamets, A. Lind, B. Tärning and P. Johansson (2013), 'How the polls can be both spot on and dead wrong: Using choice blindness to shift political attitudes and voter intentions', *PLoS ONE* 8(4): e60554. doi:10.1371/journal.pone.0060554.

4 P. Johansson, L. Hall, S. Sikström and A. Olsson (2005), 'Failure to detect mismatches between intention and outcome in a simple decision task', *Science*, 310(5745): 116–19. Reprinted by permission.

5 P. Johansson, L. Hall, B. Tärning, S. Sikström and N. Chater (2013), 'Choice blindness and preference change: You will like this paper better if you (believe you) chose to read it!', *Journal of Behavioral Decision Making*, 27(3): 281–9.

6 T. J. Carter, M. J. Ferguson and R. R. Hassin (2011), 'A single exposure to the American flag shifts support toward Republicanism up to 8 months later', *Psychological Science*, 22(8): 1011–18.

7 E. Shafir (1993), 'Choosing versus rejecting: Why some options are both better and worse than others', *Memory & Cognition*, 21(4): 546–56; E. Shafir, I. Simonson and A. Tversky (1993), 'Reason-based choice', *Cognition*, 49(1): 11–36.

8 K. Tsetsos, N. Chater and M. Usher (2012), 'Salience driven value integration explains decision biases and preference reversal', *Proceedings of the National Academy of Sciences*, 109(24): 9659–64.

9 Tsetsos, Chater and Usher (2012), 'Salience driven value integration explains decision biases and preference reversal'.

10 The literature is vast. Some classic references include: D. Kahneman and A. Tversky, *Choices, Values, and Frames* (Cambridge, UK: Cambridge University Press, 2000); C. F. Camerer, G. Loewenstein and M. Rabin (eds), *Advances in Behavioral Economics* (Princeton, NJ: Princeton University Press, 2011); Z. Kunda, *Social Cognition: Making Sense of People* (Cambridge, MA: MIT Press, 1999).

11 P. J. Schoemaker (1990), 'Are risk-attitudes related across domains and response modes?', *Management Science*, 36(12): 1451–63; I. Vlaev, N. Chater and N. Stewart (2009), 'Dimensionality of risk perception: Factors affecting consumer understanding and evaluation of financial risk', *Journal of Behavioral Finance*, 10(3): 158–81.

12 E. U. Weber, A. R. Blais and N. E. Betz (2002), 'A domain-specific risk-attitude scale: Measuring risk perceptions and risk behaviors', *Journal of Behavioral Decision Making*, 15(4): 263–90.

13 This 'constructive' view of preferences (as created in the moment of questioning) has been persuasively advocated for several decades (P. Slovic (1995), 'The construction of preference', *American Psychologist*, 50(5): 364). Many economists and psychologists have not, though, taken on the full implications of this viewpoint, imagining that there is still some 'deep' and stable underlying preference that is merely distorted by the particular measurement method.

7. THE CYCLE OF THOUGHT

1 A classic discussion is J. A. Feldman and D. H. Ballard (1982), 'Connectionist models and their properties', *Cognitive Science*, 6(3): 205–54.

2 This connectionist or 'neural network' model of computation has been a rival to conventional 'digital' computers since the 1940s (see W. S. McCulloch and W. Pitts (1943), 'A logical calculus of the ideas immanent in nervous activity', *Bulletin of Mathematical Biophysics*, 5(4): 115–33) and exploded into psychology and cognitive science with books including G. E. Hinton and J. A. Anderson, *Parallel Models of Associative Memory* (Hillsdale, NJ: Erlbaum, 1981) and J. L. McClelland, D. E. Rumelhart and the PDP Research Group, *Parallel Distributed Processing*, 2 vols (Cambridge, MA: MIT Press, 1986). State-of-the-art machine-learning now extensively uses neural networks – although, ironically, implemented in conventional digital computers for reasons of practical convenience. Building brain-like hardware is currently just too difficult and inflexible.

3 While the brain is interconnected into something close to a single network, this isn't quite the whole story. As with a PC, the brain seems to have some specialized hardware for particular problem, such as the 'low-level' processing of images and sounds and other sensory inputs, and for basic movement control. And perhaps there are somewhat independent networks specialized for other tasks too (e.g. processing faces, words and speech sounds). The questions of which 'special-purpose' machinery the brain develops, whether such machinery is built in or learned and, crucially, the degree to which such networks are 'sealed off' from interference from the rest of the brain, are all of great importance.

4 For a recent review, see C. Koch, M. Massimini, M. Boly and G. Tononi (2016), 'Neural correlates of consciousness: progress and problems', *Nature Reviews Neuroscience*, 17(5): 307–21.

5 W. Penfield and H. H. Jasper, *Epilepsy and the Functional Anatomy of the Human Brain* (Boston, MA: Little, Brown, 1954).

6 Reprinted by permission from B. Merker (2007), 'Consciousness without a cerebral cortex: A challenge for neuroscience and medicine', Behavioral and Brain Sciences, 30(1): 63–81; redrawn from figures VI-2, XIII-2 and XVIII-7 in Penfield and Jasper, *Epilepsy and the Functional Anatomy of the Human Brain.*

7 B. Merker (2007), 'Consciousness without a cerebral cortex: A challenge for neuroscience and medicine', *Behavioral and Brain Sciences*, 30: 63–134.

8 G. Moruzzi and H. W. Magoun (1949), 'Brain stem reticular formation and activation of the EEG', *Electroencephalography and Clinical Neurophysiology*, 1(4): 455–73.

9 Psychologists and neuroscientists will recognize these ideas as drawing on a range of prior ideas, from the emphasis on organization in Gestalt psychology and Bartlett's 'effort after meaning' in human memory, to Ulric Neisser's perceptual cycle, the vast range of experiments on the limits of attention, to O'Regan and Noë's theory of consciousness, to the astonishing results from Wilder Penfield's early experiments in brain surgery and Björn Merker's theorizing about the central role of 'deep' (sub-cortical) brain structures in conscious experience. My own attempt, to lock onto, and organize, these and other findings and ideas into a cohesive pattern probably doesn't correspond precisely to any previous theory, though it has strong resemblances to many.

10 Indeed, precisely because we see only the stable, meaningful world, and have no awareness whatever of the vastly complex calculations our brain is engaged in, newcomers to psychology and neuroscience are often surprised that the brain even needs to make such calculations. It is easy to imagine that the world merely presents itself, fully interpreted, to the eye and ear. Yet the opposite is the case: about half of the brain is dedicated, full-time, to what is fairly uncontroversially agreed to be perceptual analysis. But, as we shall see, the reach of perception may be greater still.

11 The question of whether we have so-called imageless thoughts was hugely controversial early in the history of psychology. Otto Külpe (1862–1915) and his students at the University of Würzburg famously reported that they experienced ineffable and indescribable states of awareness when thinking about abstract concepts. These mysterious experiences, supposedly lacking any sensory qualities, were viewed as of great theoretical significance by Külpe. Other early psychologists, including the British psychologist Edward Titchener (1867–1927), who had studied in Germany and set up a laboratory at Cornell University in upstate New York, reported that they had no such experiences. Perhaps remarkably, the resulting transatlantic controversy shook the psychological world. I, for one, have no idea what it would be like if I did have an impalpable non-sensory experience, any more than I know what it would be like to see a square triangle.

8. THE NARROW CHANNEL OF CONSCIOUSNESS

1 The role of alarm systems in conscious experience has been particularly highlighted by Kevin O'Regan's concept of the 'grabbiness' of perception – that is, if something changes in the image, it grabs your attention. J. K. O'Regan, *Why Red Doesn't Sound Like a Bell: Understanding the Feel of Consciousness* (Oxford: Oxford University Press, 2011).

2 Redrawn with permission from A. Mack and I. Rock (1999), 'Inattentional blindness', *Psyche*, 5(3): Figure 2.

3 J. S. Macdonald and N. Lavie (2011), 'Visual perceptual load induces inattentional deafness', *Attention, Perception, & Psychophysics*, 73(6): 1780–89.

4 Redrawn with permission from Mack and Rock (1999), 'Inattentional blindness', Figure 3.

5 Inattentional blindness and deafness require going 'under the radar' of the alarm system – a bright flash or a loud bang would surely be detected, however carefully we are focusing on the central cross, because the alerting mechanisms will drag our focus from the cross to the unexpected, rather shocking, stimulus. But this is not a case of locking onto two set of information – the shock of the flash (or, equally, a loud bang) would disengage our existing visual analysis of the arms of the cross and, we would presume, dramatically reduce the accuracy of our judgements concerning which arm is longer.

6. Reprinted with permission from R. F. Haines (1991), 'A breakdown in simultaneous information processing', in *Presbyopia Research*, ed. G. Obrecht and L. W. Stark (Boston, MA: Springer), pp. 171–5.

7 U. Neisser, 'The control of information pickup in selective looking', in A. D. Pick (ed.), *Perception and its Development: A Tribute to Eleanor J. Gibson* (Hillsdale, NJ: Lawrence Erlbaum Associates, 1979), pp. 201–19.

8 A wonderful update of this study, where the woman with the umbrella is replaced by a person in a gorilla suit, became something of a YouTube hit. D. J. Simons and C.F. Chabris (1999), 'Gorillas in our midst: Sustained inattentional blindness for dynamic events', *Perception*, 28(9): 1059–74.

9 The possibility that many objects, faces and words are analysed at a 'deep' level, but only one or so is then selected by attentional resources is the 'late-selection' theory of attention (J. Deutsch and D. Deutsch (1963), 'Attention: Some theoretical considerations', *Psychological Review*, 70(1): 80).

10 This does not mean that the brain processes *only* pieces of information relevant to the object, word, face or pattern that is the current focus of attention. Indeed, some amount of processing of irrelevant information is inevitable, because the brain can't always know which new pieces of information are part of the current 'jigsaw'. This point is demonstrated elegantly in experiments in which people listen to different voices 'speaking' into left and right headphones. Instructed to listen to, and immediately repeat, the voice in the left ear, people have almost no idea

what the other voice is saying (D. E. Broadbent, *Perception and Communication* (Oxford: Oxford University Press, 1958); N. P. Moray (1959), 'Attention in dichotic listening: Affective cues and the influence of instructions', *Quarterly Journal of Experimental Psychology*, 11: 56–60). For example, they can fail to notice that the unattended voice is speaking in a foreign language or repeating a single word. But suppose the messages abruptly switch ears – so that the natural continuation of the sentence heard in the left ear now continues in the right ear (A. Treisman (1960), 'Contextual cues in selective listening', *Quarterly Journal of Experimental Psychology*, 12: 242–8). In this case people frequently 'follow' the switched message to the other ear. As the brain is continually searching for new 'data' that matches as well as possible with its existing 'jigsaw', when new 'jigsaw pieces' appear to fit unexpectedly well with the current jigsaw, the brain 'grabs' hold of them. Yet the cycle of thought is rigidly sequential: we can only fit new information into one mental jigsaw at a time.

11 Of course, the brain has to figure out which pieces of information are meaningfully grouped together. Even if we are solving one jigsaw at a time, we may need to make some sense of other irrelevant jigsaw pieces in order to reject them – for example, if we are working on a jigsaw containing a rural scene, spotting that a jigsaw piece or pieces that make up a fragment of aircraft engine might lead us to put them aside. In the same way, the brain imposes meaning on information irrelevant to the meaningful pattern it is constructing just enough to reject it as irrelevant.

12 Indeed, the most popular model of how eye movements and reading work, the E–Z Reader model, assumes that attention shifts completely sequentially, from one word to the next, with no overlaps – even though there would seem to be huge advantages to being able to read many words simultaneously. Attention locks on and makes sense of one word after the next, exemplifying the cycle of thought viewpoint (see, for example, E. D. Reichle, K. Rayner and A. Pollatsek (2003), 'The E–Z Reader model of eye-movement control in reading: Comparisons to other models', *Behavioral and Brain Sciences*, 26 (4): 445–76.

13 G. Rees, C. Russell, C. D. Frith and J. Driver (1999), 'Inattentional blindness versus inattentional amnesia for fixated but ignored words', *Science*, 286(5449): 2504–507.

14 Some primitive aspects of the perceptual world may, though, be grasped without the need for attention. Indeed, such processing seems to be a prerequisite for attentional processes to be able to select and

lock onto specific aspects of aspects of the visual input or stream of sounds. We shall not consider here the vexed question of what information the brain can extract without engaging the cycle of thought – but note that it will not include describing the world as consisting of 'meaningful' items such as words, faces or objects, but rather will be closely tied to features of the sensory input itself (e.g. detecting bright patches, textures, or edges – although none of these is uncontroversially pre-attentive). See, for example, L. G. Appelbaum and A. M. Norcia (2009), 'Attentive and pre-attentive aspects of figural processing', *Journal of Vision*, 9(11): 1–12; Li, Zhaoping (2000), 'Pre-attentive segmentation in the primary visual cortex', *Spatial Vision*, 13 (1): 25–50.

15 D. A. Allport, B. Antonis and P. Reynolds (1972), 'On the division of attention: A disproof of the single channel hypothesis', *Quarterly Journal of Experimental Psychology*, 24(2): 225–35.

16 L. H. Shaffer (1972), 'Limits of Human Attention', *New Scientist*, 9 November: 340–41; L. H. Shaffer, 'Multiple attention in continuous verbal tasks', in P. M. A. Rabbitt and S. Domic (eds), *Attention and Performance V* (London: Academic Press, 1975).

9. THE MYTH OF UNCONSCIOUS THOUGHT

1 H. Poincaré, 'Mathematical creation', in H. Poincaré, *The Foundations of Science* (New York: Science Press, 1913).

2 Paul Hindemith, *A Composer's World: Horizons and Limitations* (Cambridge, MA: Harvard University Press, 1953), p. 50; online at <http://www.alejandrocasales.com/teoria/sound/composers_world.pdf>.

3 I challenge the reader to listen to a short piano piece such as Hindemith's fascinating Piano Sonata No. 3 (Fugue) and to believe that its astonishing intricacies could have been conceived, except in the vaguest and most general terms, in any sudden flash of insight. Indeed, it seems mysterious how Hindemith could have convinced himself that this dazzling web of notes, extending over several minutes, arose fully formed in his consciousness in a single moment. We shall see later that Hindemith did not intend to be taken entirely literally.

4 Left image: R. L. Gregory (2001), The Medawar Lecture 2001: 'Knowledge for vision: vision for knowledge', *Philosophical Transactions of the Royal Society Lond B*, 360: 1231–51; the right image is by psychologist Karl Dallenbach.

5 U. N. Sio and T. C. Ormerod (2009), 'Does incubation enhance problem solving? A meta-analytic review', *Psychological Bulletin*, 135(1): 94.

6 But might unconscious mental work occur when we are asleep, when the brain is otherwise unoccupied? This is very unlikely: the coherent, flowing brain waves that overtake our brains through most of the night are utterly unlike the brainwaves indicative of intensive mental activity – the brain is, after all, resting. And the short bursts of dream sleep, though much more similar to waking brain activity, are taken up with other things: namely, creating the strange and jumbled images and stories of our dreams.

7 Hindemith, *A Composer's World: Horizons and Limitations*, p. 51.

8 J. Levy, H. Pashler and E. Boer (2006), 'Central interference in driving: Is there any stopping the psychological refractory period?' *Psychological Science*, 17(3): 228–35.

9 Psychologists typically use 'detection' for tasks which require determining whether a 'signal' (a flash, a beep, or an aircraft on a radar screen) is present or not. This task is marginally more complex, requiring categorization into one or two categories (one event or two).

10 J. Levy and H. Pashler (2008), 'Task prioritization in multitasking during driving: Opportunity to abort a concurrent task does not insulate braking responses from dual-task slowing', *Applied Cognitive Psychology*, 22: 507–25.

11 E. A. Maylor, N. Chater and G. V. Jones (2001), 'Searching for two things at once: Evidence of exclusivity in semantic and autobiographical memory retrieval', *Memory & Cognition*, 29(8): 1185–95.

10. THE BOUNDARY OF CONSCIOUSNESS

1 Reprinted with permission from M. Idesawa (1991), 'Perception of 3-D illusory surface with binocular viewing', *Japanese Journal of Applied Physics*, 30(4B), L751.

2 We will see later that the brain may operate by extrapolating from vast batteries of examples, rather than working with general principles, whether geometric or not. However, this point, while crucially important, does not affect the present argument.

3 Beautiful theoretical work has analysed how this process of finding the best interpretation of the available data might work, and there are many elegant proposals for 'idealized' versions of the nervous system (and some of these proposals can be shown to carry out powerful computations). But the details of how the brain solves the problem are by no means resolved (see J. J. Hopfield (1982), 'Neural networks and physical systems with emergent collective computational abilities', *Proceedings of the National Academy of Sciences of the United States of America*,

79(8), 2554–8). Importantly, there are powerful theoretical ideas concerning how such networks learn the constraints that govern the external world from experience (e.g. Y. LeCun, Y. Bengio and G. Hinton (2015), 'Deep learning', *Nature*, 521(7553): 436–44.).

4 Although in a digital computer, cooperative computation across the entire web of constraints is not so straightforward – more sequential methods of searching the web are often used instead.

5 The idea of 'direct' perception, which has been much discussed in psychology, is appealing, I think, precisely because we are only ever aware of the *output* of the cycle of thought: we are oblivious to the calculations involved, and the speed with which the cycle of thought can generate the illusion that our conscious experience must be in immediate contact with reality.

6 H. von Helmholtz, *Handbuch der physiologischen Optik*, vol. 3 (Leipzig: Voss, 1867). Quotations are from the English translation, *Treatise on Physiological Optics* (1910) (Washington DC: The Optical Society of America, 1924–5).

7 D. Hume (1738–40), *A Treatise of Human Nature*: Book I. Of the understanding, Part IV. Of the sceptical and other systems of philosophy, Section VI. Of personal identity.

8 From this point of view, the question of *what we are thinking about* needs to be kept strictly separate from the issue of consciousness. Two people might both hear an identical snippet of conversation, but in one case, the speakers are talking about a real couple who, by sheer coincidence, are called Cathy and Heathcliff; in another, the speakers are members of a book group, discussing *Wuthering Heights*. What might be an identical conscious experience of thinking: 'Poor Cathy!' is a thought about a real person in the first case (though the hearer has no clue who this person is); in the second case, it is a thought about a fictional character (though the hearer may have no clue which fictional character, or even that she *is* a fictional character). The nature of consciousness and of meaning are both fascinating and profound puzzles, but they are very distinct puzzles.

9 For example, dual process theories of reasoning, decision-making and social cognition take this viewpoint (see, for example, J. S. B. Evans and K. E. Frankish, *In Two Minds: Dual Processes and Beyond* (Oxford: Oxford University Press, 2009); S. A. Sloman (1996), 'The empirical case for two systems of reasoning', *Psychological Bulletin*, 119(1): 3–22. The Nobel Prize-winning psychologist Daniel Kahneman is often seen as exemplifying this viewpoint (e.g. D. Kahneman, *Thinking, Fast and Slow* (London: Penguin, 2011), although his perspective is rather more subtle.

10 For example, P. Dayan, 'The role of value systems in decision making', in C. Engel and W. Singer (eds), *Better Than Conscious? Decision Making, the Human Mind, and Implications for Institutions* (Cambridge, MA: MIT Press, 2008), pp. 51–70.

11 There is a small industry in psychology attempting to demonstrate the existence of 'unconscious' influences on our actions (see, for example, the excellent review by B. R. Newell and D. R. Shanks (2014), 'Unconscious influences on decision making: A critical review', *Behavioral and Brain Sciences*, 37(1): 1–19). From the present point of view, this hardly needs demonstrating: we are only ever conscious of the outputs of thought and our speculations about their origins are always mere confabulation. A consequence of this viewpoint is that any demonstrations of the 'unconscious influences' on thought do not imply the existence of hidden unconscious pathways to decisions and actions that compete with conscious decision-making processes (although this has been a popular conclusion to draw: see A. Dijksterhuis and L. F. Nordgren (2006), 'A theory of unconscious thought', *Perspectives on Psychological Science* 1: 95–109). On the contrary, such effects are entirely consistent with the cycle-of-thought viewpoint: there is just one engine of thought, the *results* of which are always conscious, and the origins of which are *never* conscious.

Must we conclude that each of us is completely oblivious to the processes which generate our thoughts and behaviour? Within a single cycle of thought, I think this is right. But conscious deliberation – pondering different lines of attack on a crossword clue, planning ahead in chess, weighing up advantages and disadvantages of a course of action – involves many cycles of thought. And each cycle will generate conscious awareness of some meaningful organization (a candidate word for our crossword clue, an image of a hypothetical chess move, a snippet of language, a pro or a con). The output of each cycle will feed into the next – if we are to have a stream of coherent thought rather than an aimless daydream.

12 For example, K. A. Ericsson and H. A. Simon (1980), 'Verbal reports as data', *Psychological Review*, 87(3): 215–51.

13 J. S. Mill, *The Autobiography* (1873).

11. PRECEDENTS NOT PRINCIPLES

1 For analysis of the psychology of chess, see classic studies by A. D. de Groot, *Het denken van de schaker* [*The thought of the chess player*] (Amsterdam: North-Holland Publishing Co., 1946); updated translation published as *Thought and Choice in Chess* (The Hague: Mouton,

1965; corrected second edition published in 1978); W. G. Chase and H. A. Simon (1973), 'Perception in chess', *Cognitive Psychology*, 4: 55–81; and more recently, F. Gobet and H. A. Simon (1996), 'Recall of rapidly presented random chess positions is a function of skill', *Psychonomic Bulletin and Review*, 3(2): 159–63.

2 J. Capablanca, *Chess Fundamentals* (New York: Harcourt, Brace and Company, 1921).

3 For examples, see http://justsomething.co/the-50-funniest-faces-in-everyday-objects/. The third photo is reprinted by permission of Ruth E. Kaiser of the Spontaneous Smiley Face Project.

4 This viewpoint ties up nicely with the picture of brain organization described in Chapter 7. Sub-cortical brain structures are the crucible of perceptual interpretation, serving as gateways to the senses, but they also have bi-directional projections into the entire cortex. This type of two-way link between the current perceptual interpretation and the past stock of memory traces represented in the cortex is just what is required to support a parallel process of resonance.

5 M. H. Christiansen and N. Chater (2016), 'The now-or-never bottleneck: A fundamental constraint on language', *Behavioral and Brain Sciences*, 39: e62; M. H. Christiansen and N. Chater, *Creating Language* (Cambridge, MA: MIT Press, 2016).

6 http://restlessmindboosters.blogspot.co.uk/2011/06/tangram-construcao.html.

7 The idea that human knowledge is rooted in precedents or 'cases' has a long tradition in, among other fields, artificial intelligence (e.g. J. Kolodner, *Case-Based Reasoning* (San Mateo, CA: Morgan Kaufmann, 1993), machine-learning and statistics (e.g. T. Cover and P. Hart (1967), 'Nearest neighbor pattern classification', *IEEE Transactions on Information Theory*, 13(1): 21–7) and psychology (e.g. G. D. Logan (1988), 'Toward an instance theory of automatization', *Psychological Review*, 95(4): 492). Principles are also important, but they are invented post-hoc and then themselves become fresh precedents to be amended and overturned, rather than rigid rules to be applied relentlessly.

12: THE SECRET OF INTELLIGENCE

1 C. M. Mooney (1957), 'Age in the development of closure ability in children', *Canadian Journal of Psychology*, 11(4): 219–26.

2 Mooney, 'Age in the development of closure ability in children', 219.

3 It is possible that such memory storage is not completely immutable. In my experience, though, one moment of 'insight' into an image does appear to be enough to last a lifetime.

4 G. Lakoff and M. Johnson, *Metaphors We Live By* (Chicago: University of Chicago Press, 1980).

5 Almost certainly, this is something of an over-simplification. If there are some people who are good at finding answers we all agree with, then we may trust them to define the answers for more tricky problems, which leave most of us flummoxed. This is how things work in lots of areas, of course – we trust mathematicians or literary critics more than ourselves to work out what is a really exciting mathematical breakthrough or a landmark novel. And perhaps we trust these 'experts' (if at all) because they can demonstrate their competence at things we do all know something about. So maybe we should give more weight to judgements of the 'right answer' by people who do well in IQ tests.

6 The spectacular successes of contemporary artificial intelligence work by incredibly memory-intensive methods has been made possible by major advances in both computer algorithms and an exponential growth in computer memory, computer power and the availability of massive quantities of data. These successes will, I believe, change our lives fundamentally, but they will do so by assisting and enhancing the human mind, rather than replacing it. It is telling, I suspect, that in large areas of mathematics the computer is a powerful and sometimes essential tool, but almost no interesting mathematical results have been discovered automatically; and, indeed, most mathematics is still done, more or less, with a pen and paper. The elasticity of the human imagination has, as yet, no computational parallel.

7 Lakoff and Johnson, *Metaphors We Live By*; D. R. Hofstadter, *Fluid Concepts and Creative Analogies: Computer Models of the Fundamental Mechanisms of Thought* (New York: Basic Books, 1995).

Index